THEY'RE ALL NUTS

PAUL JELLINEK

ISBN-10: 1456308831
EAN-13: 9781456308834
LCCN: 2010916032

CONTENTS

To Amy, Lisa, Michael and Rob

FRED AND PETE'S: THEY'RE ALL NUTS

Looking back, I'm not sure exactly where I first got the idea to write a book about Fred and Pete's. It might have been from listening to all those stories of Dave Stout's over all those cups of coffee at the counter. Dave's always got stories—usually good ones, and some of them are even true. Or it might have been that morning that I got into a long conversation with Marvin Block, who owns a carpet business half a mile up Route 33, about his life growing up in the Bronx, about his family, and about how he'd built up his business. Or maybe it was just the reaction that I got from Annie Pecan and some of the other waitresses when they saw that I'd mentioned Fred and Pete's in my first book, *Promise to Mary*. I remember Annie in particular being excited to see her name in there, and thinking that really, there were probably as many good stories right there at the counter (and behind the counter) as there were in all those places around the country that I'd traveled to for *Promise to Mary*. Only this time I wouldn't have to buy any plane tickets or rent any cars or pay for any more lonely motel rooms. Just the cost of the microcassette tapes, the AAA batteries, and coffee—lots of coffee.

But there was another reason besides the stories that I wanted to write about Fred and Pete's—and that's the place itself. Because places like Fred and Pete's are disappearing out from under us. Like Parfait House did, which used to be across Route 33 from Fred and Pete's and where we used to take the kids for ice cream (now a bank); or the Marroe Inn on Route One, where we used to take the kids on Friday nights to hear Jerry Rife and the Rhythm Kings play fabulous Dixieland jazz (now a car dealership); or even the lovely old Tides Hotel and Beach Club down in Florida where we used to go for our family vacations (now a gated condominium complex). They're all gone, and I don't want to lose Fred and Pete's the same way. Tom Armenti, who owns and runs Fred and Pete's, told me that he planned to put in another five years and then he's going to hang it up (that was before his heart attack, although he swears that he's feeling better than ever since they put the stent in). And I guess it's always possible that someone else will buy it from him and keep the place going, the same way that Tom himself bought the place from Fred and Pete. But I'm not counting on it.

Sure, there's always the McDonald's just up the road or the Applebee's right across Route 33 where you could get something to eat if you had to, but those places, to put it mildly, don't have a soul. At least not a soul like Fred and Pete's. So I guess, now that I think about it, that's really the main reason that I decided to write this book: to try to get some of that soul on paper before it's too late.

A word about the title. Originally, I was planning just to call it *Fred and Pete's*, plain and simple. But when I mentioned that to Midge Morrissy, one of the waitresses who's been there forever and who had actually read *Promise to Mary* (which gave her added credibility with me), she didn't like it. "Call it *They're All Nuts*," she insisted. "Because they are. All of them. Me included." And she kept on insisting on it, day after day, week after week, until finally she wore me down.

So here it is, Midge: *Fred and Pete's: They're All Nuts!* Now do I get my hot turkey sandwich?

A HORN ROLL WITH JUST A LITTLE BUTTER ON THE SIDE

Wednesday, August 6, 2008. We had some rain come through last night, so it's a pleasantly cool August morning, at least for the moment. As I drive through Five Points and make a left into the big parking lot in front of Fred and Pete's, I see that they're still blacktopping it, a section at a time. They've been at it for the past couple of weeks, and there's a row of orange plastic cones blocking off the section that they're going to do today. You can still smell the blacktop they laid down yesterday, mingled with the still dripping foliage from last night's rain and the diesel exhaust from the trucks on Route 33.

Fred and Pete's is housed in the middle of an aging strip mall called the Mercerville Shopping Center, one of many strip malls here on Route 33. There's an Ace Hardware on the corner where the Acme used to be and where I now buy my furnace filters and get my storm windows repaired. Next to it is Party Fair, a discount party supply store where you can buy mylar balloons for your next birthday party. Then comes the Carvel, which I've never once been to in the twenty-five years that we've lived here, followed by the Italian People's Bakery, which has great cannoli and seeded spolettes. Next to Italian People's is High-Q Cleaners, a Chinese laundry and dry cleaner, and next to that is Fred and Pete's Deli and Luncheonette, with one old guy sitting in one of the white plastic chairs in front of it gazing out over the parking lot, probably waiting for his friends to show up.

Next to Fred and Pete's on the other side is a Rite-Aid Pharmacy, which used to be an Eckerd's and before that was something else; Accent and Designs, featuring hand-painted décor and an art studio; Alicia Boutique, which presumably sells women's clothes; The Reading Center, which sells books, magazines and newspapers; Beauty Nails and Spa; The Clearer Image for eye exams; Rock Dreams Electronics, where I used to buy CD's until they stopped selling them a couple of years ago; Tomorrow's Treasures, whatever those might be; Sleepy's, the mattress professionals; the New World Buffet; and, on the far corner where the A & P used to be, the Hamilton Farm Grocery Store.

Across Route 33 from the Mercerville Shopping Center is the post office that used to be located in the shopping center (which was a lot more convenient), as well as a Sun

Bank and an Applebee's. Across Mercerville-Whitehorse Road from where I turned into the parking lot there's a CVS pharmacy where we get our pictures developed, and on the opposite corner there's a Lukoil station where I sometimes stop for gas. Looming in the sky behind the Lukoil is a big water tower that I've never really noticed before—which is funny, because when I'm traveling, usually the first thing that I see when I drive into a new town is the town's water tower, often with the town's name on it.

Parked at the edge of the parking lot is a small trailer with the words "Fred and Pete's Catering, Mercerville, New Jersey, 609-586-7792, Catering For All Occasions" painted on its side, along with a cartoon of a smiling chef with a mustache holding out a platter heaped with cold-cuts. Nearby is what looks like an old bread truck that also says "Fred and Pete's Catering, Mercerville, New Jersey," but goes on to say "Dinners $4.98, Subs half and whole, Breakfast Specials, Home of Six Pick-6 Winners." And then there's another, smaller white Chevy panel truck that says "Fred and Pete's Deli and Catering, Serving New Jersey since 1963." I park beside it and head inside, taking my small silver microcassette recorder with me.

It's a busy morning, but there's an empty seat at the counter, across from the toaster oven, so I take it. It's warmer in here, and filled with the smell of coffee, grilled meat, and dark toast. Marie, a petite, nicely dressed older woman who is one of the regulars, sits on my left, nursing a cup of coffee. Annie, who's wearing a black Fred and Pete's t-shirt, black pants and earrings that go well with her reddish-blonde hair, sees me, brings me a cup of coffee and asks me if I want my "healthy breakfast"—a Styrofoam bowl of Raisin Bran and a paper cup of milk.

"OK," I say.

"Paul's writing a book," Annie tells Marie. "About Fred and Pete's."

"About what?"

"Fred and Pete's," Annie repeats, louder.

"Oh," Marie says, vaguely. "That should be interesting."

"How've you been, Marie?" I ask her.

She shrugs. "Good, hon. Can't complain." She turns to Annie and asks her whether she's decided if she's going to go the Columbus flea market this weekend or to the one down in Willingboro.

"Willingboro, probably," Annie tells her. "The last time I went to Columbus I hardly sold a thing all day."

I turn to the guy on my right, a younger man, in his forties maybe. I've never seen him before. "I'll tell you," I say, striking up a conversation, "these places are disappearing."

"Yeah, they are," he agrees. "It's a shame."

"Yeah, it is," I say. "How long have you been coming here?"

"Probably all my life," he replies. He squints and takes a good look at me. "You used to go to Nottingham, didn't you?"

"No," I say. "My kids did—three of them, anyway." Nottingham is one of the area high schools, not far from Trenton. "Did you go to Nottingham?"

The guy nods. "Yeah." He keeps looking at me, still trying to place me. "Did you used to work there?" he asks.

"No," I tell him. "But I used to go there for parents nights."

He shakes his head and returns to his pork roll and eggs, obviously unconvinced. He's positive that I went to Nottingham, or maybe worked there, but for some reason I don't seem to want to admit it. Strange.

Annie brings me my Raisin Bran and milk. "I've been trying to eat healthy, too," she tells me. "I'll have a big bowl of fruit for dinner, and I mean a big bowl. And you know what I do? I'll put a big scoop of Raisin Bran on top of it."

"Oh, hey," I say, "that sounds good."

"It is delicious!" she exclaims. "I had strawberries, blueberries, cantaloupe, and grapes, and then the crunchy Raisin Bran and the sweet raisins on top—and, oh my God, it was so good..."

Marie interrupts. "Annie, I gotta go," she says abruptly. "Here's that cigar box I promised you." She pulls an ancient wooden box out of a shopping bag on the floor beside her and sets it on the counter.

"Oh, thank you, sweetheart," Annie says, fondly.

Marie carefully gets to her feet, picks up the shopping bag and her purse, and slowly starts toward the door. "Thank you, babe," Annie calls after her. Marie turns and gives her a little wave.

Annie turns back to me and starts telling me about her upcoming high school reunion at Yeadon High School, near Upper Darby, just west of Philadelphia. "I'm so nervous," she says. "I haven't seen any of these people in so long."

"What year reunion is this?" I ask.

"My fortieth," she says bashfully. "I'll be sixty in March."

"You're kidding!"

She shakes her head. "Uh-uh. And no comments from the peanut gallery either," she warns sharply, turning to Jim Fennelli two seats to my right. Jim, a big man who used to be in charge of Veteran's Park for the Township and now buys and sells gold and jewelry, starts coughing. It's hard to tell if it's for real or if he's just covering up a laugh. "That doesn't sound too good, Jim," Annie tells him as his coughing continues.

Just then, Kay, the other waitress this morning, calls to her from the grill. "Your order's ready, Annie—French toast and bacon." Kay, who always seems to have a smile on her face no matter how crazy it gets, is wearing her usual waitress uniform: high-waisted black pants and a traditional white waitress blouse, with a big gold-plated letter "K" pinned to her chest. When she comes over to put a couple of slices of bread in the toaster oven, I ask her what the K stands for.

"Kay," she says, deadpan—and then cracks up. So does Jim.

Annie puts the French toast and bacon in front of whoever's sitting on the other side of Jim, and Tom Armenti, who owns Fred and Pete's, comes bustling up from the kitchen, a big tray lifted high up over his head, making a bee-line for the front counter.

"Hey, Tom," I call as he flies past me.

"Hey, Paulie," he calls back, and then he's gone.

Meanwhile, the guy from Nottingham who was sitting on my right has taken off, and an older man, big like Jim and wearing a Red Sox baseball cap, takes his seat, between me and Jim.

"How ya doing?" the man says to Jim, his voice gruff, almost hoarse. "Thought I'd stop in today, see how you're doing."

"Did you get down there yesterday?" Jim asks him.

"Nah," the man says, shaking his head, "Didn't have time. I had to get all that stuff down to Delaware…" The rest of his sentence is swallowed by the noise. There's a booth up near the front with six or seven guys crowded into it that seems to be getting louder by the minute.

Annie comes back. "That was funny with Kay," she says, laughing. "What else could it have been? Kangaroo? Kaleidoscope?" She dumps a fresh handful of half and halfs from the fridge into the green plastic bowl in front of me, next to the napkin dispenser, the sugar dispenser, the salt and pepper shakers, and the bottle of Heinz ketchup—none of that cheap stuff at Fred and Pete's.

"Hey, Annie," Jim calls, with a mouthful of scrambled egg and toast, "looks like you got yourself a fire. In the toaster oven." He points at it with his fork, and I can see the flames. The smoke is already pouring out.

"Oh, my God!" Annie cries. "Not again!" She grabs a wooden spoon and plunges it deep inside the toaster oven, prying loose the charred remains of a bagel. "These new bagels are just too big for this toaster," she says, dropping it into the trash. "I'll just have to give them to Israel to do on the grill, like the horn rolls."

The man in the Red Sox cap is doubled over, coughing from the smoke. "Sorry about that, Bob," Annie says. "It'll clear out pretty quick with that fan on."

"No problem," he gasps, still coughing.

I wait until he stops coughing and catches his breath. "So, Bob," I say, now that I've learned his name from Annie, "how long have you been coming here?"

He turns toward me, leans back a little, squints at me like he's trying to figure out if he knows me, and reaches out to shake hands. "My name's Bob Lee," he says, apparently not hearing my question with all the racket from the guys in the booth. He grip is strong and friendly.

"Good to meet you, Bob," I say. I tell him my name and that I'm planning to write a book about Fred and Pete's.

He nods. "I'll tell you, there's more stories about Tommy's father than you would ever believe," he says.

"Which one was Tommy's father?" I ask.

"Freddy," Bob says. "Very good athlete when he was young. A funny guy. He was involved in Easter egg hunts, parades—everything. I knew Tommy's father real well. His partner was a guy named Pete. A nice guy, but not as outgoing. I'll tell you, you could just *sit here and write a book about Tommy's father." And he goes on to tell me a story about the time that Fred was in the dining room of some fancy hotel down in Virginia with his friend Tony and he somehow convinced the manager that he was a famous pianist by the name of "Frederico." It was a little hard to hear the rest of the story, except that it ended with "Frederico" sitting down at the grand piano, with all eyes on him, slamming both hands down on the piano in one colossal bang, and then standing up and taking a bow.*

I burst out laughing, and so does Bob. "There's a hundred stories like that about Freddy," he says as he starts to cough again, probably from laughing so hard. "Like one time we was out and we couldn't get into a diner—it was like 2:30 in the morning. So we head home, and he says, 'Come on.' So we come back here and he opens his store up—by now it's 3:30 in the morning—and he turns on the grill and says, 'Come on, I'll cook you whatever you want.' Meantime, the cops pull up, wondering if anybody's breaking in. So Freddy gives them coffee and fixes them breakfast. He was that kind of guy."

"Yeah, he sounds like a great guy," I say. "And so was Pete just a business partner who invested in the place?"

"Oh no," Bob says. "He was here. But just ask anybody here that's old-looking, and they'll all tell you stories about Freddy and Tommy and Tommy's brother." Just then, a guy in a blue golf shirt comes up and says hello to Bob, and Bob says to me, very politely, "Excuse me, Paul, I've got to catch up on some business."

"Sure thing," I say.

Bob turns around in his seat, and the guy in the blue shirt just stands there while they're talking. Not wanting to listen in, I shift my gaze to the big Scotsman ice machine and the soda machine behind the counter, with hundreds of red and white Coca Cola cups stacked in neat rows on either side of it for easy access. I look up at the big menu board hanging on the wall, and for the first time in all the years that I've been sitting here at the counter, I actually read it:

BREAKFAST. 2 eggs, any style, $2.10. With a meat, $3.65. French toast, $3.50. Pancakes, $3.00. Short stack, $2.50. Egg sandwich with meat, $2.95. With cheese, $3.35. Cheese omelet, $2.65. Western omelet, $3.85. Soup, $1.50. Rolls, muffins, bagels, $1.50. With cream cheese, $1.85. Coffee, tea, hot chocolate, $1.00. (I laugh. In all the time I've been coming here, I never noticed what the price of a cup of coffee was—and I have it every time.) 10 oz. Juice, $1.25. 16 oz. Juice, $2.00. Milk, $1.50.

SANDWICHES. Home-made roast beef, $3.50. Ham, $2.95. Ham and cheese, $3.10. Turkey breast, $3.50. Corned beef, $3.50. Home-made roast pork, $3.50. Italian salami, $3.00. Liverwurst, $2.85. Tuna or chicken salad, $3.00. Egg salad, $2.75. Italian cappy, $2.95. Virginia baked ham, $3.50. Pastrami, $3.50. 6 oz. Hamburger, $2.65. Cheeseburger, $2.90. Baked ham, $2.95. Hot dog, $1.50. Italian hot dog, $2.90. BLT, $2.85. Grilled cheese, $2.50. Pork roll, $2.75. Reuben, $4.00. Club sandwich, $4.00. Hot open face, $4.00. French fries, $1.50.

HOAGIES: American, $4.00, Tuna, $4.25, Italian, $4.25, Roast beef, $4.25, Turkey, $4.25.

A lot of things on there that I didn't even know they had. I tell myself that I'll have to try a liverwurst sandwich sometime, and maybe the Italian cappy.

Meanwhile, Bob has finished his conversation with the guy in the blue shirt and turns back to me. "So, Paul," he says, picking up right where he left off, "you know any of these regulars here?"

"Some of them," I say. "I'm planning to talk to Richie for my book, and Dave Stout, and maybe Johnny." Just at that moment, I notice that Dave Stout has come in, looking for a seat at the counter. I call to him, but he doesn't hear me with all the noise.

"He knows a lot of history," Bob tells me, nodding towards Dave. Then he asks me if I've written anything else, so I tell him, at some length, about my earlier book, Promise to Mary, about the Faith in Action program that provides volunteer help to people who are homebound.

Bob listens attentively. "Are you born again?" he asks me when I'm done.

I shake my head. "No, Catholic."

"Sounds like my wife and her girlfriend. They're trying to knit four hundred scarves for the kitchen at St. Raphael's here—to give out to the poor people at Christmas. A lot of churches, they do a lot." Then he starts coughing again, a dry, jagged cough that he can't seem to stop.

"Are you OK?" I ask him, a little concerned.

"It's a lung disease," he says as the coughing subsides. "Not contagious."

"Emphysema?"

"I wish it was," Bob replies gruffly. "It's idiopathic pulmonary fibrosis. It's terminal—and there's nothing that can delay it. They keep working on stuff, but..."

I ask him when he was diagnosed.

"Five years ago," he says.

"That's a long time to have something like that hanging over you," I say, trying, but not really able, to imagine what that must feel like.

"Ninety-five percent of the people die in two to five years," Bob explains. "So I'm getting a little concerned."

A little concerned? Oh my God.

Bob is seized by another convulsive coughing spasm, and when it's over, he adds that his wife has cancer. "But she's OK," he assures me. "She's in remission."

"I'm so sorry," I say, and for a while Bob doesn't answer. I sip my coffee, which is cold by now, and look down at the counter. I'm not sure whether to keep the conversation going or just let him be.

Then he says, "Now, if you were going to write another religious book, I have a lot of comments on religion."

I explain that my first book wasn't really about religion so much as it was about people from various congregations who volunteer to help people in need.

Bob nods. "The goodness of people. I know. But now you've got to write about the badness of people."

"There's some of that in there, too," I say, a little defensively. *"You know, these are real people, and people are complicated."*

He nods again. *"I should've written my own book,"* he reflects. *"You know, 'The World,' by me. Any subject you can think of—politics, religion, homophobia—I'd give my ideas. I'd give it a whack."*

I ask Bob whether he's actually written anything yet, or if he's still just thinking about it, and he tells me that he's written about twenty or thirty pages. Then he looks me in the eye and declares emphatically, *"The only thing that's wrong with the world—and I mean the only thing—is greed."*

"Is that right?"

"Greed," he repeats with great conviction. *"There's nothing that's detrimental to mankind that wasn't started by greed. Even with nice people. Like let's say that lady over there wants to sell you that bottle of ketchup and it costs a dollar. But she charges you three dollars, and you're dumb enough to pay it. That's greed."*

"Right..."

"I ask people like that, if they're religious, I ask them, 'Now, would Jesus sell that bottle of ketchup for three dollars?' I tell you, Paul, people are unbelievable," Bob says, shaking his head in wonderment.

Annie walks up and refills our coffee cups. *"You want anything to eat today, Bob, or are you just going to have coffee?"*

"A horn roll," Bob says. *"With just a little butter on the side. And can you have him heat it up on the grill?"*

TOM ARMENTI

Thursday, August 7, 2008. There was never any question about who I was going to interview first. It had to be Tom Armenti. Tom not only owns Fred and Pete's, he's been there from Day One—his father, after all, was Fred—and so he knows the story better than anyone. Besides, if I'm going to write about his place, isn't it only right that I talk to him first?

But catching up with him was another story. Because Tom Armenti never sits still. He's there seven days a week, unless he's out on a catering job, and he is always on the move: from the counter to the kitchen to the slicing machine to the lottery machine to the booths in the front to the booths in the back to the cash register—and fast. I don't think I've ever seen the guy amble in all the years that I've been going there. No wonder he never puts on any weight. If I had to say what kind of animal Tom reminds me of, it would probably be a hummingbird—the way they dart from place to place so fast that you almost don't see them move.

One morning in August, though, I did finally get his attention long enough to ask him what would be a good time for us to sit down and do the interview. "How about Tuesday morning, around 9:30?" he said. "Things should be quieted down by then, and we can talk." I said OK, but when I came in on Tuesday at about 9:20 with my cassette recorder in hand, the place was in an uproar. Janine hadn't come in yet, and Kay was off, so it was just Annie behind the counter. And so of course Tom was pitching in, waiting on tables, clearing tables, putting on another pot of coffee, buttering slice after slice of toast as it piled up in the mouth of the toaster oven—meanwhile still working the register, working the lottery machine, slicing the meat... I didn't even try to catch his eye. But when I got to the register and handed him the money for my breakfast, he apologized and said, "How about Thursday morning, same time?"

But Thursday morning was just as crazy, even with Janine there, and so he asked me if I could come back at around 5:30 that evening, by which time he promised that things would have settled down.

He was right. I got there a few minutes after five, and finally the place had pretty much emptied out. There were a couple of guys still sitting at the end table under the clock arguing about the Mets, and Israel, the Guatemalan short-order cook, was still standing at the grill, as impassive as ever. The overhead TV, which no one ever seemed to watch, was tuned to a financial channel with the sound off. The crawl at the bottom of the screen reported that AIG had just had its biggest drop in history.

I took a seat in one of the booths along the wall, ordered a Coke, and a few minutes later Tom slipped into the seat across from me. He's about five foot six, bald with a curly grey fringe, and I noticed that he had a pretty good tan, which made me wonder whether he'd managed to find a few hours over the weekend to play golf. He was wearing a copper-colored short-sleeved shirt with white stripes, khaki shorts with a brown belt, and crisp white sneakers with the white socks pulled up.

"So Paulie," he said, "what's up?" Tom was not a guy to waste words—or syllables either, if he didn't have to. Too much to do.

I told him that even though I wanted him to tell me all about Fred and Pete's, I wanted to start with his own story. "And this is probably going to be the first of a couple of conversations," I warned him. "Because I imagine you're going to be distracted."

"Right," Tom nodded.

"So when and where were you born?" I asked.

"Trenton, New Jersey. 1951."

"Where in Trenton?"

"The old McKinley Hospital in North Trenton."

"And where did your family live?" I asked.

"We lived in North Trenton, on Wayne Avenue," Tom replied. "214 Wayne Avenue."

"And you've got a brother, right?" I remembered Dave Stout telling me that he used to coach Tom and his brother on his baseball team when they were kids.

Tom nodded. "I have an older brother, two years older, and a younger sister."

"Oh, a sister, too?" I said. "Is she still around?"

"She lives in L.A.," Tom replied. "My brother lives in Flint, Michigan."

"But you stayed here."

"Yep," Tom said. "Never left."

A middle-aged woman in a Long Beach Island t-shirt came in and wandered up to the green lottery machine, looking around. Tom leapt to his feet to help her, excusing himself and promising to be right back. I had the distinct impression that he was relieved to be moving again. Meanwhile, an older man took a seat in the booth right behind me, and when the waitress came over—a young woman I'd never seen before—he ordered a Coke and a cheeseburger. "You want fries with that?" she asked him.

Tom returned and took his seat across from me.

"This is going to be tough, Tom," I said.

He nodded. "Until we lock the door. So anyway, older brother, two years older..."

"Right," I said. "What's his name?"

"Fred. And one sister: Susan. About three years younger than me. Or maybe five years younger, something like that."

"And you grew up in Trenton?" I asked.

"Til I was about five years old," Tom replied. "Then we moved to California. We went to California and my father was a milkman for movie stars."

"No kidding!"

Tom shook his head. "We lived right in L.A. He used to be the milkman for Zsa Zsa Gabor, Robert Mitchum, Ida Lupina."

"I had no idea," I said, trying to imagine Robert Mitchum in his trench coat coming out his front door in the morning to pick up the milk bottles that Tom's father had left for him.

"Yeah," Tom continued, "we went out there because he said, 'If you want to be a good athlete, you have to go where the weather's warm.' So we all shipped out and went to California—and then fifteen months later he got homesick and decided to come back to Trenton."

"You're kidding...!"

"We lived in Santa Monica," Tom recalled, a touch of pride in his voice. "Right near Muscle Beach. You remember how in *Marcus Welby*, right before his show, he would always walk this path along the beach? That's where we lived. We lived right there."

"Isn't that something!" I exclaimed. "But only for fifteen months?"

"Actually, eighteen months," Tom said. "We got back here in '58, and my father went to work for the Borden's Milk Company that he was with prior to leaving. I was eight years old at the time, or maybe seven. And then in '63, he opened the deli."

I took a sip of my Coke. "So how did that happen?"

"It was an investment with his partner," Tom explained. "They lived five houses away from each other, and one night, the four of them—the wives and all—decided to go out to dinner and a movie. And on the way back, my father said, 'You know, they're gonna build a shopping strip from the Acme to the A & P,' and so they said, 'Why don't we open up a deli there?'"

"You mean there were no stores here yet?"

"There was *nothing* here," Tom declared. "There was the Acme and there was the A & P. And then Joe Cion was going to put this strip in between, so my father said, 'Let's open up a deli.' And neither of them didn't have a pot to piss in or a window to throw it out," he added.

"No money at all?" I asked, incredulous.

Tom shook his head.

"So why a deli?" I asked. "He was a milkman, right?"

"Yeah," Tom said. "You know, he didn't know nothing about the shoe business; he didn't know nothing about the carpet business—but he knew food. So…"

A woman had come in, wanting help at the deli counter. Tom jumped up and sliced her a quarter pound each of ham and turkey and a half a pound of American cheese to take home for dinner. When he came back, I suggested that maybe we should take a break until after he'd closed the doors, and meanwhile I could just hang out.

He asked me if I'd like something to eat, and fixed me an Italian hot dog on the grill—basically, a hot dog with grilled peppers and potatoes on a hoagie roll. When he brought it over, he looked tired, and I asked him what time he got up every morning.

"Four-twenty," he said. "Wake up at four-twenty, get out of bed at four-thirty, leave the house at ten to five, open the door at five—like clockwork."

I groaned. "So what time do you go to bed at night?"

"Ten o'clock," he replied. "Except sometimes when I'm watching a football game and I get stupid and get involved in it…" He sighed, and then he was off again, to help another customer.

I put some mustard on the hot dog and looked around the place, paying a little more attention than I normally did. There was blond paneling on the walls, and there were about a dozen booths, stretching from the refrigerator cases in the front to the men's room in the back. The counter, I noticed, had half a dozen seats on either side, with a gap in the middle for the waitresses to get out from behind the counter. The grill was to the left of this gap, with a double row of coffee mugs stacked on top, upside down—presumably to keep anything from landing in them.

Over by the wall clock in the back, there was a handwritten dinner menu, which, in contrast to the items on the big menu board hanging behind the counter, changed from day to day. Today's entrees included "hot roast beef, chicken parm, roast pork, marsala chicken, and spaghetti," and the sides were green beans and mashed potatoes. It sounded pretty good, and I decided that one of these days, I'd have to stop in for dinner.

There were several plaques on the wall, including a recent one dated May 3, 2008, that actually had an American flag inside the frame. It read: "This flag of the United States of America is presented to Tommy Armenti for your support of the combat operations assigned to the XXX National Corps, Iraq." And there was a framed *Trenton Times* story, dated July 4, 2008, with the headline: WITH PRIDE AND GRATITUDE, but I couldn't read the rest of it from where I was sitting.

As I was taking all this in, a retired roofer and former high school basketball star by the name of John Wilwol—known for some reason as Johnny Woo, and dressed today in a navy blue t-shirt with "Roofers Union 30 and 30-B" emblazoned across the back in big gold letters—came by my booth, quietly wiped the table with a rag, and cleared away my plate. I would see John fairly often in the mornings, and sometimes at lunch; and now here he was at dinner time, apparently helping out. We usually said hello, but John was a fairly quiet guy, and he seemed even less talkative than usual this evening, so I just nodded and said thanks.

Meanwhile, the old guy in the booth behind me had been flirting with the waitress, and now was needling Tom about closing so early.

"So what do you want me to do?" Tom asked him. "Stay open from six in the morning til one at night?"

"You could put in a pizza oven," the old man suggested.

"I *had* a pizza oven," Tom replied.

"Is it still there?"

"No," Tom said, "I've got a convection oven in there now."

"You could make pizza in there," the old man persisted.

"Sure," Tom said patiently. "Listen, at seven-thirty you could shoot a gun down this street and not hit anybody—seven-thirty at night. Everybody goes home—especially in winter. We used to stay open til ten o'clock at night at one time. How nuts was *that*?"

The old man relented. It was obviously not the first time that he and Tom had had this conversation.

Tom came back to my booth, wiping his hands with a paper napkin. "We're done now," he promised, and took his seat across from me again.

"OK," I said skeptically, not really convinced that we weren't going to be interrupted again. "So your dad saw this place, he saw the opportunity..."

"Yeah," Tom nodded. "So they went to the landlord, and when the strip opened, they opened this place. The rent was four-fifty a month back then," he added dryly. "Now it's forty-five hundred. So things have gone up a little bit."

I asked him what the place had looked like when they first opened in 1963.

"Basically the same," Tom replied. "We only had six booths instead of twelve, and we had no tables down the middle. But the counter was in the same position; the grill was in the same position. So it was the same idea as it is now."

"And how about you?"

"I was twelve—washing dishes," Tom said. "I remember one time I'm washing dishes in the back, and I have the door open. And my father comes in and says, 'What do you got the door open for?' And I say, 'I'm air-drying the dishes.'"

I laughed.

"And he says, 'Close the goddamn door and start using the towel!'" Tom concluded with a chuckle.

I asked Tom whether his brother worked here, too.

Tom nodded. "He was here a bit, but he wasn't too much into it, you know. He was more into academics.

"But you got into it right away," I said.

"Yeah, I did," Tom replied. "Right away."

He checked his watch and got up to lock the door, but before he could get there, another man came in to buy a lottery ticket. And then another. And then another woman wanting to buy lunch meat. For a moment, I almost felt sorry for Tom, and then I remembered that, after all, these were all paying customers—and that you could never have too many of those.

"When these people leave, I'm going to lock the door," Tom promised again when he returned.

I nodded. "So anyway, you started here when you were twelve, washing dishes in the back…"

"And two years later I was up front cutting lunch meat," Tom said, picking up where he'd left off. "Back then, I used to work Saturdays and Sundays only. You'd work twenty-three hours on weekends: from seven to seven on Saturdays, and from seven to six on Sundays. That was the schedule."

"Pretty demanding for a teenager," I observed. "So Tom, tell me a little more about your dad. What kind of a person was he?"

"You never met him?"

"No," I said. "And I never met Pete, either."

"Well, my father had a different personality from most people," Tom recalled with obvious pride. "He associated with rich people, poor people, gamblers, intelligent people, people with no education—he'd get along with anybody. He would say, 'I could charm a rattlesnake if I had to.' And he always liked to sing. He'd be in here, and he'd start singing out loud."

"What would he sing?"

Tom shrugged. "Oh, he'd sing some Italian song, you know. But now Pete, he was the other way—more matter of fact. You know, 'This is how we do it.' My father didn't give a shit. He just did what he wanted to do when he wanted to do it."

"So did they go in fifty-fifty?" I asked.

"Yup," Tom replied. "Fifty-fifty."

I was curious where they'd gotten the money to start the business, given that, as Tom had so delicately put it, they didn't have a pot to piss in or a window to throw it out.

"Borrowed from everyone," Tom answered. "He'd go to the milkman, go to the meat man, and he'd say, 'I need a case. I'll pay you ten dollars a week.'"

"And they did?"

"Oh yeah," Tom said. "I mean, they had nothing—just themselves. And them two were like day and night. Just two different opposites. And how they stayed in business together for eighteen years is amazing."

"Were they both out here?" I asked.

Tom nodded. "Oh yeah, they were both out here. One of them would be cooking, and the other was up front with the lunch meats. And when they first opened up, both their wives—my mother and Pete's wife—worked here, too. Back then, they didn't have delis in the Acme or the A & P. There was none of that. So if you wanted baloney, you had to go to a deli. So years ago, when I was fourteen or fifteen, we would have like four people cutting meat on Saturdays."

I was surprised. "Oh, so the deli really *was* the main business back when they started? Before the lottery?"

"Oh yeah. Before the lottery, before the catering. And now it's kind of like it's turned around." Tom looked bemused as he paused and looked around his place. "Now we have twelve booths, we seat seventy-four people, catering is much bigger... The deli is a thing of the past."

Maybe, I thought, but people still seem to come in with their orders. Then it occurred to me that my wife and I actually do get our deli meat at the supermarket, and I felt a twinge of guilt.

"So," I said, trying to get us back to Tom's story, "you started out up here when you were fourteen or so, cutting meat."

Tom nodded. "Fourteen or fifteen, cutting meat illegally. But back then," he quickly added, "they didn't have the rules they have now—at least I don't think they did."

"And then you went off to college, right?"

"No," he said, "then I went to one year of prep school in Massachusetts. My brother had gone to Brown University and I wanted to go to Brown, too, but the soccer coach at Brown said, 'I want you to go to one year of prep school first.' So I said, 'OK, I'll go to prep school for a year,' and I went to a place called Winchendon Prep, near Worcester, Mass. Four kids in a class."

"Oh, wow..." I was surprised. Tom didn't seem like the prep school type. "So that was only your second time out of Jersey, right?"

"Right," Tom replied. "L.A. for fifteen months and then a year up there."

"And you were playing soccer?"

"Yeah," he said. "And I got accepted to several schools up there—Amherst, U. Mass... But then I got a letter from Maryland, and they offered me a full scholarship for soccer. Four full years. So I went to Maryland."

I was impressed. "You must've been one hell of a soccer player," I remarked. "And you say you got accepted at Amherst?"

"Yeah," he said, as if it were no big deal, "but not Brown."

I told him that I thought Amherst was every bit as good as Brown.

"Yeah," he agreed, "they're both fine schools."

"Any regrets?"

"No, not at all. Nooo!" Tom was emphatic. "Maryland was a fun time," he added with a grin.

He graduated from the University of Maryland in 1974 with a degree in economics, and then waited two years for the next state police class to open up—the ninety-second state police class. But he didn't finish.

"At the time, I was engaged," he explained. "So I left the state police academy with six weeks to go. Pete was ready to get out—out of the deli—so I left the academy and bought the deli. With six weeks left to go in the academy," he repeated.

I was stunned. "Jeez..."

"Yeah," Tom agreed wryly.

"And your dad was still here?" I asked.

"Yeah, he was still here," Tom replied. "He'd come in at four and he'd work til seven at night so I could go home."

"But you bought it from both of them?"

"Yeah."

"So you were the sole owner at that point," I said. "You weren't splitting with your dad or anything."

Tom shook his head. "No, no. He was basically an employee."

"And where did you get the money to buy the place?" I asked, wondering how in the world a young man who had just dropped out of the state police academy six weeks shy of graduation could have raised that kind of capital.

"They were very nice about it," Tom recalled with a smile. "I didn't have a penny, so they let me pay them every Sunday for the next six years."

"No kidding!" I said. "So tell me, what made you decide to do that? I mean, that was a big change. First you got a degree in economics. Then you went to the state police academy. And then, all of a sudden, when Pete quits, you decide that you're going to do the deli. What happened?"

Tom smiled again. "There was the opportunity to make money. I mean, it's true, it's a seven day a week job, but I did quite well over the years."

"So it was economics," I said.

"Yeah," Tom nodded. "Absolutely."

I asked Tom about Viet Nam, since we were the same age and that had put us at prime time for the Viet Nam draft.

"A student deferment," he said. "And that's when they had the lottery. I don't know if you remember the lottery..."

"Sure do," I said. "What was your number?"

"Two-fifty-four," Tom replied.

"Three-sixty-one," I said.

"Oh my God!" Tom exclaimed. "My buddy was number four. He was at Villanova at the time, so he didn't have to go. But he was number four. And

I was two-fifty-four. I was at Winchendon Prep that day. Amazing how you can remember, huh?"

I nodded. "I was in New York City."

"So anyway," Tom said, getting back to the story, "then I took over here."

"And were you married at that point already?" I asked.

"Yeah, I got married," Tom replied. "Then I bought it. So they worked a little longer. They wanted to stay on a little longer, and then I bought it after that."

I was confused. "So when did you actually buy it?"

"March of '81," Tom said. "Twenty-seven years ago." Which, quickly doing the math in my head, I figured must have been about three years after he'd left the state police academy.

"That's a lot of hours," I commented.

"Yeah," Tom agreed. "And a lot of days in a row without a day off."

"So what's the best part for you?" I asked him.

"The customers," Tom replied without a moment's hesitation. Then he glanced up and noticed that the last customer had finally left. "I gotta lock up now," he told me as he quickly slipped out of the booth, pulling the keys out of his pocket as he headed for the door, "because every time..."

"Yeah, sure," I laughed. "Go ahead."

"So you paid them off over six years," I said, when Tom had settled back into the booth across from me. He finally seemed to relax.

He nodded. "Yeah. Pete was the first three years, and then my father was the next three years," he said.

"And your dad stayed on?"

"Yeah, like I said, he'd just come in for a couple of hours in the afternoon. No big deal. And then every January, February, March, my parents would go down to Florida. But Pete was out a hundred percent."

"Did he ever come by?" I asked.

"Oh yeah," Tom replied, "Pete would come in, have a cup of coffee. And we had an agreement that, you know, 'You need lunch meat, you just go cut it yourself and take it home—don't worry about it.' That was like his pension plan."

I laughed. "So you said the best part is the customers," I said, coming back to where we were before he'd locked up.

"Yeah, I think so," Tom said, smiling to himself. "Getting up in the morning is no fun, and standing on your feet twelve hours is no fun. But the customers are good. I mean, you get some pain in the asses, but ninety-five percent are good people."

"And what's the worst part of the job?"

"The hours," Tom replied. "Every morning I come in at five, and here we are, after six, and I go home after this."

"And are you really working seven days a week?"

"Oh yeah," Tom assured me. "I've got about six hundred and seventy days in a row now without a day off."

"Six hundred and seventy days?" I couldn't believe it.

"In September it'll be two years," Tom added.

"Tommy," I said, "that's crazy!"

"Yeah..."

"How does your wife feel about it?"

"She's good about it," he replied. "She knows that's how it has to be. I mean, there was days when the kids were little that I'd go to work, they'd be sleeping. I'd come home and they'd be back in bed already. So she'd bring them down here for dinner just so I could see them."

"How many kids do you have?" I asked him.

"Two," Tom responded. "My daughter Brooke, she's twenty-eight now, and my son Kent, who's twenty-three. And," he added, "they didn't want any part of it."

"Kent was here earlier, wasn't he?" I asked, recalling that I'd seen him working behind the counter many times over the years.

Tom sighed and looked up at me. "He was here because he wasn't working elsewhere, you know?" he replied sardonically. "He said if he owned a place, he'd open at eleven and close at one-thirty."

I laughed. "And Brooke? What's she doing?"

"Insurance," Tom said. "New Jersey Manufacturers—in the home-owners department."

"Does she still live here in town?" I asked, wondering whether I'd seen her here at the deli, too.

"Yeah," Tom said. "When my parents died..." He paused, and a momentary shadow of pain crossed his face. "My father passed away in '93—in fact, fifteen years ago today we buried him—and my mother died in '99. My brother and sister wanted no part of the house we all grew up in, so I bought it off of them, and she lives there."

"So you still see her," I said.

"Yeah," he nodded. "It's only two miles away."

"But neither of them wants any part of the business?"

Tom shook his head. "Nooo!"

I took a sip of what was left of my Coke, which was pretty much down to the ice melt by this time. It was strange to be in Fred and Pete's when it was so still. Even the silent TV over the kitchen door was turned off. There was only the quiet rumble of the air conditioner and the lingering fragrance of grilled meat and onions and fried potatoes that still permeated the air around us.

"So, Tom," I said, "you told me recently five more years and you're done. Is that right?"

"I hope so," he sighed.

"And then what? Do you think you'll be able to sell it?"

"Yeah," he said. "I mean, it's a turn-key operation. If somebody wanted to just come in tomorrow morning, turn the grill on, turn the coffee machine on, and do the same thing we've been doing, you'll make it pay."

But, I wondered, would anybody else be willing to put in thirteen hours a day, seven days a week, year in and year out, to stay on top of the place the way that Tom had? And if not, could a place like this actually continue to thrive? And what about the "people" side of it? Tom might not sing the Italian songs like his father had, but he knew all the regulars by name, and they all knew him. Would Fred and Pete's still be Fred and Pete's without that?

"So tell me about some of the characters," I said. "Some of the people that stand out for you as you think back."

"Oh God," Tom cried. "Well, there's been two governors that've been here. Christie Whitman and Jim Florio. And Florio was amazing. He was here four times. He came in here one time and he met my kids. And the place was crowded. I mean jammed. And then he comes in here again a month later. Two o'clock on a Saturday, I'm ready to close, and a state trooper pulls up and says, 'The Governor and Mrs. Florio are out front. They want to know if they can have lunch with you.' So I say, 'Sure, come on in.' So the three of us sit down to have lunch, right over there"—Tom pointed at one of the nearby tables—"and he says, 'How are Brooke and Kent?' I say, 'I can't believe you remember their names!' And he says, 'Yeah, I remember everybody's name.' Just a down-to-earth man," Tom concluded. "Surrounded by bad people, but a good man."

"So you had Florio, who's a Democrat, and Whitman, who's a Republican," I said.

"Yeah," Tom replied. "Both sides of the fence. Whitman was here twice. She came in with a group of people. I don't know if she was campaigning and we were a local stop..."

"And what about Alito?"

"The Supreme Court judge? Yeah, he's been here," Tom said. "He's a year older than I am, and we went to high school together at Steinert. I knew him back then, and I thought, Given a chance, he's smart enough to be a Supreme Court judge. That's how smart he was. Nice guy, too," he added. "And his mother lives right around the corner. She still comes in once in a while. Of course, now she has a helper with her—she's ninety-two or something, but still sharp as a tack."

I mentioned to Tom that Fred and Pete's used to have a reputation as a place where a lot of the local politicians would hang out, and asked him if that was still the case.

"Years and years ago," he recalled, "the school board members all met here. The local officials. It was funny because it was both sides of the fence. You had the Republicans sitting in this booth"—he pointed at our table—"and the Democrats sitting right behind you. They'd both be listening in on each other, trying to hear what the other guys were saying. But that's all changed now. Now it's more of a social club. You know, people come here, and if somebody's not here for three days, it's 'Is Jim sick?' 'Is Bob hurt?' So, you know, everybody's made some good friendships."

I nodded. I had myself.

"You know," Tom continued, "you see some of these people day in and day out. And it's funny, they come at the same time, sit in the same seats, order the same things." He chuckled. "Creatures of habit we are."

I asked him whether there were any customers in particular that he remembered from the past.

"I don't know," he reflected, taking a deep breath and slowly letting it out. "You go back to some of the older people, years and years ago. They always have one little joke to tell you or something. They're good people. They get older and older, and before you know it, they're sick and they fade away."

"I know," I murmured, and I thought of Jake Wig, a retired builder in his late eighties who had passed away a year or two ago. Jake had lost his wife of more than sixty years, and he used to sit at the counter with me most mornings and tell me about the old days in Trenton and about all the great musical groups that he used to play and sing with when he was a young man.

"We had a lady—Doris Schmidt," Tom said. "Nice old lady. She'd come in, play a couple of numbers. And Daisy used to come in here. Now Daisy's in a walker. So you see them going down hill."

I asked him how long John Wilwol had been coming in.

"Johnny that just now left?" he asked.

"Yeah," I said. "The retired roofer."

"Johnny's been coming here maybe seven, eight, nine years," Tom guessed. "Since he retired."

"Seems like he's here all the time," I observed.

"Breakfast, lunch, and dinner," Tom agreed. "And he'll help out. Like he sweeps up the floor. He's not getting paid for anything. He just likes to help out. And then there's Big Bill, he comes in and he's here breakfast, lunch and dinner every day. So when he's not here, you know he's sick."

I said that I didn't think I knew Big Bill.

"You do know him," Tom insisted. "He was in here today—a tall guy. You could interview him." He paused, trying to think of who else I might talk to. "And then there's all the kids who've been employees." He smiled to himself as he thought back. "You can't imagine how many cars and education bills this place has paid for. We had one fella, Joe, that started here when he was a senior in high school—I'm going back to maybe '64. Now he's a retired CIA agent."

"No kidding!"

"Yeah, he used to work with the Marines," Tom said. "Gary DeLorrenzo is a big shot with an investment firm in New York, and Greg Cox, who was here for twelve years—he's an eye surgeon now. Angelo Onofri, he's a lawyer in Trenton with the prosecutor's office, and then there's been four or five kids that have worked here and that have married each other."

"Wow!"

"Oh yeah," Tom said, with obvious pride. "Joe Lane and Cathy Lemming got married, Jessica Fava and Steve Nitti got married…" He paused, then shook his head. "I can't think of the others right now."

"You've also got an international cast here," I observed. "You've got the Ukrainian guy—Cash—and the other guy who used to work the grill…"

"Ostap," Tom said. "Ostap Krupa. He came over here, couldn't hardly speak English. Now he's an electrician. And when Cash first came here—Volodymyr Kush is his real name, but we always call him Cash—he weighed about a hundred and ten pounds. Now he's one-eighty and he's got arms like tree trunks."

"Yeah, no kidding," I agreed. "And then you've got Israel."

"From Guatemala," Tom said. "And Gonzalo is from Mexico." Israel was his current short-order cook, and Gonzalo, the dishwasher. It had occurred to me more than once that the two of them were like Cervantes' heroes in reverse: Israel, short and squat like Sancho Panza, and Gonzalo, tall and thin like Don Quixote.

"They don't seem to speak a lot of English," I commented. "How do you communicate with them?"

"They understand," Tom assured me. "We're not exactly doing brain surgery here. You know, a hamburger's a hamburger. Cheese, yes or no. So there you go."

I nodded.

"And as far as waitresses are concerned," Tom continued, "three hundred girls must've worked here over the years."

"Any standouts you can think of?"

"Oh yeah," Tom replied with sudden enthusiasm. "There was this one girl—Debbie Hutzel was her name—she was only maybe eighteen at the time, but she could run the whole store by herself. I remember one Fourth of July we were here; I was on the grill, and she took care of the whole store all by herself.

That's how fast she was," he said, his voice still filled with admiration after all these years.

"And Ann," he added. "Ann can really move when she wants to. She can wait on a lot of people at one time, and keep her mind straight as to who gets what."

I agreed—although for me, what made Ann a great waitress had a lot more to do with how she treated people than how fast she could work or how many orders she could keep track of. But then I wasn't looking at it from the business end.

"And then there's the Keating family," Tom went on. "They had four girls, and all four of them worked here. And the Abbott family had *five* girls and one boy, and all of *them* worked here at one time or another over the years. I mean, the older one started, and as she got into bigger and better jobs, before you know it here comes another fifteen-year-old. I ask her 'Who are you?' and she says, 'I'm *Mary* Abbott.' Then she'd leave, and later on *Susie* Abbott would come along." He shook his head and chuckled to himself as he remembered them all.

I asked him whether any of them ever came back.

Tom paused and stretched. It had been another long day. "Yeah, once in a while I'll see them," he replied, stifling a yawn. "Now they're all married with kids, you know. Some of them are grandparents."

"It's a really special place," I told him. "You know, there's not a lot of community left—not here, not most places that I've been. But this place gives people that."

Tom nodded. "Yeah," he reflected. "We've been here forty-five years now. It's the only original store in the whole center, and it's basically stayed the same. It's been a good store for everybody."

But there had been some changes—such as, for example, the fact that Fred and Pete's was no longer a political meeting place but more of what Tom called a "social club." I asked him whether there'd been any other significant changes over the years.

"Well," he said, "the store got bigger restaurant-wise and on the catering end, with less of the deli. The deli's more part of the whole thing now. You still need the deli to accent the rest of the store. And when you do a party and you do the party trays, you need a deli case that you're going to cut the meat from."

"How big is the catering?' I asked him. "I mean as a share of your business, how much is the catering, how much is the food, and how much is the lottery?"

Tom thought for a moment before answering. "The lottery used to do twice as much as it does now," he said. "Because of the demographics of the area, and the casinos. You don't hardly see anybody in line buying lottery tickets that's under forty years old anymore. They all want to go down to Atlantic City to the casinos—they want the fun down there. The older people will play the casinos, but they're on fixed incomes, so they play less. So now the restaurant is probably sixty percent of the business, and then the catering does maybe thirty percent of what the whole store does."

I was a little surprised that the lottery was such a small share of the business, given that somebody always seemed to be waiting at the green machine for their chance at the big multi-million dollar jackpot. But I knew they did a lot of catering, and that Vicki forever seemed to be fixing enormous trays of hoagies, piled high with all kinds of sliced meats, cheeses, tomatoes, peppers, onions and lettuce. I asked Tom how he'd gotten involved in the catering part of the business.

He grinned. "It started out, a lady calls me up and says, 'Can you make me a couple of trays?' I don't want to lose the business, so I say, 'Yeah, I'll make it.' I'd never made anything like that in my life, but I'd made it at home—so I just made more of it. Her name is Josephine Tancredo, and I always kid her when I see her. I tell her, 'You're the one who put me in this position.' So that's how we started, and now we've done as many as twelve jobs in one day—twelve different parties in one day."

"Wow!"

"Oh yeah," Tom said nonchalantly. "Right around Christmas, prior to Christmas, all the different state offices having their parties."

"Well, I know you've got the panel truck out there," I said. "And the bigger..."

"Right. And the regular van," Tom interjected, and then chuckled. "You know, I started out with a Volkswagen truck. A man used to come in here—Joe Carroll. Joe Carroll was a bartender around the corner, and he'd come in and say, 'Tom, I need ten dollars.' I'd give him a ten. 'Tom, I need twenty dollars.' I'd give him a twenty. 'Tom, I need a five.' I'd give him a five. Finally, we figured out he owes me about five hundred dollars. So one day he fills out the deed to his Volkswagen truck, hands me the keys and says, 'Here, the truck's yours. We're even.'"

I laughed. Pure Jersey!

"Big Joe Carroll," Tom murmured wistfully, shaking his head. "He was funny—a good man. There's been a lot of people over the years."

I wondered what Tom did when he wasn't working—besides sleep. I remembered him telling me a while back how he had bought a big new flat-screen TV along with two top-of-the-line new La-Z-Boy recliners to set in front of it, one for him and one for his wife, and how on the very first night when he'd come home from work to watch the game on his big new TV, he'd fallen fast asleep almost as soon as he'd settled into his wonderful new recliner. "Never did see that game," he'd told me ruefully.

"So, Tom," I asked him now, "what do you do when you're not working? Anything besides watching the games?"

"That, and I play golf," he replied with a sigh. "But it's so time-consuming. And right now I'm probably working more hours than I ever worked before. Before, I used to have J. R. here—Jim Valdora. When he was here, or when Volodymyr was working longer hours—he's got some other job now with benefits—I could leave the store for five hours and know that it'd be OK. But I don't have that liberty now, so I haven't played in quite a while."

"But you've got a tan," I said. "How'd you manage to get a tan?"

"We're doing a lot of outdoor cook-outs—off-premise cooking," Tom explained. "Like tomorrow we're doing one for the custodians, and Sunday we're doing one over at DiPaolo's turkey farm. Next week, I have another one for the Cranbury Mayor's Association—we'll do lunch and dinner right there. So I'm outside for those, and it's a good change."

"I can imagine," I said. "So do you have time for anything else in your life?"

"No," he said flatly. "Don't travel, don't do none of that good stuff. Just look forward to five years from now, maybe."

I asked him what was going to happen five years from now.

"I'm going to pack it in," he replied evenly.

"And then what?"

Tom shrugged. "I'll do something else. I'm sure I'm not going to sit home all day. But I want to do something that I'm off on weekends. You know," he said, "I never have Saturdays and Sundays off. Maybe I'll go to work for Sam's Club in the butcher's department. Who knows? Three days a week, enough to pay for dinner and golf." He shrugged again, then added, "If the stock market don't straighten out, nobody's gonna be retiring, you know."

I had a hard time imagining Tom taking orders from someone else in the butcher's department at Sam's Club or anywhere else, but I had an even harder time imaging him sitting still at home—or sitting still anywhere. "So you don't think you're going to miss this place?" I asked him.

"I'll miss the people," he said. "I'm not going to miss the hours—coming in at five o'clock every morning. That's the difference from Fred and Pete. They had two people then: Fred and Pete. You know, 'I'm going home, you're in charge, Pete.' 'OK, Fred, I'll work.' And they had no catering back then. And no lottery when they first started. That didn't come out until about 1980, maybe 1985."

I asked him if he remembered when they went smoke-free.

"Oh yeah," Tom said proudly. "We were the first in the county."

"Is that right? How did that happen?" I was genuinely amazed. I remembered the first few times I'd stuck my head in the door, back when we'd first moved to Mercerville in the mid-1980's, Fred and Pete's was almost as full of cigarette smoke as the bingo games we used to have to work over at Our Lady of Sorrows.

"It was December 7," Tom said. "I'm gonna say year-wise it had to be 19... 94. I'm doing a catering job that night and my wife and kids come in. They're gonna take all the pictures down to clean them. They spray, and the brown smoke's coming off. And they spray again. Filthy dirty, you know. So I say, 'If this is what the *pictures* are, what the hell am I breathing?'"

"Wow..."

"It was December 7," Tom repeated. "I'll never forget that. Pearl Harbor Day. We put up a sign that said, 'As of January 1, there will be no more smoking in this store.'"

"So before it was mandated," I said.

"Oh," Tom chuckled, "nobody even *knew* about it. Like I said, I was the first one in the county. And people told me, 'You will go broke. You won't have nobody in the store.' And I said, 'Well, either I'm gonna go broke or I'm gonna die from the smoke, and I've made my decision.' My father died of leukemia. My mother died of lung cancer. And they were both here all those years, all the time."

He shook his head sadly, then went on. "So in the beginning, some people didn't come in. But they're all back. And it's funny, because what happened is that all of a sudden people say, 'No smoking?' And so I got families coming in now—I'm talking about 1994, '95. Now suddenly I got people coming in and they're bringing their three-year-olds. Before that, they used to say, 'I'd like to come, but I can't bring my three-year-old.' But now, all of a sudden, it smells different in here."

"Now you can smell the food," I said.

"Yeah," Tom nodded. "Before that, I remember one time I walk by and Big Bill's got a cigarette in each hand. He didn't even realize it. And I say, 'Bill, you have a problem? You nervous today?' And he says, 'No, no, no,' and he puts the stubby one out."

I checked my cassette recorder and saw that there were still a few minutes left on the tape, so I decided that I might as well use it up, as long as Tom was willing and able to keep talking.

"So Tom," I said, "tell me about the chairs out front. How did that get started?" Those white plastic chairs out in front of Fred and Pete's were a local landmark. If you said Fred and Pete's to somebody in Trenton, they'd say, "You mean that place with the chairs out front?"

"The chairs started with John Delorenzo," Tom replied. "John came around—I'm going back, I don't know, twenty years ago—and he had a lawn chair in his car. And he was hanging around out front, so he puts up his lawn chair. So then other friends bring *their* lawn chairs. And I say, 'Wait a minute. This is ridiculous.' So I went and purchased six plastic chairs. I think they were three dollars each. And so the guys started hanging, and before you know it, now on a Sunday morning there's thirty-five guys out there." He chuckled softly to himself. "Some people moaned because they can't walk down the sidewalk with all the guys there. But I said, 'I'm sorry, that's the way it is.' And so it's a meeting place for a lot of people."

"Sure is," I agreed. Even when the weather was lousy, there were usually at least two or three of them out there—and sometimes a woman, too, although not too often.

"A lot of these are North Trenton people," Tom continued. "From Chambersburg. And years ago, when they grew up, that's what you'd do. After dinner, you'd go hang on the corner. Well, you can't do that anymore. What corner are you gonna hang on?"

"Five Points," I chuckled—the incredibly busy five-way intersection a block away that I drove through to get to Fred and Pete's.

"Yeah, exactly," Tom nodded. "So now they hang out at Fred and Pete's."

"And Richie can smoke his cigar," I added.

"Yeah, he can smoke his cigar, and they can all smoke their cigarettes," Tom said. "So it works."

The heavy rumble of the air conditioning suddenly clicked off, and for a moment the place was completely still.

"You know," Tom suddenly declared, leaning back in his seat, "I think the day that I retire—and I told you before I hope it's five years from now; that'll be the fiftieth anniversary—if I can pull it off, I'm gonna throw a big block party right here in the parking lot. And I'll probably end up getting arrested and everything else, but I want to throw a nice party, and everyone in the township is welcome."

"Fantastic!" I said. "Because, you know, I think the whole community's got a lot to be grateful to you for."

Tom nodded. "Yeah, well, they've been good to me."

"You've created a space for people that just wouldn't be here," I told him. "You can't hang out like this at McDonald's."

"No," he agreed, "they don't want you there."

"Or Applebee's across the street," I added. "What's their motto? Something about the neighborhood?"

"'Eating good in the neighborhood,'" Tom intoned solemnly.

"Right," I laughed. "Have those places hurt your business at all?"

Tom shook his head. "No, they're a totally different deal," he explained. "I mean, I've still got a five dollar dinner. They don't even have an appetizer over there for five dollars."

I asked him how he'd been able to keep his prices so low.

"It's been tough," he acknowledged. "Because if you look... I mean, I go to other places to eat myself sometimes, and I'm saying, 'I can't *believe* that they're charging seventeen dollars for a chicken parm dinner when I'm charging five!' Of course, I don't really make any money on the dinners. It's more that I have the help here, the store has to be open because of the lottery and everything else. So I might as well have some reason to bring the people in. And maybe they'll buy a loaf of bread on the way out."

"Any regrets?"

"No!" Tom exclaimed. "None. Although sometimes I look back and think that maybe I should've stuck out the state thing with the police," he added wistfully. "I would have retired with a pension and benefits. Skip Monyer told me, 'Go with the State.' And I told him, 'Skip, you don't make enough money.' He was head of personnel for the Board of Health. But now his son's probably making every bit of what I make—and he's off a hundred and fifty days a year."

I smiled. "Tom, have you ever spent any time in one of those state office buildings down in Trenton?" I asked him. "I mean on a regular working day?"

"Yeah," he said dubiously.

"Well, you wouldn't want to spend your life doing that, would you?" I insisted. "That's forty years of your life, day in, day out. I mean, here you may be working your tail off, but at least it's good stuff."

"Yeah," Tom conceded. "It's fun. I've had a lot of fun times here. And if you're not super, super busy, you get to sit down with... Like tonight, to sit down with those guys back there and bullshit about baseball. Or to talk about, you know, who went to the casino the other day, who lost or won."

"And the thing that amazes me," I said, "is that you'll be in the middle of a conversation like that and then, just like that, you'll turn around and take care of the person at the counter."

Tom shrugged. "Well, you grow up here, that was part of the ballgame. You know, get the customer in, make him happy, and get him out. And by keeping the prices reasonable, I get these people coming back every day."

Including me, I thought.

"I mean, if I were to say bacon and eggs is six dollars, the customer might say, 'You know what? Maybe I'll only go two days a week.' So now the waitresses get hurt, the store looks empty—and I don't make any more money," Tom concluded. "You know," he added, "I met my wife in here."

"Is that right?"

"She worked for Bell Telephone," Tom said, "and her and her friend Vicki, who now works up front, were coming in for lunch. I was maybe twenty-five, and I was working the store. And it's, 'What's your name?', you know, and we got to talking. And then, sure enough, we went out on a couple of dates, and before you know it, we're engaged. That was thirty years ago."

"No kidding!" I said. "That's wonderful. And I didn't realize that Vicki went back that far."

"Oh yeah," Tom nodded. "Vicki and my wife grew up together."

I asked him whether Vicki had been here ever since, and he shook his head. "No, she's retired from Bell Telephone after thirty-five years. She was in management with Bell Telephone. I guess she's been here about three years now."

"Speaking of Vicki," I said, "do you have any problem with me interviewing your staff?"

"Not at all," Tom replied, and then chuckled. "Put Midge on the line." Midge was probably the most outspoken waitress at Fred and Pete's. There was no telling what she might say.

Then we talked about some of customers I might want to interview. "How about Dave Stout?" I asked him.

"Yeah, Dave's been coming here for years. He was our baseball coach back when me and my brother were kids," Tom replied, and then he turned to me and said, "You know, I've paid a lot of bills out of this store."

"I can imagine."

"And when I took over, the truth is, Muzzie knew the whole story," Tom continued. He looked at me and realized that I didn't have a clue who Muzzie was. "Muzzie Primmer—Nick Primmer—who's a great guy," he explained. "Anyhow, when I took over, Fred and Pete retired. I mean, they were done. But the thing is, when they were running things, Fred would say, 'Pete, did you pay that bill?' And Pete would say, 'Yeah.' And then Pete would say, 'Did you pay that bill, Fred?' And Fred would say, 'Think so.' And so when I took over in '81, I had guys knocking on my door saying, 'They forgot about me.'"

Tom paused and shook his head ruefully. "It took me about three years to get out of the woods," he said. "And most people, let me tell you, they were good. Jimmy DeNini from Caesar's Meats, we had a mutual agreement: 'I'll give you a hundred a month until we've knocked off the twenty-four hundred they owe you.' And Jimmy said, 'Fine.' That's all—a handshake. And Thuman's Meat, he was twenty-five dollars a week, because they had let that build up so bad. So, just everybody—Public Service… It took three years to pay everybody off."

"And meanwhile, you're also paying Fred and Pete!" I cried.

Tom nodded grimly. "Every Sunday."

"Boy, that's rough."

"Yeah," he sighed, "it wasn't easy." But then, as he leaned back and looked around the place again, I noticed a quiet smile that lit up his tired face. And for a moment, I couldn't help envying the guy.

By the time we walked out and Tom locked the door behind him, the parking lot was almost deserted. You probably *could* have fired a shot and not hit anybody, just like he'd told the old man, but it was too nice an evening for anything like that. The harsh heat and sunlight of the August day had given way to the softer twilight and the cool breeze of an August evening, perfect for opening a beer and watching the fireflies from our screened-in back porch.

"Thanks again, Tom," I said as we shook hands. "You must be exhausted."

"Yeah," he said. "Think I'll go home and maybe watch the game for a little bit. And get some sleep before it's time to get up again. Have a good one, Paulie."

"You, too, Tom."

And I'm sure he did.

DAVE

Saturday, April 4, 2009. It was another eight months before I took my next crack at the book. I'd gotten busy with work in the meantime—the kind of work that pays the bills—and with some other writing I wanted to do. But finally, on a Saturday morning in April, I stuck my cassette recorder and a fistful of blank tapes in my jacket and headed over to Fred and Pete's to see if maybe I could catch Dave Stout, the auctioneer.

Dave is a friendly guy and a great talker, which I guess is probably a good thing for an auctioneer to be, and we'd gotten to know each other reasonably well over the past several years, just from sitting together and talking at the counter. I'd told him that I was thinking about writing a book about Fred and Pete's, and I'd been threatening to interview him for weeks now, so I figured that the time had finally come to make good on my threat.

And, sure enough, there he was, sitting at the counter talking to Richie, who sometimes worked with him, more often worked with Tom on his catering jobs, and always seemed to find time to watch the world go by from one of the white plastic chairs out front, usually talking with Mario or Marvin or Tony and chewing on a black cigar. Richie was just getting up, so I took the seat next to Dave and ordered a cup of coffee.

"So are you ready?" I asked him.

"For what?"

"You know."

"Oh God," he moaned. "Today?"

"If you've got time," I said.

Dave nodded. "Nothing going on today. You want to talk here?"

"It's kind of noisy in here today," I said. "Could we do it at your house?"

He said that would be fine.

It was a windy, overcast morning, with row after row of black clouds stretched across the livid April sky, like giant zebra stripes. I pulled left out of the parking lot into the Saturday morning traffic lined up at the Route 33 traffic light and watched as the remains of a *Trentonian* tumbled across the CVS parking lot and became lodged in the bushes at its edge. Dave's house was practically across the street from the strip mall where Fred and Pete's was housed, but it was behind the Sun Bank, so you could either drive through the Sun Bank parking lot or come around on Trenton Avenue and turn onto Jefferson, which is what I did.

Dave's white Chevy truck was parked at the end of the driveway, instantly recognizable because it had his name emblazoned in elegant lettering across the back:

DAVE STOUT, AUCTIONEER.
HAMILTON, NJ.

Dave himself was standing behind the truck, leaning over and calmly saying something to a small dog on a leash that was barking furiously for no apparent reason.

"You found me!" Dave cried as I walked up the driveway. Dave's got a remarkably open, friendly face, a full head of gray hair, and today he was dressed in a copper-colored sweatshirt, blue jeans, and sneakers. "Heck of a wind out here today," he said as he came up and shook my hand. "Come on in."

I followed Dave up the front steps, past what appeared to be a scarecrow, dressed in a black suit and sprawled across a lawn chair. As I stepped inside, I couldn't help noticing that the walls of the foyer were covered with paintings—and that every painting included at least one brightly colored parrot. And as I followed Dave into the living room, there was a big, very brightly colored parrot, very much alive, perched on top of his or her very large cage.

"Is it a she or a he?" I asked Dave.

"It's a *she* now—since she laid an egg," Dave replied, and then turned to the parrot and said, in baby-talk, "Somebody finally laid an egg after thirteen years."

I laughed and asked what her name was.

"Becky," Dave said. "Used to be Bucky. I bought her in 1995, so she's about fourteen now, but she'll live to be eighty. Outlive me, probably." Dave, I knew, had had a triple by-pass more than ten years ago after a stent that they'd put in the day before collapsed, leaving him, as he put it, "dead on the table." It had taken him three months to recover from the surgery.

I'd been to Dave's house once before, but I'd forgotten how chock full of paintings and antiques it was. It was almost like a small museum—the kind of place you could spend a whole day and still not take in everything there was to see: a pair of giant snowshoes from the Yukon, a Peruvian blow-gun, a display of fancy door-knockers, a ceramic bulldog with its paw in a sling, a display of Boehm porcelain—you name it. We moved into the kitchen area and sat at a big wooden table, just behind a large ceramic pig in a chef's hat that faced into the kitchen. There was an adding machine and a stack of papers near Dave's seat, and a jumble of items that appeared to be antique was scattered across the table.

"I just picked up some of this oddball stuff," Dave told me, picking up a child's doll in a faded velvet dress. "This is like an 1885 sleepy-eyed doll. See the eye?" The eyeball moved as he gently shook the doll. "It's rare because of the teeth. See the teeth?" He tilted the doll's head back so that I could see the small ivory-colored teeth. There was something vaguely disturbing to me about the teeth.

"Where'd you get it?" I asked.

"Bordentown. And then these are those medals I was telling you about," he added, as he pushed a box full of old medals across the table toward me. I vaguely remembered him saying something about medals in one of our recent conversations.

I asked him what he thought he could get for the doll.

Dave shrugged. "A doll like that should bring about a hundred and a half. They used to bring three hundred, but the doll craze is kind of down now. But that's OK," he added, as if he half-expected that some day it might come back.

It was time to start.

"So, Dave," I began, "were you born...?"

"In Trenton," he replied before I could finish the question. "At St. Francis."

"And you have one brother, right?"

Dave nodded. "Four years older," he said.

I'd met his brother at Fred and Pete's, and seemed to remember that he was into antique guns. But maybe we could get to that later. First, I wanted to get Dave's take on Fred and Pete's. "So let's talk about Fred and Pete's," I began, and before I could even start my question, he said, "First day they opened."

I looked at him.

"First day they opened, I was there," Dave declared.

"Is that right?" I was impressed.

"This was my grandfather's house," he explained. "I bought the estate when he passed away. I didn't live here then, but I was visiting the day they opened, and he took me over there for lunch."

"No kidding! Do you remember what you had?"

"Hamburger—common person that I am," Dave deadpanned. "Or maybe it was a cheeseburger."

"And you've been going there ever since?"

"Yeah."

"And what do you normally get for breakfast?"

"At Fred and Pete's? Bacon and eggs," Dave replied. "Even with my cardiology problem, I have bacon and eggs."

"That's a lot of bacon and eggs over all those years," I said.

Dave nodded. "And I know," he added, "when they serve me coffee, every day, they give me a plastic spoon to stir my coffee. I don't put anything in my coffee. I've been going there roughly forty years. Over twelve thousand spoons they have wasted."

I burst out laughing.

"I keep telling them," Dave said, shaking his head, "but..."

"And why do you keep going back?" I asked him. "Not for the plastic spoons..."

"It's the camaraderie. Charming people, mostly. Even some of the waitresses." He chuckled. "They had this one, you could order whatever you wanted, you got whatever she felt like giving you. You remember her."

"Oh yeah," I laughed. "She chewed me out once when I asked for a fresh cup of coffee."

"Well, I remember I told her one time that I wanted half a cup of coffee," Dave recalled. "I told her I wanted the top half, not the bottom half, and she just couldn't figure that out."

I asked Dave how long he'd known Tom.

"Let's see," he said, "I knew Tommy when he was thirteen. I drafted him on my Babe Ruth League team. I had his brother on the team, who is now a heart surgeon. And his father was *right* behind me—*every* game," he added dryly.

I laughed. "So what was he like as a baseball player?"

"Tommy? He was good," Dave allowed. "He was like me—always the shortest guy on the team, so you become very effervescent."

"What position did he play?"

"Second base."

"So how about you?" I asked. "Did you play a lot of baseball as a kid?"

"Oh yeah," Dave grunted. "I've played probably three or four thousand games in my life."

"Wow," I said. "That's about one game for every three plastic coffee spoons. And what position did you usually play?"

Dave thought for a moment. "Well, because my brother had a first baseman's glove, I started out as the first baseman—for one game. Then I played second for a long time, like Tommy; then short-stop. All that time," he added, "I was pitching fast-pitch softball for older teams. So, over the years, I migrated on to the fast-pitch game, and I probably pitched five hundred to a thousand games there. Plus slow-pitching, I don't know how many games. Plus college, I played hardball. Played ball with a great bunch of guys that still come in to Fred and Pete's. As a matter of fact, a lot of great pitchers were over there with me at Trenton Junior."

"Is that right?"

Dave nodded. "Ed Steckley, Nick Marino... They all come in off and on. And Forrest Parker, he was a catcher. As a matter of fact," he added, "Danny Napoleon ended up playing for the Mets"—although it turned out that Danny, who had indeed played for the Mets in 1965 and 1966, wasn't one of the guys who still came in to Fred and Pete's; he had died in 2003.

"And what was your best batting average?" I asked.

"Fast-pitch?" Dave said. "Probably three-forty, three-twenty—something like that. I actually was a better ball player than I thought I was at the time. You know, I'd get on a team, and they would bat me clean-up. And it never hit me til later in life that I must have been better than I realized."

He sounded pleasantly surprised.

"So you were born in Trenton, right?" I said, backing things up a bit. "Where did your family live when you were born?"

"When I was born, we lived on East Brown and Hutchinson in Trenton, just off of Chambers Street," Dave replied. "When I was four, I moved to White Horse Avenue. And that's where I grew up."

"OK." I was struck that he'd said "I" rather than "we" about the move, but I didn't pursue it just then. "So tell me a little about your parents. What was your dad like?"

Dave lit up. "My dad was the greatest, most outgoing person you ever met. Him and the original Fred Armenti—Tommy's father—were great friends. They would sing all the time together, and he always sat at the same table at Fred and Pete's. He was an insurance man all his life. It was his only job, and he never missed a day of work for sixty years; then he retired."

"Was he an independent or did he work for a company?"

"He worked for Metropolitan," Dave replied. "As a matter of fact, Fred Wright, who eats at Fred and Pete's, was the mailroom boy that distributed the mail." He shook his head in amazement, adding, "He still remembers my father's number."

"No kidding!" Fred Wright, who was about Dave's age, now ran a legal services firm down in Philadelphia, drove more than one Mercedes, and was often at the counter in the morning, dressed in an elegant suit and wisecracking with Annie and Dave and whoever else was around.

"And my dad loved kids," Dave continued. "He actually raised my brother and I. When my mother left when I was four, he raised the two guys, right? And I don't know if I became a ball player because he wasn't much of a ball player, but he'd take me out—now this is where I really appreciate him—he'd take me out to Hamilton High: one ball and a bat. And he'd pitch to me, and I'd hit the ball. I never thought about this til later, but he'd go and get the ball, walk all the way back, throw one pitch, and go get the ball..."

"Oh my gosh..."

"Then he had this little old worn baseball glove, all beat up," Dave went on, "and I'd pitch to him—and I was pretty fast. And I'd hear an 'Ouch' every once in a while, but he never complained. Never."

"He sounds like quite a guy," I said.

"But then he went on," Dave continued. "I went into the Little League—I played in the first Little League game in Hamilton Township, which was way back in '48, I guess it was—and when I graduated, he took over a team in the League. He never would manage in the same league that I was in, but he worked with kids all the time. Anyhow, from there I went to the Babe Ruth League, and I played for a team that was undefeated for four years—probably the greatest team ever put together in this league, including Al Bonacci, who was a big politician guy in this area—and then when I left, my father became president of the league for eleven, twelve years. I'd cut the grass and he'd drag the field when there was no help at all. So we actually helped the Babe Ruth League to keep going."

Dave smiled as he remembered those days with his father. "Then I managed teams off and on, and I was very proud of myself because we kept winning the League—and we'd get last pick. And then come in first place."

"Wow..."

"Now you think about that," Dave chuckled. "But the key was I had a good guy, Gene Beiger, who worked with me, and he was very good with kids. He was down on Locust Avenue, but he passed away. Real nice guy. As a matter of fact, Rich Giallella played for him, and the following year, after Rich played for him, we took over a team together, and we would go down and scout in a little place in Sunnybrae—a little field that they had there, we'd get the players there, and nobody even knew about that place. So we were pulling guys that nobody even knew about—and winning the championships."

"Pretty nice," I remarked.

"I can remember we picked a fella—his name was Mark Cubberley, who's now a lawyer here in Hamilton—and nobody wanted him because his feet were too big. He was a big kid, but we saw a potential, and from his first game pitching in the Babe Ruth League right on through high school, I don't think he ever lost a game."

"No kidding..."

"Yeah," Dave grinned. "Little things like that. Then they gave me a team... I get a call from a guy named Len Wattley. He was an umpire for years and years; everybody knew him. He worked with Fran McManimon, who had a great recreation department. 'Dave,' he says, 'we have a problem. We have a Saturday morning league of younger kids from the Babe Ruth League who don't get to play much—thirteens and fourteens—so we have a league specially for them.

And we have a team that's 0 and 6, and a lot of the kids have quit because they couldn't win a game, so now there's only six kids left. Can you do anything with them?'

"So I went down to the Maple Shade School playground and I watched the kids playing there, and I got five or six of them to come out and play—and we ended up 13 and 6. So we won thirteen straight games, and we won that league," Dave concluded proudly. "Just doing little things that added up to something big."

I was duly impressed, and asked Dave what he thought the key to his success as a coach had been.

"I think maybe because I was always the smallest guy—the shortest on the team," he replied. "I mean, I'm about five-nine now, but I was five-one when I was a freshman. So you're always a little more aggressive. These little challenges, you kind of..."

"Yeah," I said.

"And then later I was the first to bring black ball players into the township to play in my team," Dave added.

"Really?" I said. "And what was that like? Was that a problem?"

"No," he said, smiling. "Because they were good."

Back when we'd first moved to Mercerville in the mid-1980's, I'd become fascinated by the history of the area, especially the Revolutionary War period. After all, Washington's historic crossing of the Delaware and his subsequent victories at the battles in Trenton and Princeton, generally regarded as a crucial turning point in the Revolution, had all taken place within a few minutes of where we lived. In fact, Washington and his troops—including then-Captain Alexander Hamilton, for whom the township was named, and Hugh Mercer, the brigadier general for whom Mercerville and Mercer County were named and who died from the wounds he received on the Princeton battlefield—had reportedly marched very near the spot where Fred and Pete's now stood on their way from Trenton to Princeton.

Most people's eyes glazed over whenever I brought any of this up, but not Dave's. As an auctioneer who handled lots of antiques, he had an obvious professional interest in the history of the area. But it turned out, as I'd discovered in some of our conversations at Fred and Pete's, he also had a personal interest. I decided to ask him a little more about that now.

"OK, Dave," I said, "I want to back up now for a minute. Because you've told me that the Stout family goes back to the Revolution..."

"*Pre*-Revolution," he corrected me. "We were the first Caucasian family in the Delaware Valley."

"And that goes back how far?" I asked.

"It's hard to say exactly," Dave replied, "but it was the early 1600's. The ship she was on came to Stony Point and wrecked, and they swam ashore. Most people went to New York, but her and her husband ended up in New Jersey, and he was killed by Indians. She was mortally wounded."

"What was her name?"

"Penelope von Princess," Dave said, and then, seeing the skeptical look on my face, he added, "I can show you books on that. It's well documented."

"OK," I said, still not wholly convinced that he wasn't pulling my leg. But I checked afterwards, and sure enough, it *was* well documented—and her name really was Penelope von Princess.

"Two Indian women found her hiding inside a rotted tree," Dave continued, "wounded and, I believe, partially scalped, because for years she wore a scarf. The Indians brought her back to health and took her to New York for a reward, and she ended up marrying a Stout. Then they migrated down to the Hopewell area"—about twenty minutes drive north of Mercerville—"and they had ten children, seven boys and three daughters, who mushroomed out and founded Pennington and Lambertville and the whole area."

"No kidding!"

"And from there, it mushroomed out to John Hart," Dave went on. "John Hart was, I think, the forty-third signer of the Declaration. He lived in Hopewell. As a matter of fact, the farm is still there—the Hart farm."

I asked whether John Hart was married to a Stout, and Dave said it was something like that, although he wasn't sure of the details. When I looked into it later on, it appeared that it was one of John Hart's sons, Edward Hart, who had married a Nancy Ann Stout. Close enough.

"But then later on in the Revolution," Dave told me, "there was the Fighting Forty from Lambertville. They were mostly Stouts, and they came down to help Washington. They were actually the first group to get near the barracks in Trenton where the Hessians were stationed. As a matter of fact, probably the boats that Washington's troops crossed the Delaware in belonged to our relatives."

He said that there were all kinds of books about this stuff, and even some movies, that I might find interesting, and then he thumbed through some of the papers piled on the table alongside the sleepy-eyed doll and the medals.

"I can't find the flyer," Dave said as he continued going through the stack, "but one of the groups came down here, and so we were one of the nine founders of Hamilton Township, too. In fact, some of the family still live down in the Crosswicks area," he added, referring to the small unincorporated town south of Hamilton Township. "They just sold the big farm down there by the little creek you would cross over before you went up the hill."

"So you go *way* back," I observed.

"Yeah, you can't go much further," Dave agreed, but then corrected himself. "Well, I could go further. My grandfather on my mother's side was quarter Indian. I'm trying to track that down, because his father came over from Germany when he was nineteen, so it wouldn't be on his side unless he married someone who was part Indian—or something like that. And then my grand-mother on my mother's side, she came from Philadelphia. She would travel on the paddle-wheeler that came from Philly, and it blew up one time and blew her into the river."

"Quite a family," I said.

Dave nodded. "And actually," he remarked, "I've had a relative die in every war in the history of the country."

"Including Iraq?"

"Has to be," Dave said. "There's so many of us now."

That took me where I wanted to go next, which was Dave's own military service. I knew he'd been in Vietnam, and asked him whether he'd been drafted after his stint at Trenton Junior College.

"Yeah," he said, "I was drafted because I didn't go back to college my next year. They drafted me in '64. Which was the big build-up for Viet Nam. So I went to basic training at Fort Dix, went to radio school, and I had taken some German in college, so when they asked where I would like to transfer to, I put in Germany. So naturally, I go in to look at the list of where people were going, and they had me down for Hawaii."

"Close," I laughed.

"Anyway, I figured, 'Oh, that's great. I'm going to Hawaii,' right? And the sergeant looks at me and says, 'I'm really sorry about that, but you're going to Hawaii.' And I couldn't figure out why until I got there: the counter-guerilla outfit, Twenty-fifth Division. Spent most of the time in the mountains, training constantly, very specialized survival stuff. We actually went through training there, in case we got caught, where they had a prison up in the mountains. And when I say mountains up there, it's nasty because it rains—and you can't believe how hard."

I shuddered, imagining it.

"And they had Vietnamese people working as prison guards who were nasty," Dave continued, almost in a monotone "Like you had no food for four or five days, no water; they made you do all kinds of weird stuff, they'd give you shocks with little electrical things; no sleep for two days..."

"Jeez."

"It was part of our survival training," Dave explained. "Remember, we were supposed to be a counter-guerilla outfit. In case someone attacked the West Coast, we would be behind them," he added with a straight face.

I laughed.

"So after about a year, we were happy to leave from there," Dave concluded, "and off we went to Vietnam."

I asked Dave where in Vietnam he'd wound up, and he said that they landed in a place just north of Saigon. "And we rode on a ship, we didn't fly over," he added. "Thirteen days on a ship, and believe me, the Army doesn't travel well on a ship. I was never sick, just a little queasy, you know, but everybody else..." He shook his head. "It was terrible, really."

I nodded. I'd been seasick myself, and knew all too well what he meant.

"But now for some reason," Dave went on, "they had put me in charge of the Division safe. Now I don't know who's going to steal this three-thousand pound safe, but it was down by the kitchen with the door open all the time. This big massive door was open for fresh air for the kitchen, right? I sat there with this safe, and I read every James Bond book ever written. And I always had oranges and muffins, because I was there round the clock, twenty-four hours a day."

"You're kidding. The whole thirteen days?"

"Oh, it was weird," he replied. "And then we go to get off the ship, onto these landing crafts. They put the safe up on a high spot on this landing craft, and all our troops are down in these landing areas. So then the captain of this little landing barge, he says to me, 'Get down off of there, soldier.' I say, 'I can't. The commanding officer told me to stay with the safe.' And he says, 'I command this ship. I'm going to send these men to come up and get you.' And I say to him, 'Sir, before you come up, I should tell you that I'm the only one with a loaded weapon.'"

I laughed.

"I tell you, I got away with murder," Dave chuckled. "I was never going to shoot nobody. But anyhow," he continued, serious again, "now we're coming up to the beach like it's Iwo Jima or like we're landing at Normandy. Everybody's locking and loading and getting ready to run out onto the beach; they drop the front, and it comes down right on the beach"—he paused for effect—"and here all these little kids are, selling Pepsi Cola and sandwiches."

I burst out laughing. Between his superb timing and his bone-dry delivery, Dave was a natural.

"It was really something," he chuckled. "Anyhow, then they were going to put us in a place called Cu Chi, which you can see on the History Channel all the time. That's the big show they put on sometimes, because it was all tunnels."

"OK..."

"So they fly in with planes and drop Agent Orange on the one square mile area," Dave continued, "and burned everything flat. They take our whole division, and drop it on top of this one-mile area of Agent Orange—not knowing, right?"

"You're kidding…"

Dave shook his head, and went on. "Now, we put tanks all around the perimeter," he said, "but somehow, Viet Cong kept popping up and stealing stuff. And we find out later, they had dropped us on the largest complex ever made of underground tunnels. Right on top. We found that out because we had a ditch-digger that would dig like ten or twelve feet deep all around this one-mile area, and they flooded it with gas and lit it." He paused and looked across the table at me, his eyes narrowed. "So we got rid of anybody that was down in there," he said, making sure that I fully comprehended the horror of what he was saying.

I did.

"But that was right at the entrance to Cambodia," Dave went on. "It was a trail from up in North Vietnam that came through Cambodia, right into Vietnam. And I was there for the rest of my tour, from January til November."

I asked him whether he'd had any particularly scary moments while he was there, and he said there was one, just before Christmas, when he went to pick up the mail for the guys in his unit. "So I came back to the guys with the mail," he said, "and just then they launched rockets—the Viet Cong—and hit the postal area. One guy was there working overtime; it blew him up. Christmas cards and letters all over the place."

"So that was close," I murmured.

"Yeah," Dave agreed. "And then, about a month later, a young fella in one of the line companies who would go out and build roads and stuff, his mother died. We only had two radio operators in this whole company, so I told him I would go down and take his twelve hours, too, so he could go back for his mother's funeral. So while I'm there, we get hit with gas. And I'm in the little bunker, and I could smell it. I don't know what it was, but I went out and started beating this big shell to wake everybody up. So the guy comes out who was in charge of the gas masks—he can't find the key to the lock."

"Unbelievable…"

"So I go into the bunker to call Division headquarters, and this gas is everywhere. I can't breathe; I actually burned my lungs…" Dave paused and took a deep breath, as if he were reliving it. "So then they said, 'Well, you'll have to clear the area out there where they're launching the mortars.' So I called Division airfield, and they sent a plane up called 'Puff the Magic Dragon,' which has four or six Gatling guns, each of which fires three thousand rounds a minute. And they came up and fired over twenty or thirty thousand rounds at this one-mile area—and completely did away with it. There was no more sounds."

Dave was silent for a moment, and it was absolutely still, except for the sound of that poor dog still barking in the driveway.

"But that's basically it," he said. "Except for one thing that really bothered me. I was really friendly with the people in the town. I would go down with the dirty clothes, and I would sit there and have nothing to do while the clothes were being washed, and you get to thinking, 'What are we here for?' I mean, you're not accomplishing anything…"

Dave's voice trailed off for a moment, and I could vividly imagine him being friendly with those villagers, in exactly the same way that he was with everyone at Fred and Pete's.

"But anyway," he said, resuming his story, "I see this tank coming in that we had lent to the Vietnamese military, and it's loaded with Viet Cong, presumably—guys dressed in black, dead. Now the weather's a hundred and ten degrees, so the surface of that tank had to be… whatever. So it was just like these people were frying. And they dumped them in a pile in the middle of the little town—as a symbol type thing, you know?" Dave frowned, sighing heavily. "It really bothered me," he muttered.

It turned out that there was something else about the Vietnam war that bothered Dave, which came up in a roundabout way when I asked him what he thought about the state of the nation these days.

I said, "What do you think about what's going on in the country?"

Dave thought for a while before answering. "I think the publicity that's been brought out about the well-to-do structure in this country and how it's so far out of line—it's phenomenal. What this president has done… I mean, with the banks and all that—it's just mind-boggling. I think Obama, because of his position and because he's black, he's more aggressive to a point, because they've been down-trodden so long that there are things that surface now that they might be more aware of than we are. I mean, we're a little more affluent than they are, and so we would overlook a lot of it."

I nodded.

"I think the war's a joke," he added emphatically. "I mean, you can see my family crest on my truck—they were in the Crusades and everything. And we've never been able to do anything with those people."

"You mean Iraq?"

"Iraq, Afghanistan, any of those areas," Dave said. "I don't think you're gonna change them. The financial end is bad enough, but the loss of lives is just ridiculous. And the worst thing is, the ones you're losing now are a higher echelon of troops. They're all volunteer, a lot of college graduates, where before, with the draft, it was a different group of people."

He paused, shaking his head. "I don't know why anyone would volunteer for this war. And as a Vietnam veteran," he added, "I don't understand why they're all heroes coming back. I mean, I'm more than happy to see people come back, but being one of the forgotten people—nobody cared when we came back—you just wonder why the parade now when Johnny comes marching home."

"Maybe they're just making up for it," I said. "I think people realize now..."

Dave cut me off. "But these are the people now—I mean the parents—that when it was us didn't give a damn. They were against the war, but when we came back, they didn't care," he said bitterly. "Everybody was demonstrating against the war, blah, blah, but when you came back, who cared?" He took a sip of his water and looked across the table at me. "There's some ill feelings about that, you know."

"Sure," I said.

"I mean, Jane Fonda," Dave muttered. "Nobody really cares about Jane."

"Yeah," I said, "you come back and you feel like..."

"Oh, God." Dave just groaned and was silent for a while. Then he brightened and told me about the Vietnam Memorial over at Mercer County Park. "It's great," he said. "In fact, I know two or three of the people whose names are in there. Like John Szymanski, who I played trumpet with at Hamilton. It's kind of touching, you know. Of course," he added pointedly, "it was the Vietnam veterans that put that there."

Dave came back from Vietnam at the end of 1966. After a short detour that involved a bizarre and grueling two-week war game at Fort McClellan in Alabama with a group of Green Beret National Guard recruits that was designed to determine whether they were ready to be deployed to Vietnam, he went back to teaching at Hamilton High, which he'd started doing before going into the Army. He was teaching drafting and printing, which he said he knew enough about to stay one page ahead of his students. At the end of that school year, based on the strength of his teaching experience in the field, Dave was hired as an illustrator by a firm in Princeton called Aerochem Research—a job he held for the next four or five years.

"We worked with NASA a lot," Dave recalled. "On the Space Shuttle and some other things. So I got to know some of the astronauts. It was fun."

"Which ones? Do you remember?"

He sighed and shook his head. "No," he said. "I had the coveralls from one of them, but my first wife threw it away, because she thought it was for the garage and that I didn't want them anymore. And I have one of their autographs, but I can't read it."

I laughed.

Eventually, the contracts at Aerochem dried up, so Dave found himself another job in Princeton, this time as an illustrator in the geophysical unit at Continental Oil, which he thoroughly enjoyed. And when they relocated to Houston a few years later, he did the same thing for Mobil Oil—also in Princeton at the time—but he didn't enjoy that job at all. "They were the complete opposite," he recalled with a frown. "You were like second-class people."

Meanwhile, going back even before his tour in Vietnam, Dave had started to become involved in the auction business. It was really pretty much of a sideline, until one summer day in 1976.

"I remember the exact date," he told me. "It was a week before the Fourth of July. I was going to have an auction at the State Fair Grounds. They had given me a big building for nothing to use for my auction, to try to draw people for a flea market they had established at this site. So a friend of mine—Carney Rose, who used to rent horses to ride over in the White City area—he was going to hold an auction next door to mine, sort of like a tailgate auction where the trucks drive through and you sell junk, and then I was going to have the antique sale alongside of it."

"So what happened?"

Dave grinned. "He and I bought the entire 1776 caravan that was coming across the country."

"You're kidding!"

"It was for the Bicentennial," Dave explained. "They had driven all the way across the country in these wagons, with oxen and cattle and horses and everything, and they just wanted to sell it. So we bought the whole caravan. Animals, wagons, livestock—even the costumes that they wore. Hats, bonnets..."

"And then auctioned it off?"

Dave nodded. "Auctioned it all off. And it was so festive," he recalled, smiling. "The governor was there, the newspapers, everybody was there. It was just a big show. We even had a Dixieland Band... It was cool."

"So how does that work?" I asked him. "Where did you get the money to buy all that stuff?"

"We told them we would pay them the following week," Dave replied. "We gave them a check and told them, 'Hold the check.' Then we sold the stuff, made some money, and paid them."

"But meanwhile you're on the hook," I said.

"Yeah."

"And do you remember how much you paid for all that?"

"Thirty-eight hundred dollars," Dave replied without a moment's hesitation, as if it had been yesterday.

"And did you *have* thirty-eight hundred dollars?"

"No way," Dave chuckled. "But I would've gotten it somehow."

From that point on, Dave was in the auction business full-time, although, he said, that first year was tough. "As a matter of fact," he recalled ruefully, "it was so bad that first year that the government sent me two-hundred-sixty dollars for what they called 'small business subsistence.' It was that bad."

But then, Dave said, came a lucky break. "There was a place at the Independence Mall down on South Broad called the Big C, and they were going out of business. It was a big place, like a Sears-Roebuck, and they were giving like thirty percent off this, seventy percent off that. So I go over there to get some Christmas stuff for the kids, you know. And they have these big display cabinets of perfume and after-shave lotion and whatnot, and people are offering them like twenty-five, fifty dollars—and I say to myself, 'That's crazy.' So I'm talking to the guy that's in charge of the liquidation, and I say to him, 'What would you take for the whole place?' And he says, 'Give me an offer.'

"So I'm looking around, and I tell him, 'A thousand dollars'—as a joke. He says, 'Let me go in the office.' He comes out and he says, 'You got it. But you gotta be outta here by tomorrow night.' He says, 'I'll get my personnel to box everything for you tonight, and you come in and pick 'em up.'"

"Hell of a deal," I murmured.

"Yeah," Dave agreed. "But now this is Saturday night. Where are you going to get a thousand dollars? He wanted cash. So I went down to the bowling alley, talking to my friends. I used to bowl down there like three nights week, so I have lots of friends. And this young fella, Bobby Davis, says, 'Oh, I got six hundred.' The other guy says, "I got fifty." Well, by the time I got done, I've got a thousand dollars. So I say, 'I'll give you guys ten percent tomorrow'—but they didn't care about that They said, 'Well, how are you gonna get it outta there?' I say, 'I don't know.' And they all volunteered. 'We'll work for you.' So I got six guys, right?"

"Not bad," I said.

"The funniest thing," Dave continued, "is we go up early Sunday morning, and he's got one hundred boxes. Just think, for a thousand dollars, that's only ten dollars a box. And these boxes are three by three, and like one of them is all Timex watches—just ten bucks for the whole box of watches! Anyhow, so I'm talking to the guy, paying him, and these guys are starting to load. Well, it turns out there's some sporting equipment in some of the boxes, and when I come out, they're all dressed in catcher's outfits with hockey sticks, going all through the place playing hockey!"

It sounded like a Marx Brothers movie.

But over the course of the following year, Dave said, he'd break open those boxes each week and take out a few items from each box—which had cost him practically nothing—and then every Friday he'd have a sale. And by the time he'd sold it all, he had made his thousand dollars back at least ten times over. "And what's more, it put me in business with merchandise," he added. "And from that, I started getting the consignments in, and now I basically work off commission. I don't even have to advertise all that much anymore—other than my truck, which is a landmark."

Actually, he told me, not long ago somebody had stolen the original hand-painted sign from his truck, and he figured that one of these days he might see it hanging on the wall in a Cracker Barrel somewhere. "But I wouldn't mind that at all," he chuckled. "It'd actually be pretty cool."

I asked Dave to tell me a little more about the auction business. For instance, how many did you have to do to make ends meet?

He said that he'd started out doing about one every week, but it got to be too much, so now he was down to one or two a month. "But a big one," he added. "You have to be more selective so you can be more profitable. And it's still a lot of work. You have to hire more people, and you have to have a mailing list—now we have e-mail, too."

Dave said he'd placed an ad in the *Trenton Times* for a big auction that he was holding next week. He had checked to make sure that they got the spelling right, and discovered that the ad wasn't there. "I called, and they said they'd put it in on Sunday," he said, "but Thursday is the day that everybody looks. But I've got over a thousand selective buyers already notified, so it might work out."

I asked him if he remembered his best auction ever.

"Oh yeah," he said, "without a doubt: Bordentown. It was a mansion, and I got called by Sovereign Bank. They said, 'Dave, we have an estate down in Bordentown. We've had an appraisal done locally at five thousand nine hundred dollars. Do you want to go down and take a look?' So I went down there with a young lady from the bank. It was over on Farnsworth Avenue, between Route 130 and Route 206, close to the Hungarian restaurant: a big green mansion."

I nodded. It was half a block from where I used to take my Saturn.

Dave took a sip of water and continued. "So she says, 'Here's the key, and I'll just park the car.' So I walk up, open the door, walk into the foyer, come back out and say, 'OK, let's go to lunch. I'll treat.'"

"You're kidding!" I said. "Just like that?"

"And she says, 'Well, we'll have to go through and see if you see anything...' And I tell her, 'I'll give you a hundred thousand dollars—right now.' And she laughs. So we went to eat. We didn't go in the house at all."

I didn't understand. "How did you...?"

"The reason was," Dave explained, "I looked in there, and there were paintings—oil paintings and stuff. And I know the one painter from New Hope who had started the New Hope Guild of Painters, back in the late 1800's—his name was Daniel Garber—I saw one of his paintings. So there, guaranteed, is ten thousand dollars right there—for just one painting. And I looked around, and I could see at least a dozen more paintings. Plus, the place is *loaded* with antiques—I mean quality antiques. A beautiful place, all inlaid oak panels..."

"Wow..."

"So, to make a long story short," Dave continued, "the old lady was there—we almost adopted her as our grandmother, she was such a lovely person—and she took me through the house. And I told her that I had told the bank that I would do it for twenty percent, thinking that at five or six thousand dollars, by the time I paid for the labor, I'd get three or four hundred dollars, which is a good day's pay. So she talked to her son, who was a lawyer down in Texas, and he OK'd the whole deal. And I come to find out that these people were the well-to-do people of Bordentown. They had owned the company that dredged the Delaware River for the ships to come in, and this house had been built by exclusive Baltimore builders—gorgeous wood, not a single knot in thousands of feet of oak or anything." He shook his head in wonder, as if he still couldn't believe it. "And we found twenty-eight paintings in there. The daughter had been promised this one painting, and she thought it was worth eight hundred dollars. And I said, 'Well, if you want to put it in the auction, it'll do fairly well.'"

"And did she?"

"Yeah, she let me put it in," Dave said. "So anyhow, I had advertised really well all over the country—I had one man actually fly back from *Italy* for the auction. And then on the day of the auction, I look outside—and there's over five hundred people in the front yard!"

"Oh my gosh!"

"Now, it's ninety-something degrees in the morning," Dave continued, "and there's trees all around. So by noon they're all standing around where it's cooler, and I'm standing in the middle, in the sun—I lost seven pounds that day. But the dollar signs were kicking up, you know."

I laughed.

"I knew it was going to be a good day, because we went out in the back to the garden area," Dave recalled, "and there were these big concrete statuaries. First one brought three hundred dollars. By the time we got out of there, I'd sold a full-size ship anchor out there that brought twelve hundred or something, a grist-mill wheel—a big full-sized stone wheel... all kinds of stuff. Then I walked around front, and the old lady is sitting in her rocker, and I had a friend of mine, Bob Coyle from Coyle's Gallery up on the porch with all the paintings, and so we start auctioning the paintings. Then we get to the better paintings. And all of a sudden there's a hush."

Dave paused for dramatic effect. "And I say to myself, 'Well, I'm going to just see what happens and start this one at five thousand dollars'—just for the heck of it, you know? It was just a country scene in Pennsylvania, and it looked almost like a child had done it. And at five thousand dollars, ten hands went up."

"You're kidding!" I laughed.

"And I said to myself, 'Whoa! Something's going on.' So I said, 'Fifty-one hundred, fifty-two hundred—hundred dollar bids, you know. And hands are flying up all over the place. So I'm up to six, seven thousand dollars, and I start taking *thousand* dollar bids—and it's still going up and up. I get to twenty-nine thousand dollars, and sell it."

"Not bad!"

"And remember this," Dave said. "It was twenty percent. It took me one minute. So I just made five thousand dollars in one minute."

"Not bad at all," I laughed.

"So now I put the other big one up that the daughter had wanted eight hundred for, and I started it at a thousand. The hands all went up again. By the time we got to twenty-one thousand, I sold it. Fifty thousand dollars in two minutes—I made ten thousand dollars in two minutes!"

And then, Dave said, he started selling some of the furniture and clothing from inside the house, including several uniforms from the Revolutionary War and a Civil War uniform that he said was in mint condition—"like you just got it today." And again, he said, the money was phenomenal. "And so at the end of the day, I went up to the old lady and I told her, 'I can't charge you twenty percent.' And she says, 'My contract reads that you receive twenty percent. That's what you're getting.'"

"Fantastic!" I said. "Do you remember what you cleared for the day?"

Dave remembered—to the dollar. "How's that for a day's work?"

"That's a good day," I laughed. "And a lot better than twenty percent of fifty-nine hundred dollars."

"Ain't that the truth," Dave said, grinning happily.

Dave told me about another interesting job—this one in Princeton—in which, among other things, he'd come across papers from the famous Lindberg kidnapping case that had never before come to light. In fact, he said, the client— once again, an elderly woman—had actually attended the final day of the famous trial, and could still be seen in the film of the trial as a nine-year-old little girl, sitting in the front row.

"That's pretty neat," I said.

"Yeah," Dave agreed. "You never know what you're going to find in this business."

We then talked a little bit about his family—how, after twenty years, his first marriage had ended, and how he had two daughters, Debra and Kim. He had remarried about twelve years later, in 1998, and he and his current wife Sue now had twelve grandchildren between them, ranging in age from seventeen to one—plus, he said, two dogs, two cats, and two parrots.

Then there was his mother-in-law, Heidi Kral Preece, who had once been a famous soprano at the Metropolitan Opera. Dave had once brought some old news clippings and pictures of her to Fred and Pete's, and it was obvious that in her day, she had been a stunning beauty. "Even to this day," Dave said, "she resembles the 1930's and 1940's-type movie stars—and she's almost ninety. She loves to cook. You know, she'll say, 'I just made a little red cabbage—you want some?'"

"And she still comes in to Fred and Pete's, right?"

"Oh yeah," Dave answered. "She likes Cash—you know, Volodymyr. And she buys all her scrape-offs there. You know, those chance things up at the counter? Sometimes she can't figure them out, so she asks Cash. Well, Cash might be a rich man by now, I don't know."

I laughed.

"And what about this place?" I asked, looking around. "How has this area changed since you were a kid?"

"Where we are now, this used to be called the Thirty-Acre Farm," Dave replied. "My grandfather owned all this area, all where Applebee's is, the post office, the bank... And then of course across Route 33, where Fred and Pete's is now, that was a horse farm. As a matter of fact, they just tore down that white house behind the bank—that was the farm house."

It was a little hard to imagine a horse farm or any kind of farm here, now that just about every square inch had either been built on or paved over. "What did your grandfather farm here? Do you know?"

"Just nominal stuff," Dave said. "He worked for General Motors over in Ewing as a machinist. And actually, my mother worked there, too, during the war, building planes. Like Rosie the Riveter, you know."

"By the way," Dave said, "speaking of the scrape-offs, I was one of the first winners of the scrape-off: I won fifty thousand dollars there in 1995."

"Is that right?" I exclaimed. "I didn't know that!"

Dave seemed a little surprised. "OK, well, they came out with this new thing for the twenty-fifth anniversary of scrape-offs," he explained. "John Pennacchi and Mario are playing this five-dollar scrape-off. They're sitting at the back table where Lefty used to sit. They buy the whole three-hundred-dollar book: win, lose, win, lose, win, lose. They played the whole book. And I'm sitting there, I've never played one of these things in my life.

"Now the catch is, I was going to the bank," Dave continued. "I stopped in, and I only had eight dollars. So I bought coffee and a bagel—cost me two dollars. So I had six dollars. So we go up to the counter to pay, and at the time, there weren't a lot of different scratch-offs to choose from. They would hang one of each kind from the side of the counter. I said to John and Mario, 'Hey, you didn't buy the last one.' They said, 'We're not buying any more of them.' So I paid my two dollars and I had six dollars left, so I said, 'Give me that last one.' And I said, 'You guys want half of this?' And they say, 'Hell, no.'

"So I start scraping. Now on the top is a little round circle that says 'Anniversary,' and if it says 'Twenty-fifth Anniversary,' then whatever it says under it, you win. So I scrape it, and it says 'Twenty-fifth Anniversary.' And I say, 'Look at that, guys, I got a winner.' And they say, 'Yeah, five dollars.' So I scrape it, and yeah, it's a five… and a zero… zero…zero. Five *thousand*."

"Nice!" I chuckled.

"So all of a sudden they're yelling, 'Hey, Tommy, he's got a big winner. Five thousand!' Tommy comes running out. He says, 'Give me that. I'm gonna run it through the machine.' I say, 'You ain't touching it, Tommy.' So he says, 'Well, scrape the other little boxes off and see if there's three matching numbers.' I scrape, and there's three matching numbers—that's worth five thousand. So now I got ten thousand.

"Now on the bottom," Dave continued, "there's eight numbers, and you've gotta match your two numbers to the eight numbers—any one of them. It was 7 and 13. I started to scrape, and it's 7, 13; 7, 13… all the way down. And each one was worth five thousand dollars. Fifty thousand dollars. And that was the first big winner."

"Oh man," I said. "That's not bad for a morning. That's even better than your take on that Bordentown auction."

"It was hanging on the wall until he painted the place," Dave said proudly. "He made a copy and blew it up, and it was hanging in a big plaque. But now the catch is that I had the six dollars left. If I'd had the bacon and eggs like I usually do, it would've cost me more and I wouldn't have had the five dollars."

"That's true…"

"And then after that," Dave added with a grin, "Mario and Pennacchi wouldn't talk to me for two weeks. Wouldn't talk to me at all."

JOHN WILWOL

Monday, April 6, 2009. *Two days later, on Monday morning, I was back at Fred and Pete's for breakfast, eating another bowl of Raisin Bran. I was a little surprised that Annie wasn't there, until Midge told me that Annie's mother had passed away over the weekend. It wasn't a real surprise—her mother was in her nineties and hadn't been doing well, so Annie had been expecting it for some time now—but I knew that that wouldn't make it any easier for her. Annie and her mother had been very close.*

"She said she was coming in tomorrow," the young waitress, Theresa, said when she heard Midge telling me why Annie was out. I guessed that Theresa was probably subbing for Annie, and that maybe she had talked to Annie.

"Is that right?" Midge said.

"The funeral's not going to be until next week," Theresa explained.

"I think they had it all planned out," Midge told me, "so I don't think Annie even had to worry about it."

It was relatively quiet this morning, but that was partly because I'd come in a little later than usual. I looked around, and noticed John Wilwol, the retired roofer and former high school basketball star, sitting over at the next counter by himself. Tall, slim, and still sporting a full head of curly grey hair, he was wearing his green Mercer County Anglers jacket with a big fish embossed on the back. John was a pretty quiet guy, soft-spoken, but he'd always said hello to me when we passed each other in the parking lot, and I wondered whether he might be willing to be interviewed.

He was.

I asked him if he'd mind if we moved to the booth in the far back. It was right by the restrooms, but it was probably the quietest place for us to talk, so he said that would be fine with him.

"My name is Paul, by the way," I told him as we shook hands and slid into our seats. "I don't know if you actually knew my name."

"I've seen you here," John said. That seemed to be sufficient.

I asked him how he spelled his last name, so he spelled it out and told me it was a German name—and then added, "They call me Woo for short—Johnny Woo."

I nodded. That's what Tom had called him.

John told me that he was born in Trenton, on Valentine's Day, 1933.

"The same day as our grandson!" I exclaimed—and, as it turned out when I later did the math, exactly seventy-five years earlier. "And did you have any brothers or sisters?"

John shook his head. "I'm the only one."

"So tell me a little bit about your parents," I said. "What did your dad do?"

"Roofing, just like me," John replied. "I followed in his footsteps."

"And what kind of guy was he?"

John shrugged. "Sociable guy," he replied. "Nice. Nice to people. He was with the fire department for many years, and they loved him like a brother up there, you know. And then he passed away in 1972."

"Were you close to your dad?"

"Yeah, pretty close," John said. "We did a lot of fishing together."

"Oh yeah?"

John nodded, and a rare smile crossed his face. "A lot of fishing on the beach."

I asked him where.

"Island Beach State Park," he said. "Montauk, Long Island. And Nantucket."

"All the way to Montauk and Nantucket?" Montauk, I knew, was at the far eastern tip of Long Island, at least two or three hours drive from Mercerville, and Nantucket was several hours by ferry from the Massachusetts coast. "What did you guys do—surf fishing?"

"Surf fishing, yeah," John replied. "But you can't afford to go up to Nantucket now," he added with regret. "It's very expensive."

I asked him about his mother.

"Oh," he said, "everybody *loved* her. We lived at Marshall and Lalor, and the police would stop over in the morning, get coffee and cake from her—everybody just loved her. But she had medical problems—rheumatic heart, rheumatic fever—and she passed on in 1965. But she was a nice person, nice to everybody."

"Were your parents from Trenton, too?"

John nodded. "Dad was my mother's first courting date, and that was his first, with my mother."

"Is that right? Unbelievable!" I exclaimed. "That's true love."

"Yup," John said.

"Now how about you?" I asked. "Have you been married?"

"Nope," John replied, shaking his head. "I come close, but it didn't work out, so hey..." He shrugged, and I felt a fleeting stab of sadness, although I couldn't tell for sure whether it was his or mine.

I changed the subject. "Now I heard you were a basketball player," I said. "Did you start playing as a young kid?"

"Yeah," John replied. "At the parochial school. I played for Holy Angels, you know, against St. Joachim's, St. James, St. Hedwig's. And then I started in high school. I didn't go to college. Then I started playing with the Trenton Colonials"—one of the teams in the Continental Basketball Association during the 1960's—"until 1962. It started out as the Colonial Social Club, and I came over with the big guys, like Charley Ross here. But then I just gave it up. You know, the guys that were coming up, they were taller, faster, and quicker—so I just gave it up."

"But you were on a championship team at one point, right?" I asked. Dave Stout had mentioned something about that to me, but I wasn't sure of the details.

"In 1953," John said. "In high school."

"And you guys were state champions that year?" I asked.

"Hmm..." John thought for a moment. "I'm pretty sure we were state champions, yeah," he said, although it didn't seem to matter much to him.

"What position did you play?"

"Center."

"Well, you must have been good," I said.

John shrugged. "I enjoyed it."

I asked him whether he'd been watching the NCAA play-offs this year, and he said he had. The championship game was scheduled for that night, between North Carolina and Michigan State, and I asked him who he thought would win.

"I think North Carolina," he said. "That's what I say—but hey, you never know."

Of course, it turned out that John was right—by a score of 89 to 72. The closest that Michigan State ever got to Carolina after the first few minutes of the game was thirteen points.

While we were talking, a family with a couple of young kids had settled in two booths behind John, and because he was so soft-spoken, I had lean forward a little now in order to hear him over the chattering of the kids. One of them was insisting that he wanted the ketchup *right now*, and his mother warned him in no uncertain terms to behave.

"John," I said, "I know that you said your father was a roofer. When did you start with roofing? Did you used to go with him when you were a kid?"

"Yeah," he said, nodding. "Like a helper. I went into the service in '53, and then I got a job at Roebling's—I don't remember how long that was. After that, I went to apprentice school for roofing."

Roebling had for many years been a very big name in Trenton—and a world-famous company, renowned for its wire and wire rope. John Roebling, the company's founder and a world-class bridge-builder, had planned the Brooklyn Bridge, and when he died very early in the construction process from tetanus, his son Washington Roebling took over the momentous task—although after contracting the bends during the sinking of one of the bridge's massive foundations, he almost didn't make it either.

"What were you doing at Roebling?" I asked John.

"Started in a labor gang," he answered. "Then I wound up in the carpenter shop. And then I took the test for roofing, and I got my journeyman's card in June of '59. I've been roofing ever since, and I retired in..."—long pause—"Gosh, I can't remember now..."—another long pause—"About seven years," he said at last.

I wondered whether it was harder to keep track of the years when every day was pretty much like every other day—much of it spent at Fred and Pete's. I asked John whether he remembered the toughest job he'd ever had as a roofer.

John shook his head. "It was all tough. All of it. Nothing was easy. Like tearing a roof off is pretty tough. You get all that dust all over you..."

"I can imagine," I said. "And if you're working in the summer..."

"Oh God," he groaned. "Buttoned up real tight, you know, and sweating..." He grimaced, like he was remembering a bad dream.

I asked John whether he'd ever worked on any really tall buildings, and he said that he'd worked on the Labor Building in Trenton—which, I later discovered, was thirteen stories tall. "But the tallest ones there," he added proudly, "my father did those."

"Now John," I said, "you mentioned earlier that you were in the service. Did you stay here in the States or were you shipped overseas?"

"Germany," he replied.

"What was that like?"

"I was lucky to go there, because else I would've been shipped to Korea—and it was 1953. They were still fighting over there. But in Germany I didn't see any action. I was an ammunition supply specialist—that's what I went to school for. And I went to NCO academy for a year while I was there."

"So how long were you in the Army?" I asked.

"Five years."

"And did you volunteer, or were you drafted?"

"Drafted," John said, frowning. "You didn't have a choice back then. They were drafting people then. You registered, and they grabbed you. Now it's nothing."

"Now it's all volunteer," I said.

"Yeah." He sounded unimpressed.

I wanted to hear more about John's experiences as a roofer—since it had been such a big part of his life—and so I asked him what the best part of being a roofer was. He gave me a quizzical look, so I added, "Were there *any* good parts to it?"

"Well, yeah," he said after thinking it over. "We used to have the local here—Local 108—over on Clinton Street. Then we merged with Local 30 out of Philadelphia, because we couldn't supply them with enough manpower when they came in. We always had to bring in other men."

"So you figured you might as well merge with them?"

"Yeah," John replied. "We wound up going to Local 30. That's who I retired from—Local 30. And I wound up being the shop steward—in New Brunswick, with Universal Sheet Metal and Roofing."

"Is that right?"

John nodded. "I was there for about twenty-seven years as the shop steward, and I retired from there," he declared with obvious pride.

"No kidding!" I exclaimed. "Twenty-seven years? And what does that involve—being a shop steward in a roofers union?"

"Well, you control everything," he explained. "You make sure everybody does the right thing. You do the right thing. If not, you send him down."

"So you liked being shop steward," I said.

"Oh yeah," John said. "Most of the time you didn't have to work—just go check out the job, you know."

"Sure..."

"Because I worked," he said, defiantly. "I worked a lot."

I nodded, and said, "But you still haven't told me what was the toughest job you ever worked on."

John frowned. "The toughest? The toughest was tearing the roof off. Tearing the roof off and throwing the stuff off, and getting rid of it, and sweeping and dusting—oh! That's about the toughest. I don't know what else it could be."

"Yeah..."

"I mean, when I first started out," he said, "you used to have to pull that stone up onto the roof—slag; they called it slag. That was done by *hand*. Then it was mechanized. Belt conveyor to shoot it up on the roof, put it in a wheelbarrow, and push it—so now it's easy. But when I *first* started... forget it!"

I chuckled.

"That's what my father used to say. He'd say, 'This is hard work. So if you can't do it...'—you know?"

"So why did you want to do it?" I asked John. "You knew it was hard work."

"Well," he said, "I like being outside. But the thing my father didn't like was that I had a chance to be a state trooper. I went halfway, and that was it. He didn't like that."

I was confused. "How come?"

"Because I didn't go through with it," John replied. "He said, 'What do you wanna do this for?'"

"And what made you decide not to go through with it?"

"It's hard to say," John said. "But he said to me, 'Roofing is a weak mind and a strong back—that's what you gotta have.' But I just stayed with it, and that was it. If I'd stayed with the state troopers, I would have probably had a better hour rate. You can't do much today as a cop, I'll tell you that—no way!"

He stopped to cough. "That's about the hardest, though," he said. "When you tear roofs off, it's dirty. You get that stuff in your eyes—what they call 'pitch eyes.' Your eyes are all bloodshot, and a lot of times you ride home, and you might get stopped by the police, and they'll think you've been drinking..."

I asked John whether he'd ever fallen off a roof while he was working.

"No," he said. "But my dad did—twice. My father was lucky. He didn't get hurt that badly. But I seen guys go down."

"That's gotta be tough," I said. "It's gotta be tough to stay up there. You've got the steep pitch on some of those roofs, and I don't know how you guys stay up there."

"I worked on mostly flat roofs," John explained. "I didn't do much shingle work. I worked on flat roofs—like this place. But a lot times, guys would back up, and if you don't watch yourself, the first thing you know, you're gonna go over." His face was grim, and I wondered what he was remembering. But I didn't ask. Instead, I asked him if he still went fishing.

"Oh yeah," he said, brightening.

"Where do you like to go?"

"Island Beach," he replied. "I don't travel much anymore. We used to have seven or eight guys that would travel to Montauk, Martha's Vineyard—even Nantucket. But all of them are deceased. My father's gone. One fella's still living, but he's down in Florida."

"Anything else you like to do?" I asked. "Do you bowl? Do you play golf?"

"Naw," he said, almost scornfully. "I never play golf. I just go fishing and relax. That's about it."

"And what was your best catch ever?"

"A thirty-five pound striper," John replied instantly. "I caught that at Montauk. The biggest one I caught here was twenty-six—and I won a five hundred dollar gift certificate with that, way back when they used to have the Tournament of Fish. That's all deceased now," he added. "They don't have that no more."

"Now wait a minute," I said. "Speaking of winning, didn't you win something here at Fred and Pete's? A lottery ticket or something?"

John thought for a moment. "Oh yeah," he said. "The Cash Five."

"How much did you…?"

"Twenty-six thousand."

"Twenty-six thousand?"

"That was small—very small," John said. "Everybody said, 'That's small.' But what was I gonna do? Complain?"

"Exactly!" I cried. "I mean, how much did it cost you?"

"Well," John said, "these are the same numbers I always play—my parents."

"And it finally came up?"

John smiled. "Yeah."

John told me that he'd been coming to Fred and Pete's for a long time. In fact, he used to come in with his father. "I didn't know Tommy that well back then," he said. "But I just kept coming in periodically, and we got to know each other pretty good. And once a month we used to go over to Antonio's, maybe fifteen, twenty guys, have dinner, and that's it. And I've been here ever since."

"All day?" I'd actually seen John there at breakfast, lunchtime, and dinner on different occasions.

"Not usually," he replied. "But at night I'll usually come in and have supper. And I give him a hand here. Everybody thinks I work here, but I tell them, 'No, I don't. I don't work here. I give him a hand, that's all.' I just hang around, and that's it."

"And what do you like about this place?"

John shrugged. "The people are all nice in here, you know. Sociable, talkable. The girls are nice."

I asked him if he had a favorite waitress.

He didn't hesitate. "Meghan," he said. "She's the baby sister I never had. But they're all nice," he added tactfully.

"And you've known Tommy all these years," I said.

"Yeah," John said. "And in fact, how it came about, was his cousin—Carmen Armenti, who used to be the mayor here at one time—he had a restaurant down at the shore. We used to live down at the shore—my parents and me—a long time ago, and I used to go in his restaurant and help out, clean up and everything, just so's we could get a carton of beer. Remember them days? Any little kid could go in and get it. Anyhow, I used to help out over there, and I told that to Tommy, and he says, 'I don't remember you.' And I says, 'I don't remember you either. But I did that.' And he says, 'How about that?' And that's how things got to going here."

I wasn't sure I understood. "You mean Tommy used to be out there?"

"Well, I guess he used to come see him, you know," John said. "And when they started out here, it was all politicians. Sometimes you couldn't even get in here, there was so many people. I remember my father says, 'Look at all them people in here—politicians.' And then Tommy just took it over from his father, and that was it. And now he caters and everything."

I asked John how the place had changed since he'd first started coming here.

He gave it some thought before answering. "Well, most of the politicians don't come in here like they used to," he said. "It gets kinda slow. Right now," he added, looking around and lowering his voice, "it's *very* slow."

It was quiet at the moment—the family with the kids had gone, and there were a only a couple of guys still sitting at the counter, and one elderly woman eating soup in one of the front booths.

"But he does all right," John assured me. "Of course, then he found out he'd had that heart attack."

Tom's heart attack had given everybody a scare. One morning recently when I'd come in, all the waitresses had been talking about it: that Tom hadn't been feeling well, that he'd finally gone in to get checked out, and that it turned out that he'd had what they called a silent heart attack.

"He didn't know it had happened," John told me. "Then last Thursday or Friday he had a stress test. I was here with him. When he took the stress test, he came back and he was fine, he says. And I say, 'Good, Tom. Good.' Then a little later he gets a phone call and they say, 'Would you mind coming back? We detected something.' So Tom called his wife and he went back—he locked the front door here until he came back—and then he comes back here and I say, 'Well, Tom, what is it?' And he says, 'It doesn't look too hot.' That's all he says."

I nodded. That sounded like Tom.

"Well anyway," John continued, "Friday morning he went to the hospital where he had the procedure done, and Monday morning I took his wife Noreen, because I said, 'How are you gonna bring him home? I'll gladly pick him up for you.' And she said, 'Well, I'll go with you.'"

"So you took Noreen over there?"

John nodded. "I took Noreen in my car, picked up Tommy, and brought him right back here," he replied, clearly pleased that he'd been able to help out. "And he's been doing fine."

"Yeah, he has," I agreed. "He says he feels better now than he did before. He had like ninety-five percent blockage or something."

"Yeah," John said grimly. "In the one to the heart."

I asked John what he thought about the state of the world.

He sighed. "I don't know what's gonna happen," he said. "I mean, I've seen a lot in my time, but I feel sorry for the young kids now. I don't think they're gonna have too much of a good time of it. But you know, I just take it day by day—just listen, that's all. I don't think you can cure everything. The new president, I don't think he can cure everything that's gonna happen. No way. People with money—you look at the stocks, they're losing all their money."

"Has it hurt you with your retirement?"

John shook his head. "No, it comes right from our local. It's all retirement—it's all pension."

"So you don't have stocks or anything?"

"No, none of that stuff," John replied thankfully. "We never got that."

"So you're doing all right."

"So far."

He told me that lived by himself in Trenton, on Central Avenue over by Hamilton High West, and that he still attended Holy Angels Church, just a block or two from where he'd grown up. "Not as much as when my parents were alive," he admitted, "but I pop in there every now and then." And his health was still good, he said, apart from a couple of hernia operations two or three years ago. He still mowed his lawn and he still walked a lot—he didn't want to just sit around the house and fall asleep in front of the TV.

"And what did you do with the twenty-six thousand you got from the Cash Five?" I asked him.

"I didn't get it all," John was quick to point out. "Part of it went to taxes. I got nineteen thousand five hundred."

"And what did you do with that?"

"Put it in the bank," John replied dryly. "All but five hundred of it—I used five hundred to put new windows in the basement."

We shook hands when we finished, just as we had when we started, and I thanked John for talking to me.

"Glad I could help out," he said. Then he got up and joined Tom's wife Noreen and Theresa, the waitress, who were at the back table under the clock. As I walked by a few minutes later, it sounded like he was telling them about the interview. I wondered what he'd thought of it.

Tom was up at the front counter. As I paid for my Raisin Bran and coffee, I asked him how he'd been feeling.

"All right," he said.

"Still feeling good?"

"Yeah."

"You gonna watch the game tonight?" I asked him.

"Yeah."

"Did you watch the play-off Saturday night?"

"We had company so I had to go away for dinner," Tom said. "Half and half I watched—the first half of one and the last half of the other. But that's a lot of points they're giving tonight, you know," he added. "Ten and a half points? Shouldn't they all be just about equal by now?"

It was another rainy day when I walked out—just like last week. I turned around and studied the front window. I'd walked past it at least a thousand times, but I'd never really stopped to read all the signs: BREAKFAST, LUNCH AND DINNER... LOTTERY TICKETS... CATERING FOR ALL OCCASIONS... LOTTERY CLAIMS CENTER... PLAY HERE, WE PAY HERE... DAILY SPECIALS... STARR TOURS TO ATLANTIC CITY... TAYLOR PORK ROLL... ASK US ABOUT TAYLOR BURGER... ARIZONA ICED TEA SOLD HERE... HOME OF THE WINNERS... LOEFFLER BRAND QUALITY DELI MEATS... and a blue New Jersey vanity license plate that read FRED 1. What a guy he must have been.

There was an old man with a baseball cap sitting in one of the white plastic chairs in front of the window who told me how happy he was about the rain because it meant that he couldn't paint the house or cut the grass today. "Hope it keeps raining like this all week," he added cheerfully.

I nodded and thought of John, who I'd seen out here many times sitting in one of these white plastic chairs, not saying much, just peering across the parking lot. And for a moment I was reminded of the lone blue herons that I'd see down on the beach in Florida, standing motionless and majestic at the edge of the surf, silently scanning the water for hours on end, looking for fish and taking life one day at a time.

MARIE

Tuesday, April 14, 2009. At first, Marie didn't want to talk to me. Well, she'd talk to me, but she definitely didn't want to be interviewed for the book. But then Dave Stout talked her into it. The three of us were sitting at the counter one morning—Dave, Marie and I—and Dave was telling me how one day Marie had told him that she was out of scotch.

"No, no, I didn't," *Marie protested.*

"She said, 'I'm out of scotch,'" *Dave persisted.*

"I didn't say that," *Marie told me indignantly.* "He said, 'What do you usually drink?' I said, 'Scotch,' and he bought me a bottle."

"What kind?" *I asked.*

"Cutty."

"Boy," *I said approvingly,* "that's a decent brand."

"Yeah," *Marie agreed.* "But so what do I have to do for this book of yours?"

"First, you gotta put your thumb-print on file," *Dave deadpanned.*

"Ask John," *I urged Marie.* "I just interviewed him the other day." *John Wilwol was sitting two seats down the counter, quietly eating his poached eggs and toast and minding his own business. He didn't even look up.*

"It's fun," *Dave assured her.* "Just talk to him. Don't tell him about any of your sexual encounters, though," *he added with a wink.*

Marie scowled at him, but she finally agreed to be interviewed, as long as she could stay right where she was at the counter. She definitely did not want to go to the booth in the back where I'd interviewed John.

"So what do you want to know?" she asked me, taking a delicate sip of her coffee. For some reason, Marie always got her coffee in a paper cup, even though she usually seemed to finish it before she left.

"About you," I said. "I don't even know your last name."

She told me, but asked me not to put it in the book.

"And you're from Philly, right?" I said, remembering an earlier conversation that I'd had with her.

"Yeah," Marie replied. "South Philadelphia. Well, I'm originally from North, but we moved to South Philly when the baby was seven." She went on to tell me that she'd had two brothers and one sister, but that her older brother had died.

"Are your other brother and your sister still in Philly?"

She nodded. "You ever hear of the Boulevard in Philadelphia?"

I wasn't sure. "Which one?"

"You know, the *Boulevard*," Marie said, trying to be patient with me. "There's only one Boulevard in Philadelphia."

I got it. "You mean Roosevelt Boulevard?"

"Yeah, that's it," Marie replied. "Roosevelt. They live off there. Both of them. And the nieces and nephews, they all live there, too."

"But you live up here," I said. "How did you wind up coming up here?"

"My husband worked for Hyatt-Clark, and to travel from Cherry Hill to here took like two hours," Marie explained. "So he said, 'Marie, go look for a house up here.' So I did, and I bought the house. And maybe two months later, Tommy, he came to look at the area, and he bought around the corner from me."

"Is that right?"

"Yeah," Marie said proudly. "I bought it first. When I bought it, there was only two houses in Golden Crest. And so then when I bought it, we had a party, and Tommy did the catering. And he said, 'Oh, I like it.' But," she added, "he got a bigger house."

"He didn't mind living close to you?"

"No," Marie laughed. "But he lives like two blocks away."

I asked her what kind of a company Hyatt-Clark was—the place where she'd said her husband worked.

"Well, it's a bearing company," she explained. "Actually, he'd retired. He'd worked at SKF Bearing Company on Frankford Avenue. He ran two factories."

"Oh, he *ran* the factories," I said, duly impressed.

"Yeah, two of them," Marie said. "So he had to go back and forth, back and forth. But anyway, then he retired, after thirty years. *Then* he went to Hyatt-Clark, because he was really too young to retire. And he worked there about five years."

"OK," I said, not sure I fully understood yet. "So when did you move up here? About what year was that?"

"I'm here about twenty-eight years," Marie replied.

About three years longer than we'd lived here, I thought to myself—although it was hard to believe it had been that long. "And how long have you been coming to Fred and Pete's?" I asked her.

"Well," she said, "I came here the first day I moved here. For breakfast. Fred was here then—you know, Tommy's father."

"What was he like?"

Marie smiled. "Oh, I liked him," she said warmly. "A nice fellow. He was—how do you say?—happy-go-lucky. You walk in and he would start singing. Remember that?"

I confessed that I hadn't ever met him.

"Oh yeah," Marie continued. "I used to walk in, and he'd sing that song 'Way Marie, Way Marie.' And I'd say,"—she dropped her voice to a fierce whisper—"'Stop singing that! Everybody's looking at me!'"

I laughed.

"Yeah," she said. "In fact, we had a party, and I have pictures that I gave to Tommy of his mother and father in the kitchen."

"That's great," I said. "So you've been coming here since you first moved up here. And you still come in pretty much every day, don't you?"

"Yeah, I usually come in and have coffee," Marie replied, taking another sip from her cup. "I come in and see Annie, and I give her things, you know."

I nodded. She and Annie seemed pretty close. In fact, she had once told me that Annie was the reason she still came to Fred and Pete's.

"Didn't you once tell me that you used to work for Nabisco?" I asked her, changing the subject.

Marie carefully dabbed the corner of her mouth with a paper napkin. "National Biscuit, yeah," she said. "But I worked there back when it was on Glenwood Avenue. Then they moved to the Boulevard. And that's where my sister lives, not far from there. But that was my first job. I worked on the conveyor..."

"Like Lucy!" I cried. "You know that episode of 'I Love Lucy' where she's working on a conveyor belt in a chocolate factory..."

"Yeah," Marie said absently. "But anyway, we used to go dancing. And in order to get an hour of dancing in, I gave the boss a meatball sandwich one day. He said, 'You make good meatballs.' So one day, we said, 'We want to go to the dance.' And he said, 'What do you mean, you wanna go to the dance?' And I said, 'Well, if you'll let us off at eleven o'clock, we can get in an hour's dancing.' So he said, 'Well, you bring me a meatball sandwich every day, and every Friday you can go.'"

"Son of a gun," I laughed.

Marie chuckled. "So then three or four of the girls, they started to bring him meatball sandwiches. But he says, 'Nah, I like Marie's better.'"

"So where'd you learn to make the meatball sandwiches?" I asked her.

"My mom," she replied. "I used to like to cook. And my sister, she liked to sew. But I was the cook in the family—and I'm still the cook," she added proudly.

"Well," I said, "I've got to figure out a way to get you to make me a meatball sandwich some time."

"You can get Tommy to do that," she said—after all, I wasn't in a position to let her off work to go dancing.

"I don't think it's on the menu here," I said, wistfully.

Marie tried to console me. "Well, Israel can make you a hamburger," she said, but I told her that a hamburger—no matter how good it was—just wasn't the same as a really good meatball sandwich.

She nodded in agreement. But now that we'd started talking about hamburgers, Marie didn't want to talk about meatballs anymore. "You know who has the best hamburgers?" she asked me knowingly.

"Rossi's, down in the Burg," I replied, without skipping a beat. Rossi's was an old neighborhood bar in the Chambersburg section of Trenton where Joe DiMaggio used to eat when he was in town. Their hamburgers were legendary.

"Nah," she said dismissively. "To me, it's the one down by Washington Liquors."

"Which one's that?"

"On 33," she said. "You know Washington Liquors?"

"Yeah…"

"Well, you go down a little further, and on the right-hand side there's a bar."

"And they've got good burgers?"

"Aw," Marie sighed, "to me, they got the best."

"Do you remember what it's called?" I asked her, ready to try any place that could compete with Rossi's.

"No," Marie said impatiently, "but you can't miss it. It's on the right-hand side. The owner died," she added, "but the wife's still living. And she goes to Marrazzo's, gets the best cut of meat, and you get a hamburger like *that*." She held her small hands far enough apart to hold a football.

"No kidding!"

"Yeah," she said, "you oughta try it. Sometimes we go in, have a drink, and we get a hamburger. To me, it's the best around."

"When you say 'we,' is your husband still living?" I asked cautiously.

"No," Marie replied. "He just died."

"He just died?"

"Yeah," she said, "a month ago."

I was stunned. "Oh, Marie," I said, "I didn't know. I'm so sorry." Suddenly she looked so frail, like a small bird. I wanted to reach out and hold her, but instead I just put my hand lightly on her arm.

She blinked and looked up at me. "Thank you," she said. "He went to the doctor faithfully, but he never told him that his back hurt him. See, he had high cholesterol, and he always took care of that. The last year he had it down to one-fifty."

"One-fifty!" I marveled.

"From four hundred," she added.

"Oh my God!"

"His brother's was *five* hundred," Marie declared. "And his other brother's was *six* hundred. They both died. But anyway, like I said, he always took care of his cholesterol, and he always went to the doctor faithfully. And this time, he said that for about a year, his back had been hurting. And he said, 'Maybe I'm working too hard'—because he always does things for people. Like he just did an electrical job in the basement for some friends of ours. He ripped the whole ceiling down and did it all over."

"Wow..."

"Because he said, 'If you don't do that, you're going to have a fire.' Anyhow," she continued, "he always came home and said his back hurt, so this time he finally told the doctor. So the doctor told him, 'Go get a blood test and an X-ray.' So he went, and the doctor called him in and said, 'You have a tumor on your lung, and one on your liver.'"

"Oh, no..."

"And he said, 'Nick, how long has your back been hurting?' And Nick says, 'About a year.' And the doctor says, 'But Nick, every two months you come to me. Why didn't you say something?' And Nick said, 'Well, I just thought I'd been working too hard.' So in one month, he died."

"Oh Marie," I said, "I'm so sorry. How long were you married?"

Her voice was faint. "Sixty-one years."

"Sixty-one years!" I exclaimed. "Did you get married when you were five years old?"

She smiled. "I was twenty-one," she said.

"Are you telling me you're eighty-one years old?"

"Yeah, sure," Marie retorted. "Sure I am."

"That's amazing," I said.

"Well, anyway, that's the story," she said with a deep sigh. "For about three or four weeks, he didn't want to eat no more; he didn't want to drink no more. And the doctor said, 'Just leave him go.' So we got a hospital bed one day, and the next day he was dead."

"Oh my gosh..."

"My son, he lives in Chicago," Marie continued. "He stayed three weeks. My son knew it, but they didn't tell me. He told him, 'Nick, I'm dying. Take care of your mom.'"

"Oh boy," I murmured. "And he didn't tell you?"

Marie shook her head.

"He didn't want to worry you, right?"

She shook her head again, blinking back tears. She didn't say anything.

"Oh Marie, I'm so sorry," I said, putting my hand on her arm again. "Those were good years, weren't they?"

She nodded vaguely, as if I weren't there. "Yeah."

Neither of us spoke for a few moments, and then, to change the subject, I asked Marie how long she'd known Annie.

"Oh, I don't know," she replied. "Maybe ten years, something like that..." She broke into a ragged cough and took another sip of coffee.

I waited until she'd caught her breath. "So it looks like you do stuff with her with the flea market," I said.

She frowned and shook her head.

"You just bring her stuff?"

"Rich people give it to me," she explained, "and I give it to her."

"Why do rich people give it to you?" I asked.

"For presents," she said patiently. "Instead of throwing it out, they say, 'Marie, you want this? You want that?' And I give it to her, and she sells it."

"Right..."

"And then I've got three or four jackets of mine," Marie added. "I thought maybe they'd fit her daughter. I give her a lot of stuff—a chair, a microwave, all that stuff—and then she sells it. It's good stuff; I don't give her junk. The junk I throw out." She paused and reflected. "I believe in giving," she declared quietly. "It's better than taking. Like when Dave gave me that bottle, he said, 'What are you drinking?' And I said, 'I like scotch once in a while.' He brought a bottle in the next day. So I said, 'Annie, I'll pay for his breakfast.'"

I nodded.

"Because, you know, *I* didn't want him to do that," Marie insisted. "So now he kids me about it. And I tell him, 'Shut up, or I'll bring your bottle back.'" She chuckled and added, "But he's a nice guy. He's a real nice guy."

I agreed, and then asked her about her son. "Now, you said you've got a son out in Chicago. How many kids do you have?"

"Just the one," Marie replied.

"Any grandchildren?"

"Oh yeah!" she exclaimed. "I got *great*-grandchildren. I'll show you." And out of her purse came the pictures, a whole book full of them. She started with her nephew, who had just become a fireman down in Baltimore. "Ever since he was born, he wanted to be a fireman," she told me.

Then her grandson with his wife and two beautiful little babies; her son; all her nieces; her daughter-in-law; her granddaughter; her sister-in-law and *her* grandchildren—it was quite a family. "They're all precious," Marie murmured as she turned the pages.

"It's a beautiful family," I remarked.

"This is my son again," she said proudly. "He looks just like his father."

"What's he doing out in Chicago?" I asked.

"He's retired," Marie replied. "He worked for the government; he was a special agent in charge. He worked for thirty years. He's got a degree in teaching, and I told him he was too young to retire, but he told me, 'Mom, I traveled so much. Right now, I'm taking it easy.'"

In charge of what? I wondered, but I didn't ask. Instead, I changed the subject from her family back to Fred and Pete's, and asked her what her favorite item on the menu was.

Marie didn't hesitate. "I like the roast beef with the fried onions," she declared with great enthusiasm.

"You mean like a cheese steak?"

"Yeah, that's right. We used to come, a couple of girls, we'd sit back there"— Marie gestured toward one of the booths in the back—"and I'd get it. But then I'd go, 'I can't eat all that.'" She chuckled. "It lasted me three days."

"You're kidding!"

"And I still eat here sometimes," Marie said. "With Mario and Kathy. I'll have an egg or something." She took a sip of her coffee. "I didn't feel like getting up this morning—it was too early. But they said Mario was here, and Kathy."

"Well, it's good you came in," I said, although as I looked around I didn't see any sign of Mario or Kathy.

Marie nodded absently, and then asked me, "So what are you gonna do the rest of the day?"

"Oh," I said noncommittally, "I have to go to the store, and then I've got some work I've got to do…"

"I've been cleaning the house," she said briskly. "Because we're going to show the house."

"Oh, are you?" I said, wondering whether she really meant "we" or whether that was just force of habit after being married for sixty-one years.

"Yeah," she said. "I'm going to move to Chicago."

"To be with your son?"

"Well, yeah," she replied. "I mean, I'm not going to *live* with him, but I'll be closer to the whole family. Of course, I still have a sister and brother here, and nieces and nephews—I'm gonna miss them. But they think nothing of getting on a plane. They tell me, 'Oh, we'll come and see you, Aunt Marie.'"

I nodded. "I'm sure they will."

Neither of us spoke for a few moments, and then I told her, "Well, we're sure gonna miss you here."

"Yeah... Yeah," Marie stammered. "I'm gonna miss it, too. You know, everybody's been saying, 'Don't go, don't go.'"

"Well, I'm not going to tell you that," I said. "You've got to be with your family."

"Yeah," she agreed. "My son says, 'Mom, you know if something happens— if you get sick or something—I've got to come all the way down here.'"

"But also," I said, "you want to be around your grandchildren, don't you? And now you've got great-grandchildren. You don't want to miss that."

"Well, see, I really didn't spend much time with my grandchildren," Marie explained apologetically. "My son traveled a lot, so I really didn't see them growing up. But now I'll see these little guys growing up," she said fondly, gazing down at the picture of her great-grandsons that was still on the counter next to her coffee cup.

"There's nothing like it, is there?" I said.

"No," Marie agreed with a smile, fingering the silver chain on her glasses. "They keep you stepping, though, don't they?"

"They sure do," I said, thinking fondly of our grandson, who was just turning fourteen months old today.

Marie and I finished our conversation, and when I stepped outside a few minutes later, it was raining again. No one was in the white chairs, but Vicki, wearing a black Fred and Pete's shirt, was standing alone on the covered sidewalk, quietly smoking a cigarette as she gazed out across the parking lot.

"Can't believe all this rain," I said. "And it's supposed to rain tomorrow, too."

"Friday and Saturday's supposed to be nice," Vicki remarked.

"That'll be nice," I said, taking a moment to gaze out across the lot myself as I pulled the hood up on my jacket. The cars had thinned out some since I'd arrived. "Well, take it easy, Vicki."

She nodded. "Have a good one."

YOU GOTTA FIGHT IT

Wednesday morning, April 15, 2009. *Another rainy morning like it was yesterday—sure hope we get some May flowers out of all these April showers we've been having. I get to Fred and Pete's a little later than usual because I'm putting in more time on the treadmill. Dave Stout is sitting at the same two-person table where he was sitting yesterday, having what sounds like the same exact conversation he had with me twenty-four hours ago—only this time it's with Tom instead of me. It's about the parking ticket he got last week when he parked his truck in front of Suzanne Dunn's store a few doors down from Fred and Pete's, and the question is: should he fight the ticket or just pay it?*

"I'm afraid it might be as much as two hundred dollars," he tells Tom, the same as he told me.

"You gotta fight it," Tom says. "Tell the judge there's no place to park in back of her store, so you gotta park out front."

"Plus I was doing her a favor," Dave says. "I mean it was charitable, not business."

"Well, I'd fight it," Tom repeats, and then takes off for the front counter where a heavy-set woman is waiting to buy scratch-offs.

"You still worrying about that ticket?" I ask Dave as I take a seat at the counter.

He tells me again how the problem is that he doesn't know the Township cops and the judges like he used to. It's a whole new generation down there now, he says. Most of his friends on the force have long since retired by now. "And now you look at that Tasty Cake truck," he adds indignantly, pointing at the big blue and white truck parked against the curb right in front of Fred and Pete's. "He's been there at least half an hour already, and I ain't seen nobody giving him any ticket." Then he chuckles and says, "Maybe I should make a citizen's arrest—for comparison purposes when I go to court. What do you think?"

Fortunately, Kay comes to my rescue and asks me if I want anything to eat. I order a cup of coffee and what I call "the international plate"—a Swiss cheese omelet with an English muffin on the side. Meanwhile, Dave is already deep into another conversation with some guy in a blue Yankees jacket who I've never seen before, telling the guy in no uncertain terms that he thinks A-Rod is way overpaid, and that the thirty-three million he gets is more than the entire Marlins roster gets paid. "And he's not even a good third baseman," Dave maintains. "Plays so deep he's practically in the outfield." The poor guy in the Yankees jacket just nods and looks glum.

There are about half a dozen people lined up at the lottery machine, and Joe is working the machine as fast as he can, printing out ticket after ticket for the big red-faced guy at the head of the line while the blonde in the flowered blouse behind him is obviously running out of patience.

As I'm eating my omelet, Tom walks by several times on his way back and forth from the kitchen, and I notice that he's hitching up his pants. Knowing that he's just had a stent put in after his heart attack, I ask him if he's been losing weight.

"Nope," he says, shaking his head. "Haven't lost a pound." Then he grins and adds, "I just bought bigger clothes."

NOREEN

Thursday, April 23, 2009. I was interviewing Midge in one of the booths, although she later decided that she didn't want her interview in the book because she didn't want everybody knowing her business. "I'm basically a very private person," she told me, and I respected her wishes. In any case, after we'd wrapped up, she joined Noreen and Brooke and Theresa at their table for a few minutes, where the four of them talked and laughed a lot—something about women in red hats—and then Brooke and Noreen got up to leave. I decided that this was my chance. Ever since my interview with Tom, I'd wanted to interview Noreen to find what it was like being married to someone who worked thirteen hours a day, 365 days a year, year after year for twenty-seven years. So I jumped up out of the booth where Midge and I had talked and caught up with Noreen at the lottery machine. I asked her if she had a few minutes for an interview.

"How long do you figure it'll take?" she asked, not sounding especially thrilled at the prospect of talking to me.

"Maybe half an hour," I guessed.

Noreen shrugged. "OK," she said, and she followed me back to the same booth in the back. Her sandy hair was short, with a few highlights, and she was wearing a black North Face jacket over a blue t-shirt.

I introduced myself—since, even though I'd probably seen her there a thousand times, we'd never actually met—and I told her that I'd already talked to Tom. "He told me how you guys met here..."

"Yes," she replied vaguely.

"And you were working at the phone company up on Route One at the time..."

"Yes," she said again, a little impatient—as if to say, If you already know this, why are you talking to me about it?

So I switched gears, and asked Noreen if she was from Trenton.

She was, and so were her parents. They'd lived on Mulberry Street when she was born, although later they'd moved out to Ewing. She had two brothers and two sisters. Her older brother and her two sisters were all in their seventies, she said, and her younger brother, who had just turned sixty, was three years older than she was. "So it's a two-family kind of thing," she explained.

Her father had worked for a number of different companies over the years, she said, including Trenton Pottery and Delaval Turbomachinery, but each time, it seemed that after he'd been there a few years, the company would close. "Well, Trenton's lost a lot of businesses over the years," I said, and Noreen nodded bleakly.

We talked some more about how she and Tom had first met here at Fred and Pete's when she and her friend Vicki used to come down from their job at the phone company on Route One for lunch. She'd been waiting at the door while Vicki paid the bill, and while Vicki was paying, Tom asked her what her friend's name was. He wound up inviting her to a party, and they started going out together.

"And was he going to the police academy at that point?" I asked.

Noreen nodded. "We were going out when he went into the police academy. But then he decided not to do that and to come here instead."

"So how did you feel about that?"

"I was glad!" Noreen exclaimed. "Because I wasn't real thrilled with the whole trooper idea. Of course, a lot of things happen to deli owners, too—and he's right there. Coming out of here at night by yourself in the dark in the back... You don't really know... A lot more deli owners get shot than troopers."

"But he's not open late at night," I said.

"No, but he used to be," Noreen retorted, her face clouding as she remembered all those anxious nights. "He used to be open a lot later back then."

I asked her what it was like being married to a guy who worked thirteen hours a day, seven days a week, fifty-two weeks a year.

Noreen took a deep breath. "The way we worked it out, it had to be that he did this and I did that. I was home with the kids, I did the schools, the sports, the dancing, the doctors, the dentists—and," she added, "I always brought the kids here for dinner. They wouldn't have been able to see him otherwise. When he left in the morning, they were still in bed, and when he came home at night, they were *back* in bed. So I tried to bring them down here almost every night. Besides," she laughed, "I don't like to cook anyway!"

She said that back then, when a guy by the name of J.R. was working for him, Tom could take off sometimes in the afternoons, maybe play some golf or work out in the yard. "He likes yard work," she said. "It relaxes him. Of course, now that he's just had that heart attack..."

"Boy, that was a scare, wasn't it?" I said.

Noreen nodded grimly. "Yeah," she said, "a big scare. At first, you know, you don't even realize. But his brother's a heart surgeon, and his brother did say,

'That's a widow-maker.' That's what they call it—a widow-maker. So yeah, that was a scare." She paused and for a moment her gaze dropped to the table-top; but then she looked back up at me. "You know, everybody sits here and tells me, 'You gotta tell him to slow down, you gotta tell him to do this, you gotta tell him to do that.' I can't—besides the fact that they don't realize that you have enough stress with what you already have going on. I had the family at home and he had this, and if I start hounding him about how to do this..."

"It's just going to make the stress worse," I said, finishing her thought. "Yeah, sure."

"Sure, there was times when I wished he was home more," Noreen acknowledged. "But this is how we worked it out, and we did what we had to do. We did it the best we could, that's all I can say."

I nodded.

"He's a hard worker," she declared. "And," she added fondly, "he's a good man. He's generous, and he's a good man."

I nodded again. "That's why this is a good place," I murmured. "If he wasn't the person he is, this'd just be a business."

"It's *way* more than that," Noreen cried adamantly. "Like *Cheers* on TV: everybody knows your name." She shook her head. "I can't imagine what all these old people would do if he wasn't here: some of them are here three times a day!" She looked around and lowered her voice. "This is their family."

I told her that I'd once walked past the original Cheers in Boston, on the edge of Beacon Hill, a very upscale section of town that was nothing like Mercerville. Busloads of tourists came by to take pictures of the place.

Noreen was surprised. "Is that right? It seemed on TV like it was just a neighborhood place where everybody went—and here it really *is* that way. This is what it is, and this is what they do. People just come here looking for other people. They don't have anybody, a lot of them. They don't have *anybody*."

"I know," I murmured.

"One year, we had one of the ladies here over for Christmas," Noreen recalled. "To your house?"

She nodded. "For Christmas dinner," she said with a sad smile. "Because there was nowhere else for her to go..."

At first, she couldn't remember the woman's name, and I told her that a doctor I knew who specialized in geriatrics had assured me that forgetting people's names was *not* an early symptom of Alzheimer's.

Noreen laughed. "It's a good thing, because I'm terrible at it!"

I told Noreen about my recent conversation with John Wilwol, and how he had told me that he'd taken her to pick up Tom at the hospital in Trenton after his heart attack.

She nodded. "Such a nice man," she said. "Yeah, he took me to pick Tom up. Because I figured if I drove to get him, first of all, I'm not so good at finding my way around Trenton—and besides, I'm not that crazy about the area. But secondly, Tom would want to drive home." She chuckled. "You know, he's not one you can hold down too long. But if somebody *else* came to pick him up in their car, he'd have to get in the back and let them drive him home."

"Pretty smart," I said.

"Yeah," she said with a grin, and then repeated, "That Johnny Woo, he's a very nice man."

I asked Noreen whether her kids had ever worked here.

"My kids both did," she replied. "Kent started working here when he was seven, standing behind the counter and everything. He loved it. He used to love to come down here with his father then. He still comes in, but..."

She shrugged.

"He doesn't love it as much any more?" I asked.

Noreen laughed. "He doesn't love it as much any more," she agreed. "But he did a picnic with him this morning, actually," she added. "Kent works 2:30 to 10:30 for the Township, but Tom had a couple of catering jobs, and one of them was this picnic. So Tom'll get him when he can for the catering jobs. Or sometimes he gets him in here on Saturdays, especially on the holidays when it's booming."

I nodded. The place was often a madhouse on weekends.

"My daughter Brooke, she works here, too," Noreen continued. "She's worked here for years before she started working for New Jersey Manufacturer's"—an insurance company. "But she needed benefits. You know, you need to get into something. Because this is not..."

Noreen paused, and then said softly, "I really didn't want this for them, because it's not going to always be here."

"Plus you have to work thirteen hours a day," I added.

"That's right," she said. "It's one of two things: it's either very intriguing to you and you want to take it over because you think it's really booming—which, in past years it was. But it's not what it was. There's too much competition. The younger people, they want one-stop shopping, like the big Shop-Rites or whatever, where they can get everything they need in one place."

"Right..."

"And you know," she went on, "everybody always says, 'Your kids are crazy! This place is a goldmine!'" Noreen laughed, shaking her head. "But Tom says, 'It's a coal mine.'"

We talked some more, and then Noreen said she had to get going. I thanked her for taking the time to talk with me, and then I noticed that John Wilwol had come in while we were talking. He was sitting at the counter by himself eating what looked like tomato soup. Noreen waved to him on her way out, and I stopped by and said hello. He looked up from his soup and nodded.

Tom was working the lottery machine as I was walking out, his red baseball cap pushed back from his forehead.

"Well, Tom," I said, "you done good. Your wife's a very nice person."

"Oh yeah," he answered. "I think I'll keep her a few more years." He paused and grinned. "I think I'd better."

KATHY

Friday, April 24, 2009. It's sunny and windy, a perfect April morning. The flowering trees are beginning to shed their blossoms, their petals scattered across the edge of the parking lot as I drive in. The news, on the other hand, is not so good. According to this morning's paper, the Taliban has now moved within seventy miles of Islamabad, the capital of Pakistan, and Pakistan, as we are constantly being reminded, has a nuclear arsenal. Not good at all.

As I pull up in front of Fred and Pete's, it strikes me how surreal it is to realize that these two very different realities actually co-exist at the same time on the same planet: that at the same time that I'm pulling up to this blissfully peaceful little neighborhood deli on a sunny morning in Mercerville, New Jersey, there is a murderous army of fundamentalist extremists just seventy miles from the capital of Pakistan, dead set on getting their hands on nuclear missiles with which to destroy us.

I've scheduled an interview with Annie for this morning, but she tells me she can't do it today. Her adult son Bryan, who lives with her over in Hightstown, has severe diabetes, and Bryan's doctor has changed his medication. She's picked up the new medication, but now she has bring it home to him because he's going to need it as soon as he gets up. "But you can interview Kathy," Annie tells me. "She really wants to talk to you."

I'm disappointed that Anne can't do it today, but I see that Kathy Kapp is here, just a few seats down from me by the lottery machine. So I get up and ask Kathy if she has time to be interviewed this morning. She smiles and says she does, so after each of us finishes our breakfast, we head to the back booth where I now seem to be doing most of my interviews— even if the odor from the restrooms is a little pungent at times.

Kathy, who had short dark hair and a bright smile, didn't even wait for me to ask my first question. "I feel a little funny with that," she said as I put the microcassette recorder on the table between us and snapped it on ("You'll get used to it," I assured her), "but I'm really happy to be part of this. Because I've been coming here about ten years now, and sometimes I'll wake up in the morning and think, 'Oh, maybe I'll just eat at home...' But no—because you miss the camaraderie, you know? Talking to the people—to Anne or Kay... I mean, it really is part of what I like to do. And it's comfortable here. I mean, look at me. I wake up in the morning, throw a comb through my hair, brush my teeth, and put on my old clothes—because I don't work until twelve-thirty. So I can look any old way I want..."

She paused to take a breath.

"And my husband appreciates that, too," she went on. "Because he has a full-time job, but he works on lawnmowers on the side. So of course he's all greasy and grimy and smelly, and so when I come home, he doesn't want to go to any other place. And plus the food here—it tastes like home cooking!"

I asked Kathy what she usually got for dinner.

"I like the pork," she said. "Or I like the chicken. And I *love* when he has the whole potatoes. Oh my gosh, they're my favorites!"

"How about breakfast?"

"For breakfast, I like to get my eggs clean scrambled, over light or whatever. Israel always cooks them the way I like them. Once in a blue moon maybe they don't come out right, but usually they're perfect."

Kay called over to us from behind the counter: "You two need anything back there? Any coffee? Anything to eat?" We waved to her and assured her that we were doing just fine.

"So it's just a very warm, comfortable place," Kathy continued. "The food's delicious—and it's cheap. You really can't beat it!"

I agreed.

"My mother and sister passed away a number of years ago," she went on, "and Tommy catered both funerals. And the food, people just raved about it. The rolls, fresh and nice, and the potato salad was like home-made..."

"So Kathy," I interrupted her, "are you from around here? Did you grow up here in Hamilton Township?"

"Well," she said, "I was born in Dunellen"—a small town just north of New Brunswick—"and then my family moved down to Kendall Park, so that's where I grew up. Then my husband and I bought our first condo in Grandville Arms here in Hamilton, but then we sold it and bought our house where we live now out on Old Trenton Road. I'm still close, and I shop here as opposed to the West Windsor stores—so I guess I still consider myself a Hamiltonian," she laughed.

"So how long does it take you to get over here in the morning?"

Kathy thought for a moment. "Ten minutes? I just come the back way all the way through, rain, snow, whatever—it's worth the trip. Of course, I've been a little more sporadic this past year because of other things going on. Like my brother needed help. It seems like every time I turn around, somebody needs help," she added with a chuckle.

I asked her what kind of work she did, and she told me that she worked at West Windsor-Plainsboro High School North. "I'm what they call a secretary," she said. "I didn't always do that. I used to work at Boehm Porcelain Gallery."

"Oh, no kidding!" Boehm was a legendary Trenton-based porcelain company that made all kinds of high-end porcelain statuary: birds, animals, religious figures, flowers—you name it.

"I was a computer operator there for years," Kathy said, "and then I worked my way into the gallery, where I became the manager... But you don't want to know all that."

I assured her that I did. "This isn't just about Fred and Pete's. It's also about the people who come to Fred and Pete's and the people who work here—who they are, what their lives are like, what they think of what's going on in the world. So let me ask you, Kathy, what *do* you think of what's going on in the world?"

"It's scary," she said grimly, her voice losing its ebullience for the first time. "It's very frightening. And I feel—and I'm sure *everybody* feels this way—we just feel helpless. We're just everyday people. The most we can do is vote. I mean, what else can we do?"

I asked Kathy what in particular was scary to her.

She took a deep breath. "Well, you never know from day to day if you're going to lose your job," she replied. "I mean, right now I feel pretty secure. They do want to lay off some secretaries, but they're doing it by attrition. And there are people with lower seniority than me, so I feel pretty safe. My husband and I are OK, I think, but my daughter's job—and her husband's—we're just not sure at all. So I worry about them—and they have four kids to boot," she added anxiously.

I nodded. It seemed like most of us were living that much closer to the edge these days, especially after the big financial meltdown. It was amazing to me—and tragic—how the irresponsibility of a handful of selfish Wall Street clowns could directly affect the lives of someone as far removed from that world as Kathy's daughter and her family. Maybe Bob Lee was right about the perniciousness of greed.

I asked Kathy about her job. "What do you do, exactly?"

"I work in the library," she replied, "but only part-time."

I was puzzled. "I thought you were a secretary."

"They call us all secretaries," she explained, "but I work in the library. I check out books, and when new books come in, I process them. I put them on the shelves, help kids find things..."

"So you're a librarian," I declared.

Kathy shook her head. "No. It *sounds* like it, but the librarian has the education. So he's the one who orders the books... I mean, you're right; we do a lot of his duties. But I don't want to mislead you. I'm not a librarian. I wish I was," she chuckled. "I'd be making more money. But I have no college. The position at Boehm I kind of worked my way up to, you know. I've been lucky like that all my life. When I was younger, after I'd had my older daughter, I started working at a data processing place because I knew how to type, and I worked my way into the computer room. I guess that's how I work: instead of education, I kind of ease my way into places."

"So you must be a good worker," I said.

"I guess I am," Kathy acknowledged. "I'll give myself that. I'm a very dependable person. And I'm an honest person—I wouldn't steal as much as a bobby pin from you, you know. That's just how I am."

"That's worth a lot," I said.

"Especially in this day and age," Kathy murmured.

THERESA

As I start walking out after my interview with Kathy, one of the waitresses—a lively, petite young woman by the name of Theresa Carney, tanned, wearing fashionable glasses, and dressed in tight blue jeans and a brightly flowered top—comes up and asks me if I'd be willing to interview her, too.

"I'd like to be in the book," she says bluntly.

"Sure," I say, a little surprised. "When would be a good time for you?"

"How about right now?" she asks.

"Sure thing," I laugh.

"I don't know if I'm that interesting, because I've only been here for a few years," Theresa said as we settled into the back booth, facing one another, "but I guess I'll tell you what I can and then you can decide."

"Fair enough," I said.

"When I started coming here, I was only fourteen—I'm nineteen now," she began in a rapid-fire delivery that never slowed down the entire time we talked. "Anyhow, I used to come in here every day, and I would always annoy Tommy." She laughed. "They'd make me baloney, turkey and ham sandwiches, and he'd say kids are over-rated and why do I need three lunch meats on my sandwich. He would always yell at me about my sandwiches, and I would have to wait. I was in love with the worker Cash, so I would come in and talk to him every day—although he's married now, which obviously spoiled my little crush—and also I would have dinner with Tommy Suits—Tommy Pyle. Have you interviewed him yet?"

"Not yet," I chuckled, trying to keep up.

"He's quite a character," Theresa said. "He's here like every day. So we would eat pretty much every night together."

"OK..."

"So I would come here to eat," she continued, "and everybody came to love me. I would always be yelled at for the clothes I wore here."

"Why?"

"They were too tight or something," she laughed. "Inappropriate. So anyhow, I started asking Tommy if I could work here, and he always said, 'You're not working here. You don't dress right.' So he never gave me a job here. And then one night I remember I came in here—I was already working next door at Carvel for like three years—and I came in here and there was no waitress that night. Cash was leaving, and I was just in here talking to all the old people. And so I said to Tommy, 'Let me help you clean off the tables. I'm a hard worker.' So I started wiping down all the tables; but it was weird, because then I started wiping down all the chairs. And so Tom looked at me and he said, 'Are you wiping down all the *chairs?*' And I said, 'Yeah, why?' And he said, 'You're next in line.' And so the next Sunday, I started working here. And of course I already knew a lot of the people—not like a new waitress starting out. Plus I'm friends with his daughter, and we play tennis. I have Thanksgiving dinner at Tommy's house," she added. "I'm close with his family now."

"Sounds like it," I said, still trying to keep up.

"So anyhow," Theresa continued, "I've really, really enjoyed it. I mean, the people here are kind of insane. I've been the one that has had some... problems with people here," she admitted bashfully, and then laughed. "I mean, they're old-style. Tommy always tells me, 'Can't you wear baggier pants? Maybe that'll help.' And I'm like, 'Well, they might as well die happy.'"

I cracked up.

"Fred and Pete's is my hangout," Theresa said. "It's like a family place. I mean, I loved working at Carvel, and my mom works at Rite-Aid, but here... I mean, I get along with old people really well. I just became friends with everybody. I mean, I'm like glue. You tell me to go, and I'm staying. I love working dinner here, because it reminds me of when I first started coming here. They think I'm going to be here forever, and I'm like, 'I want to graduate college.'"

I asked her if she was going to college now, and she said that she was. "I go to F.I.T. in New York;"—the Fashion Institute of Technology—"I want to be a buyer. But I plan to stay here for a while."

"So what are your hours here?"

Theresa thought for a moment. "I work on Mondays, 1:00 to 6:00. Tuesdays I work the morning shift with Anne, 8:30 to 3:00. On Thursday I work 1:00 to 6:00. And I work Saturday and Sunday. Wednesday and Friday I'm in New York. And I'll fill in for anybody whenever they call me."

"And you want to be a buyer?" I asked.

"Yeah, hopefully," she said. "But here's like the best experience. There's nowhere else you can go, and like eat off people's plates. " She laughed. "And like John, he brings me Easter candy."

"You mean John Wilwol?"

She nodded. "Woo-Woo. I love him," she said fondly. "I used to eat dinner with him all the time, too. Or like Meghan, the other girl who works here. She's been here much longer than I have, for like four years, and we're just *close* to these people. They're kind of like our grandfathers, in a way."

I asked Theresa whether she had any brothers or sisters.

"Yeah," she said, "I have two sisters—who *won't* come in here. I finally got my one sister to come in here for the first time, and she's like, 'The French toast is pretty good.' But I guess the outside appearance... You know, it's not their thing. I'm like, 'Let's go into Fred and Pete's.' And they're like, 'Eww, no... You've got the old men out front, and sometimes they're loud.' But I tell them I just come right up and join right in. They all know me, or they'll call me..." She paused. "I have a nickname," she said.

"What's your nickname?" I asked her.

"Lushka."

"Lushka?"

"My mom's name is Lucy," she explained. "Nobody here really calls me Theresa besides maybe the other waitresses. Tommy's family basically calls me Lushka. Cash made my name."

"Cash came up with Lushka?"

Theresa nodded proudly. "I was called Little Lushka forever. And I will respond to it. If they call me Theresa, I might not hear it, but if they say 'Lushka,' I'm like 'What?'"

"So you actually have your own Fred and Pete's name," I said. "Does anybody outside of Fred and Pete's ever call you that?"

"My mom, sometimes."

I asked her whether she was able to make decent money here as a waitress.

"I put myself through school," Theresa said proudly. "And I commute. So I do pretty well. Of course, I clean houses, too. I've always had more than one job. But I was able to quit Carvel and still put myself through school without Carvel's help."

I was duly impressed.

KAY

I come back around 1:30 that afternoon to interview Kay Neutzman, who gets off at 2:00. I take a seat at the counter and Midge brings me my lunch: a liverwurst sandwich on soft rye with mustard, onions, lettuce and pickles—a great sandwich for $3.50. Midge is in a good mood because Meghan has just arrived, which means that she gets to leave at 2:00. Midge is always going on about how she hates waitressing—hates it!—but of course nobody believes her.

The place is quiet at the moment. A couple of other guys are at the counter eating their lunches and reading house copies of the Trentonian. Tommy stops by and tells me he just finished reading a John Grisham book last night. He says he doesn't have much time to read, and he usually falls asleep after three pages, so it takes a while to get through a book. But he says it was pretty good.

Joe's working the lottery machine, selling tickets to a heavy-set blonde in a shiny red, white and blue striped blouse. The jackpot is $156 million today. "That's a lot of liverwurst sandwiches," I remark to Joe, who doesn't hear me.

I pick up a copy of the Trentonian and leaf through it until I get to the police blotter on page 8, which they call "Law and Disorder." The first item is titled **Yo, Adrian**: "Police said they found Adrian McFarlane, 25, of Franklin Township, Somerset County, in possession of trace amounts of marijuana subsequent to a motor vehicle stop on Route One at North Harrison Street early Tuesday at 1:35 a.m."—that's by Larry's Sunoco, where I used to stop for gas once in a while back when I worked up on Route One.

Next item: **Suspected shoplifter busted**: "Alleged shoplifter Nancy Nicholas, 25, was busted while trying to walk out of Nassau Park's Wal-Mart with $35.71 worth of women's clothing, which she didn't pay for, police alleged. Incident occurred about 7:20 p.m. Tuesday. Police released Nicholas from custody after processing her..." Looks like Tuesday was not a particularly good day for 25-year-olds. Imagine winding up with a criminal record for $35.71 worth of women's clothing.

It's 2:00 now. Midge picks up her stuff and says goodbye, and Kay tells me she'll meet me in the back booth in a minute. As I head back to the booth, the wall calendar beside the kitchen door catches my eye. It's from Johnny-On-The-Spot, New Jersey's Finest Portable

Restroom Service. The crawl on the TV overhead says that the results from the bank stress tests are supposed to be released today. Can't wait!

"So, Kay," I began, "you know what I'm doing, right?"

"Not really," she said.

"I'm trying to write a book about Fred and Pete's," I explained. "There aren't a lot of places like this any more, where everybody knows each other."

"A corner bar without the booze, that's what I always think," Kay chuckled.

"That's about right," I laughed. It occurred to me that this was probably the first time in all the years I'd been coming here that I'd actually seen Kay sitting down. She was always on her feet, always on the move—usually with a coffee pot in her hand—and always dressed in the same high-waisted black waitress pants and starched white blouse that she was wearing today.

"So how long have you been here?" I asked.

"Going on eleven years," she replied. "But I only work two days a week— Wednesday and Friday."

"Is that right?" I was genuinely surprised. "It seems like you're here a lot more."

Kay laughed, a wonderful, full-bodied laugh. She said she'd started working here after she'd retired from Cricket's, a restaurant in the Chambersburg section of Trenton that had since closed. "I sat home for about a year," she recalled, "and then I decided I wanted to work. So I called Tommy up, and I said, 'Do you need any help?' So he says, 'Yeah, I'll give you two days a week.' I've had the same two days since I started."

"No kidding!" I said. "So you knew Tommy before."

Kay nodded. "Yeah, because he used to come in to Cricket's, and he used to come in to the Heidelberg. I worked there, too."

"Had you been in here before?"

"Not too much," she said. "I'd come in a couple of times to buy numbers, but I don't buy that many tickets. I used to come with a couple of girls from the Heidelberg on our lunch break to buy tickets."

"Now Kay, I've got to ask you a question," I said. "You're the only waitress here who actually wears a waitress uniform. What's the story?"

"From my days at waitressing," she replied. "You know, I've been a waitress almost fifty years, and so other than the Heidelberg, where we'd wear the jumper and the blouses, I've always worn this. So when I came here, I just wore this. And everybody said, 'We don't wear that.' And I says, 'Well, I do. I'm used to this.'"

"So you don't wear the black t-shirt."

"Never."

We both laughed.

"I just think that when you're serving food, you should be dressed in white," Kay said. "That's my opinion."

I asked her how she'd gotten started on waitressing.

"It was years ago, when I was married," she answered. "My husband had been laid off, and my neighbor says, 'Come on and be a waitress.' I started out in catering, actually. And then the boss needed a waitress on a Saturday night, and my neighbor says, 'Why don't you do it?' And I said, 'I can't. I never did it before.' And she said, 'Take it.' So I did—and I liked it better than the catering."

"So that was it?"

Kay nodded. "I've been doing it ever since."

"Do you still like it?"

"I love it," she replied enthusiastically.

"What's the best part of the job?" I asked.

She didn't hesitate. "The best part is being around the people," she declared. "Trying to make them happy and content. I always get very nervous when they get up, because I feel that when you go out, you should be served. You shouldn't have to get up to get your ketchup or another cup of coffee. So I get real nervous when I see people get up to get stuff. I think they should be treated like a king and a queen when they go out, you know?"

"And you do," I told her.

"I don't make a lot of conversation, but I try to…"

"You're very friendly," I interjected. "You're always very friendly. And you must know a lot of these people."

"Oh, I do," Kay affirmed. "From when I started waitressing. A lot of them from when I started at Villa Capri; and then a lot that I know from the Heidelberg and Cricket's. A lot of them are from North Trenton." Like most of the people I'd talked to so far, Kay was a Trenton native, although she'd grown up in Ewing and had lived in Hamilton some forty years now.

I asked her what she did on the days that she wasn't working at Fred and Pete's.

"Well, let's see," she said, pressing her fingertips together. "Mondays and Tuesdays I babysit my grandchildren. Of course, they're getting bigger now, but I pick them up from school, take them home, cook their dinner. Then when their mother and father come home, we'll sit down and eat. And I take them to dancing lessons," she added. "But that's just Mondays and Tuesdays. Thursday I shop, and Saturday and Sunday I clean."

It sounded like a very full and well-organized life to me. "And are you living on your own?" I asked her.

"I live alone, yes," Kay replied. "Of course, when you're a waitress, there's no pension, so you've got to work. I do get Social Security, but if you want to go shopping and buy some things, you've got to work a little bit." She chuckled.

"But I love it anyway. I want to work until I die. I don't ever want to quit. Unless something should happen," she added soberly. "Like if I get sick or something."

I nodded. "You don't have health insurance, do you?"

"Oh yeah," she said. "I have it through Medicare."

"Medicare?" I exclaimed. "I didn't think you were old enough for Medicare!"

Kay laughed. "Oh sure," she said. "I'm seventy-six."

"Are you serious?" I was genuinely surprised. "Well, just for the record, you don't look it. I would have guessed maybe sixty."

"Oh," she laughed, "I like you!"

"So what's the hardest part of the job?" I asked her.

"The hardest? *Here?*" Kay replied in disbelief. "Nothing here is hard. Really. It's all easy. Tommy's very easy to work for. I mean, he doesn't ask anything of you other than that you come in to work. I mean, I try to clean up. But he doesn't tell you to. I do that on my own." She smiled. "I'm sure he appreciates it, though."

"I'm sure he does," I said.

I asked Kay whether she ever got together with her co-workers outside of work, and she said that she did once have some of them over for dinner, around the holidays. "But not often enough," she lamented. "I should do it more often."

"I was just curious," I said. Then I asked her whether there were any customers in particular that she was particularly fond of.

"Oh, a lot," Kay replied, beaming. "There's lots of them. Lots of them that are my friends. Midge always goes, 'Here comes your husband,'" Kay added with a laugh.

"A different guy each time?" I asked.

"Oh yeah," Kay nodded. "One guy, he says to me, 'You got so many husbands, I'm afraid to talk to you—afraid I'll get hit in the mouth!'"

I burst out laughing.

"She's always teasing," Kay said fondly. "I tell her, 'Why don't you find me somebody *nice*, Midge?'" She laughed, shaking her head. "Anyhow, it's a lot fun. Anne and I both love it here"

I asked her how long she and Anne had worked together.

"Well, she started right after me," Kay replied. "So almost eleven years now. We're a good team."

"Better than the Yankees," I said.

Kay looked thoughtful when I asked her what she thought about what was going on in the world. "I kind of have faith in our president, and I think he's going to bring things around," she said cautiously. "I don't know. I don't know that much about politics. I really didn't want to vote for him; I wanted to vote for

Hillary Clinton. But I think he's going to do a good job." Then she smiled and added, "But not too many people do in here. It's a real Republican restaurant."

"I kind of noticed that," I said dryly.

Kay laughed.

"Then as far as television," she said, going back to my question, "there's too much sex on television, don't you think? It's too plain. It's too out in the open. And I get nervous when my grandchildren watch, because it'll be on a show that you don't think it's going to be on."

I asked Kay what her favorite movie was.

"My favorite is *Sweet Dreams* with Jessica Lange," she replied instantly. "That's my very favorite. It's the story of Patsy Cline."

"Oh sure," I said, vaguely remembering now.

"That, and *Goodfellas,*" Kay continued. "That's another favorite. I could watch *Sweet Dreams* and *Goodfellas* every night."

"How about *The Godfather?*" I asked.

"I like *The Godfather*, too," she replied, "but not as much as *Goodfellas.* Because when I first started waitressing, it was very much like that in the restaurants—like it was in *Goodfellas.* It brings back a lot of memories."

"Oh really?" I was intrigued. "Say a little more about that."

Kay chuckled. "I mean, guys would come in one night with their girlfriend and another night with their wife. And the boss would say, 'You don't know nothin', got it?' But they were good to us. They were very friendly guys; they were a good bunch."

"You mean they were good fellas?"

Kay laughed. "Yeah, I guess. But that movie is very much how it used to be. That's why I like it."

We talked some more about her family life. Kay said she'd married young— at age eighteen. "I lived in Ewing for a while, til I could work," she recalled. "Then I moved to Hamilton. So I was in Ewing til I was about thirty-six."

"And that's when you divorced?"

"Yeah," she said.

"And you never remarried, right?"

"Never remarried," Kay murmured. "I've got three kids."

"Do they ever come in here?"

"On occasion, my one daughter does. That's because her kids like to come in. But you know, they work during the daytime. They used to come in back when I used to work nights, but not here. Because they're working during the day."

I asked Kay what her kids were doing now.

"My two daughters and my son-in-law are with the state," she replied. "My son is laid off right now; he worked in a plastics factory."

"How long has been laid off?"

"Since last June."

"Last *June*?"

Kay nodded heavily. "Now he's trying to start a new occupation," she said. "He's going in for truck-driver, learning to drive the big trucks." She sighed. "Hopefully, that'll work out."

"How old is he now?" I asked.

She thought for a moment. "Let's see, he's in his fifties. Fifty-three."

"That's tough, to be laid off at that age," I said, remembering my own experience at age fifty-one.

"And my oldest daughter is fifty-seven," Kay said.

"So I guess you're really not sixty," I said. "That wouldn't make sense."

"No," she said, laughing heartily. "I guess not."

She really did have a wonderful laugh.

It was mid-afternoon when Kay and I wrapped up. The place was very quiet. There was an overweight guy in a tight knit shirt muttering into his cell phone at the counter, and an older man by the name of Mike scowling in one of the booths. Meghan, the only waitress working the floor at that hour, asked Mike if he wanted anything.

"Yeah," he growled. "A million dollars would be nice."

Wouldn't it though? I thought as I made my way through the parking lot back to my car. There was a bumper sticker on the car next to mine that said "Real Men Don't Hit Women." I wondered whose it was.

RICH

Monday morning, April 27, 2009. "The old knees are giving out on me," Rich Erkoboni told me without a trace of self-pity. We were in my usual interview booth. Rich, who has curly grey hair and a neatly trimmed mustache, was wearing a sporty green checked shirt and green shorts. He'd been sitting out front on one of the white plastic chairs, along with John Wilwol, Dave Stout, and Marvin Block, peacefully smoking his usual morning cigar, when I'd asked him if he'd be willing to be interviewed. Somewhat reluctantly, and after being assured by Dave Stout that he wouldn't feel a thing, he'd agreed.

"Well, you look like you're good shape," I said.

He nodded. "For seventy-four."

"Really? When's your birthday?"

"August 15," Rich said. "I was born August 15, 1935."

"In Trenton?"

"Yeah, at Helene Fuld Hospital—but it was called McKinley then. My parents lived in Lawrence Township, in Eldridge Park."

"You remember it?" I asked.

"Oh yeah, quite vividly," Rich replied.

"Any brothers or sisters?"

Rich grinned. "Eight brothers and one sister. We had quite a large family."

"I'll say. And where were you in the line-up?"

"Next to the last," he said. "I have a younger brother."

"And what did your dad do for a living?"

"My father, when he first came to this country, he was twenty-two years old and he was in the construction business," Rich said. "Then he went to work for General Electric—worked there for quite a few years. And he worked for Acme Rubber, and he had many, many side jobs because he had a big family to support."

"You say he came to this country. He came from Italy?"

"Yes," Rich said. "My father was from Rome, and my mother was from a little town called Polino." Polino, I learned later, is indeed a very small town in the Umbria region of Italy, about fifty miles northeast of Rome, with a population of about 275 people—although it used to be closer to 500 in the early years of the twentieth century when presumably Rich's mother had lived there.

I asked Rich if he'd ever been to Italy.

"Yes, we have," he said proudly. "Been there twice. The last time we were there, we visited the area where my mother was from. They had a grocery store, and they were also in the restaurant business."

"You still have family there?"

Rich nodded. "My mother had a sister there. That was basically the last of them. But it was funny," he said. "When we first went there, it was this little town on the side of a mountain. And when we pulled up—it was five of us brothers with our wives—they had no idea who we was. And all the windows got shuttered up and everything else. And then, little by little, after they found out who we were, they all started coming out and started talking and conversing with us."

"Do you speak Italian?"

"Enough to get by on," Rich replied. "Before it was all over, we had several invitations for dinner and for breakfast. They really took to us. I mean, they didn't want us to leave. They wanted us to stay overnight. It was big."

"That's terrific," I said. "And so you grew up in Trenton."

Rich corrected me. "Lawrence Township," he said. "All my life. Although I went to Trenton High, because Lawrence didn't have a high school—and they didn't have a junior school either. I went to Junior Three, and then from Junior Three I went to Trenton High. Then I spent a year and a half at Rider"—then Rider College, now Rider University, located in nearby Lawrenceville. "Then I didn't want to go to school anymore, so I had to go to work. I went to work for Heinemann Electric Company and I was there for thirty-six years. I only went there for the summer months because I was going to go back to school again..."

"But you wound up staying?"

"Yeah," Rich said. "And I ended up being a supervisor. I was the youngest supervisor that they had there. When I first went there, I quit twice. But they called me back in again every time I quit—and promoted me!" He chuckled. "They told me they wanted me there, and they sent me back to school again. They paid for all my schooling," he added proudly.

"No kidding!" I exclaimed. "What kind of schooling?"

"Well, I went to the A.M.A.—the American Management Association—for management training. For two years I did that. And each time I graduated from different schools, I kept getting promotions. Ended up as a supervisor, and I was in charge of shipping, receiving, warehouse, traffic. I ended up, I had about two hundred people under me."

"Wow!"

Rich pulled his wallet out of his pocket, thumbed through it, and handed me a worn business card. Sure enough, under the Heinemann Electric Company name, it said "Dick Erkoboni, Supervisor," and listed all the departments Rich had just mentioned.

"And so you retired from there?" I asked.

"Yeah," Rich said. He told me later that he retired after the company relocated down to Maryland—mostly because of what he considered to be irrational and excessive demands by the local union. He actually did work down at the new Maryland plant for about a year and a half—staying there during the week and coming home on weekends—but in the end he decided it was too much. For family reasons, he and his wife didn't want to relocate, and so, at age fifty-six, he took the retirement option.

"Then from there, I stayed home for two years," Rich continued. "I'd been selling used cars at night for my brother who was in the car business, so I did that for a while until I got tired of it, and then I went to work for the Hamilton Township School Board. When they built Crockett School, they hired me as the head custodian there." He looked up at me. "They didn't call it custodian then. 'Engineer' they called me."

I nodded.

"I stayed with them for five years. This was back in the '90's," he said. "They were still building the place when I went over there. They wanted me to learn all the electronics and their whereabouts in the building. And with the background I had with Heinemann Electric, I was in charge of maintenance, too," he added. "So I fell right into place."

Our daughter Amy had gone to Crockett shortly after it opened, and for a moment I wondered whether my wife and I might have passed Rich in the hall back then on one of our visits to the school.

Changing the subject, I asked Rich whether he had been in the military.

"*Oh* yeah," he said sardonically, shaking his head. "I played in the Seventh Army Corps, and I traveled all over Europe playing ball."

"Is that right?" Now we were onto what I knew was one of Rich's favorite topics: baseball. I asked him when he'd first started playing.

"Oh Jeez..." He scratched his head. "I guess I was about eleven, twelve years old. When I was fourteen years old, I had my birth certificate changed so I could play Legion ball. I wasn't old enough to play Legion ball. You had to be fifteen, and I was only fourteen. First I played one year with the Schroths, but I couldn't play with the Schroths because I lived in Lawrence Township. And Lawrence

Township, they had Post 414; I had to go with them. So I left the Schroths and played three years with Lawrence."

"OK..."

"And like I say, I don't know if you remember, but years ago, all the major ball teams used to have try-outs here locally in Trenton," Rich continued. "I don't know if you're familiar with Dunn Field or not—remember Dunn Field and the Trenton Giants?"

I shook my head. "No, I didn't live here back then." In fact, I later learned, I didn't live *anywhere* back then: Dunn Field was demolished in 1950—a year before I was born, far away in Wisconsin.

"Anyway," Rich went on, "that was a Double A pro team, and it was the New York Giants' farm team. And they played here in Trenton at the Brunswick Circle, at Dunn Field. They used to have tryouts there. They also had tryouts at Edsel Field. Well, the first time I went and tried out, I think I was sixteen or seventeen years old, and the guy asked me if I was still in school. So I told him, 'Yeah, I got one more year.' And he says to me, 'Well, when you're done with school, we can talk about baseball.'"

Rich paused and gave me a meaningful look, as if to underscore the wisdom of what the man had told him. "My father was a baseball fan," he said, "but he didn't want any of us guys to do that as..."

"As a living," I said.

Rich nodded. "But the last tryout for the Giants was at Dunn Field. I went down there, and the guy took all my pertinent information. He says, 'I'm gonna come over and talk to your parents.'" Rich sighed. "Well, my father didn't want no part of it. So I'll never forget it: Saturday morning, the car pulls up and the guy comes up on the porch, and he introduced himself. And I'm in the back-yard; I always had a baseball glove on my hand. And my mother says, 'Hey, Mr. So-and-so's here, and he wants to talk to Rich about playing ball.' And my father says, 'He's not gonna *play* no ball. There's two things that are gonna happen to this boy. He's gonna go to work—or he's gonna go back to school again. But baseball: no. He's not gonna be a bum.' Because in those days...."

"No thirty-three million dollar contracts," I said.

"He wanted her to ask the man to leave, and I was pissed," Rich recalled. "And my mom says, 'Well, let's give him a chance.' But my father was dead against it. So that was the history of my ball-playing career."

"What about the burning of the glove?" I asked him, remembering that Dave Stout had mentioned something about it at one time.

Rich frowned. "He took my spikes, he took my glove, and threw them into an outside pit we used to do barbecue in. Threw them in there and he said, 'That's where you're gonna play ball.'"

"That was right after the guy came over?"

"Yeah."

"Oh Jeez..."

"Yeah, he didn't want no part of it," Rich said. "I very seldom got mad at my father, but I was really pissed."

"And do you think he was wrong now, looking back?"

"Oh yeah," Rich said, without a trace of doubt. "And I'm not bragging, but I think I could've made it. Because I compared myself with some of the guys who were playing then. You know, I had the opportunity to play with Willie Mays."

"You're kidding!"

"Oh yeah," Rich said nonchalantly. "Willie Mays played for the Trenton Giants. Well, they took the two best guys from every Legion team, and we played the Trenton Giants as an exhibition game. And I did quite well. Mo Cunningham, who was the first-baseman for the Trenton Giants, when the game was over, comes over and he asks—I was the smallest guy on the field—he asks me, 'Son, I don't know *where* you get your power from. What the hell do you *eat?*'" Rich laughed. "I drove one off the center-field wall. And I'll never forget the pitcher, who played pro ball with the Trenton Giants and later moved on up to the New York Giants. Look it up, and you'll see. His name was Al Corwin. That's the guy I hit the ball off of."

Rich was beaming.

"What position did you play?"

"Third base," he replied. "I had a fairly good arm."

"That's what I heard," I said. "In fact, I heard you've *still* got a good arm."

Rich chuckled. "Not like the old days," he said ruefully. "The thing that used to amaze them was the power I had for such a small guy. I don't know where I picked it up at, but I did have some power for a guy my size. I was the smallest guy out there; I used to bat clean-up."

"Is that so?"

"I would have liked just to have had a shot," Rich said quietly. "See what I could've done, you know?"

We talked a little bit about the state of the world, which Rich didn't think was very good at the moment. He was particularly concerned about all the money that the federal government had been spending in response to the recession. He acknowledged that some of that money was being used so that police and teachers wouldn't have to be laid off, which might be a good thing.

"But in many instances," he maintained, "there's a lot of overkill—in local government, in local police forces, and in your local schools, I think the job can be done with fewer people. You take Hamilton Township: you got twenty-one schools, and there's a principal in each one of those schools, and an assistant, and *another* assistant. You go back and look at the same structure with your Catholic schools: you got *one guy* that's in charge of all the Catholic schools. So how come one guy can do that in the Catholic system and we need ten thousand guys to do the same thing in the public system? Which leads me believe there's room for improvement."

I nodded.

"But no one will fight that system," Rich said angrily. "Because they say, 'Oh, you're against education.' No, I'm *not* against education; I'm *for* education. But let's streamline it and let's make it more efficient."

"Well, you've been on the inside of the system," I said, "so I guess you've seen it for yourself."

"Listen," he said, "when I went to school, if you wanted to play baseball, you bought your own glove, you bought your own bat—because that's what you wanted to do. If I wanted to do it that bad, then I'd save and scrape up money to buy my glove. Well, that's all *given* to kids today. And a lot of kids do not appreciate it anyway. Whereas if a kid had to go out and fight for it and work for it..."

"He'd value it much more," I said.

"Exactly."

I asked Rich my usual question about what his favorite movie was (*The Godfather*, in part because Mario Puzo's brother used to work for him at Heinemann Electric), but what he really wanted to talk about was how important family had been in his life. "Family was a big thing with us," he explained. "There wasn't a Sunday that went by at home that we didn't get together. Everybody had to go to my mother and father's house. It was ritual. If you didn't go, you got scolded. My mother would call and say, 'What's a matter? What's the trouble, boy?'"

"Was she a good cook?"

"Oh man!" Rich exclaimed. "Tremendous! There'd be maybe thirty of us with the kids and all, and she would go down to the cellar—we had a kitchen in the cellar—and in a half hour, she would prepare a meal for everybody. Unbelievable!"

"What was her specialty?"

"I really liked her ravioli," he said fondly. "It was the best!"

I asked Rich how long it had been since his parents had passed away.

"My mother passed away," he replied, "and four months later, my father passed away. He actually died of a lonely heart."

"Is that right?"

"Oh yeah," Rich said emphatically. "They were married sixty-something years. He didn't even want to go to the funeral. He couldn't bear it. They argued—but they were tight."

"So talk to me a little bit about Fred and Pete's," I said. "When did you first start coming here?"

"Oh God," Rich laughed. "It's got to be—what? Ten years ago? I was doing some work with Dave Stout—you know, I work with him sometimes, too—and he says to me, 'Meet me over at Fred and Pete's.' And I say, 'Fred and Pete's? Where the hell is that?' So he told me, and that's how I got here."

"Was Fred still here?"

"No, Tommy was just starting to take over," Rich recalled. "The reason Tommy took to me was because of sports. Because Tommy's a sports guy, too, so we had that in common. And it was like, 'Hey, you wanna help out with a cooking job?' And so I started out just helping him out from time to time. But then it turned into like part of the factory!"

"You help out with the catering, right?"

"Yeah," Rich said. "And he does quite a few. I would venture to say that right now his catering business is as good or better than the store."

I asked Rich how much he actually worked for Tommy these days.

"Well, I would say I do almost all of his cookouts," he replied. "And he'll ask me, 'Who do you want to take with you?' And I'll take Mario sometimes, or Joe. Or if the guys aren't available, I'll take one of the girls. And it's gotten to the point where he'll send me out on jobs by myself, where he's not even involved. I like to think that I've promoted his business a little bit. We've had people come back and say that they want me to do it, so evidently I must be doing something right."

"That's terrific," I said "So you like this place, huh?"

Rich shrugged. "It's a home away from home. Certain people come, you know, and they get along. Other people come and no one likes them, and they can't get along. I have no problem getting along with people. It's all what you make it, isn't it? You can make life miserable or you can make it good. And like I say, I enjoy coming here. It's like if I *don't* come, Tommy'll call me on the phone: 'Are you sick?' If I don't come for a couple of days, he calls. He's concerned."

"Right..."

"Even these guys in here will call me at home: 'We ain't seen you, man.' And whenever I'm home for a couple of days, my wife'll say, 'You didn't get a phone call yet?'" Rich laughed. "She'll say, 'I don't know what's going on down there, but these guys are more concerned about you than you are about me!'"

I cracked up.

"She's also threatened to have my mail sent down here," he added, laughing. "She says, 'Set up your bunk-bed down there, and I'll have your mail sent down. That way you'll save money on gas; you won't have to go back and forth.'"

I WAS WONDERING WHY THEY PUT THOSE ARROWS THERE

Tuesday, April 28, 2009. John Wilwol and Tom Armenti are sitting out front on the white plastic chairs and, having just had my breakfast inside and not being in any particular hurry to get back to my current consulting project, I decide to join them. It's probably the first time since my interview with him last August that I've actually caught Tom sitting still. It's a beautiful Spring morning: a nice breeze, a clear blue sky.

Tom's talking about how this recession has been tough on a lot of businesses, so I ask him how business has been here at Fred and Pete's. He says he hasn't been hurt by it, but his costs are up. Everything costs more: the utilities, the food, everything. But business has not slacked off at all—so far.

"That's good to hear," I say.

We sit without talking for a while, just gazing out at the parking lot, when Tom notices some guy driving his car the wrong way up one of the aisles in the parking lot—against the white arrows that are painted on the blacktop.

"Yeah," he says, "I was wondering why they put those arrows out there. Probably had some paint left over and they didn't know what to do with it, so they just decided to paint some arrows."

John nods in agreement.

Then, spotting an old, old man very slowly making his way across the parking lot, Tom shakes his head and says, "He's still driving."

"Yeah," John says.

Another couple of minutes go by, and Tom spots another guy, but at first John and I can't see him. "You'll see him in a minute," Tom says. "He's wearing a blue shirt. He's going to come around the back of his SUV."

And sure enough, a guy dressed in a blue polo shirt and shorts steps out from behind a Mercedes SUV, talking on his cell phone.

"He's always on his cell phone," Tom says. "He's always talking to somebody about baseball. I don't know how the guy does it. I mean, here it is, ten o'clock in the morning: how can the guy not be working? Every time I see him, he's on that cell phone talking baseball. How does he make a living?"

I ask John if he's done any fishing yet, and he tells me no, the water's still too cold. I ask him whether he ever goes out to Montauk anymore to fish, and he says, no, not since his father died.

Tom asks where Montauk is, and I tell him it's at the eastern tip of Long Island.

John says, "Yeah, we used go out there, and sometimes we'd go out to Nantucket and Martha's Vineyard, too. Great fishing. But the ferries have gotten so expensive, I can't do it no more."

We sit for a few more minutes without talking, and then I get up to go back to work myself. After all, I've got to make a living.

FRED WRIGHT

Thursday, April 30, 2009. I'm at the counter, having my usual Swiss omelet and English muffin and coffee. Anne and Midge are both here. I ask Midge how her dachshund George C. is doing, and she tells me that she only gave him three hundred kisses this morning before coming into work, so she has to go back home and kiss him some more as soon as she off from work. "I just love him to death," she says.

A guy I've never seen before with long, stringy white hair comes up to the counter and orders an Italian hoagie. Seems a little early for something like that, but then again, maybe he's been up since five and this is his lunch.

I notice that Fred Wright is here this morning—how can you not notice Fred? He's a big guy, definitely one of the regulars, always kidding Anne and the other waitresses; and when he laughs—which he does a lot—you can't miss it. You can't miss his Mercedes in the parking lot either; in fact, he's got several of them, all in mint condition. Fred's the kind of guy I could easily imagine leading the fox hunt, hounds baying, horn blaring— and definitely getting his fox.

At the moment, he's sitting by himself at one of the two-person tables, sprawled across the chair, in animated conversation with a couple of guys in suits who are sitting in one of the booths with papers spread across the table. Fred's wearing a red windbreaker and a baseball cap, so it doesn't look like he's going in to the office today. I interrupt his conversation to ask him whether he's got a few minutes to talk to me after breakfast; he says he does.

Meanwhile, Kathy Kapp comes in and takes a seat at the counter, so I talk to her while I finish my breakfast. "Everything OK at the school?" I ask her.

"Yup," she says. "You look around anywhere else and you worry what's going to happen, but at least they've told us right now they're not going to lay anybody off. Just by attrition, when people retire or move. So that's OK. Of course, the kids get very rambunctious this time of year. I mean, after they get back from Spring break, they should just close the schools. The kids are nuts."

She asks me who I've already interviewed for the book and has several additional suggestions. I mention to her that I'm going to interview Fred Wright as soon as I finish my breakfast. Tom Armenti, who's coming by with another tray of sandwiches, overhears me. "Oh, man," he says, "you're gonna learn a lot!"

I started by telling Fred about the book, and some of the people whom I'd already interviewed, including a number of the customers.

"Like who?" he demanded.

"Well," I said, "I started with Dave Stout..."

"Did you ever finish?" he asked, breaking into a big laugh. He loved to bust Dave about what a talker he was.

"So, Fred," I said, "How long have you been coming here?"

He thought for a moment. "I would say... early eighties. I go back to his father; Tommy wasn't here. I had a good rapport with his father—Freddy—because he was a golfer. Him and I and some other people would go different golf places. We'd go to Myrtle Beach, Pinehurst, and we'd play for a weekend or a few days at a time. We got along well."

In fact, he said, it was golf that first brought him to Fred and Pete's. "I would come in here with a group of other people before we'd go golfing—especially if we had an early tee time, because they'd be open here at six o'clock in the morning or whatever."

"So that's how you first met Fred Armenti?"

"Yeah," Fred replied. "And he was also a member of one of the golf courses that I used to be a member of."

But although he'd first started coming to Fred and Pete's almost thirty years ago and was still very much of a regular, Fred told me that there was a period of about four or five years when he'd stopped coming in because of, as he put it, "certain customers who were here."

"So what got you back?"

"Tommy would call me," Fred recalled, "because we would always have card games at my house—Tommy was one of the card players—and he'd talk to me at the card games, so finally I said, 'Oh, I'll bite the bullet.' And I'm glad I did, because I shouldn't have let that length of time go by because of a disagreement with someone."

Fred was originally from Lawrenceville, but his family had moved to Hamilton when he was in tenth grade. Like Tom, he'd gone to Steinert High School, but he said Tom had been several years behind him. "Tom's like fifty-eight or fifty-nine, and I'll be sixty-two. I knew his brother, though. His brother was only a couple of years behind me."

I asked Fred whether he'd known Alito, the Supreme Court Justice, who had also gone to Steinert, but he said he'd been a senior when Alito was a freshman, so he didn't know him back then. "I've had dealings with him with my job, though," he added.

"I thought you might have. Talk a little bit about your job, Fred."

Fred leaned back, his arms folded across his chest. "I'm the proprietor of a legal appellate services company which specializes in assisting attorneys who are appealing and going through the appellate process. So our office assists that attorney with the preparation and documentation in compliance with the appellate rules and procedures of that court, either state or federal. I've been doing it, I guess, about thirty-two years."

I nodded, not sure I fully understood what Fred had just said. Just his description sounded like it came out of a complex legal document. "And you're based in Philly, right?" I said.

"Now," he replied. "I mean, I opened up my offices perhaps eleven years ago in Center City Philadelphia, but prior to that I was with competitors—or ran their programs—for many years." In fact, he said, before he'd started his own business, he'd been in charge of operations for another firm, and he'd been running six offices—including something like a hundred staff, and seventeen attorneys. "It was getting out of control," he said, shaking his head.

I asked him how his business was going, now that he was on his own.

"When I went on my own—of course, you had your growing pains, you know—and I opened with just a two-office suite," Fred recalled. "Now I have a seven-office suite. So things went well, over time. Even with the economic situation today, business is still not bad. A lot of firms who had not done work with me before, now I'm getting work from them, because it's cheaper for them to farm out the work than to have someone on the payroll constantly, like associate partners, or legal secretaries or paralegals. Especially with the cost of benefits."

"Makes sense," I said, remembering that I'd just heard somewhere that health insurance premiums for small businesses were expected to go up an average of 15 percent next year—an *average*.

Fred said that the accountant he'd just talked to had asked him the same question—how business was going—and he'd asked him when he was planning to retire, given that he was almost sixty-two. "But I don't know," Fred mused. "You know, I have expensive tastes. I like to buy stuff. And I think that by going out that early, it may reduce some of that aggressive spending. But another three years is the max," he declared emphatically.

"And you know," he added with a sigh, "the court systems are changing. They're going to e-filing, and that may eventually put an end to services such as ours. In fact, the federal courts are going that route now, but the state courts will probably be another three to five years, because state courts are always behind. Of course, I don't have a crystal ball, so we'll see."

The two guys in suits who Fred had been talking to when I'd come in were putting their papers into their briefcases and getting ready to leave, and I realized that one of them was probably the accountant whom Fred had just mentioned. It reminded me that a lot of business still got transacted here at Fred and Pete's.

"Now you mentioned that you have expensive tastes," I said to Fred. "Do you remember when you bought your first Mercedes?"

"Nineteen-eighty... six."

"And how many have you had since then?"

"Probably ten," Fred replied. "I have three now."

I chuckled. "That's just wild."

"I had four, but I got rid of one."

I asked him which ones he still had.

"I have the S-550, which is the large one," he said, ticking them off on his fingers. "I have the SL-55 ANG, which is the roadster sports-car, hardtop convertible. And then I have the SUV ML 350. And then I have a couple of other cars," he added. "A Chevy King Cab—that's a '71 pickup truck. And then I have a Mazda Six."

"Have you always liked cars?"

"Yep," Fred said.

"Do you work on them at all?"

"Just wax 'em," he said.

"So you're not into the mechanical side," I observed.

"No, not at all," Fred replied, shaking his head. "And now I have a motorcycle, too," he added with a grin. "I like the toys. I'm a believer in the toys. And I think that's one of the reasons probably that I'm not going out at sixty-two. Because I'm a believer in the materialistic concerns."

I asked Fred about his family.

"I have one brother; he's a hair-stylist," Fred replied. "My mom passed on maybe seven years ago; my dad died twenty years ago. I'm married thirty years—no kids. My wife's retired."

"Does she come in here with you?"

"No," Fred said. "If she's been in here, it's for a lottery ticket." He smiled. "My wife doesn't believe that I come in as often as I do."

"What do you mean?"

"Because she knows that I like fancy, classy operations," he explained, and added with a chuckle, "This is not for the food or the décor."

"So why *do* you come here?" I asked.

"Oh, because everybody knows me," Fred replied expansively. "I bullshit with everybody, argue with everybody—you know, laughs!"

We'd talked for about twenty minutes, and I'd promised Fred that I wouldn't take more than twenty minutes of his time. But he seemed to be enjoying the conversation, so I asked him if he had a few more minutes to tell me about some of the cases he'd been involved with over the years.

"Oh sure," he said. "One of the more interesting was the Glenn Miller case. I don't know if you've ever seen the movie."

I had, but I didn't remember anything about it.

"Anyway," Fred continued, "we assisted the family. The son and daughter were adopted. And for many years, the lawyer representing the estate was collecting royalties from all the music and records being played—for many, many years. Because when Glenn Miller—whose name was Alton—when he died, he was a resident of Bergen County. So the probate was in New Jersey. Because he was never found. His body was never found."

"Is that right?" I said. I'd forgotten that, too.

"Never found," Fred repeated. "Back in 1947. So anyway, the adopted kids took the lawyer to court. Because they said, 'Enough's enough. How long does he have to continue collecting these royalties?' See, he was getting a percentage."

"Is that right?"

"So they took him to a lower court and they lost," Fred continued. "And then they appealed it. And the firm that I was with at that time—I was involved in handling it—we had all the originals, because this was in the early '80's and they didn't have the high-speed Xerox and copying services back then. So we had to mark all the original manuscripts—like "Little Brown Jug," all the music—so that they weren't copied and replaced."

I nodded, not sure I completely understood.

"So we assisted in that appeal," Fred said proudly, "and I met the son—Steve. And we were successful in overriding the lower court. So they did sanction the attorney, and there were some fees involved. The purpose of the litigation was just to stop him. And it did, in the appellate court. Then *his* attorney—the attorney for the lawyer—filed for the Supreme Court of New Jersey, but they didn't want to hear the case. So that was the end of that."

"Right..."

"And then I had one with Gotti," Fred went on, barely pausing to take a breath. "And that went to the Supreme Court. But they refused to hear it."

"The federal Supreme Court?" I asked.

Fred nodded. "The Supreme Court of the United States," he said. "It *was* in the Second Circuit Court of Appeals—that's when we got involved."

I remembered having heard about the Gotti case at the time—it had been front-page news—and asked Fred what the issue had been on that one.

"Well, first of all, one issue was they wouldn't allow him—he had the lawyer, Bruce Cutler, representing him—and they said he can't represent him. Because every time he went to court, he would get the case thrown out—because he's a pretty sharp guy," Fred explained. "But then they came out and said he was being paid for his services with mob money. So the bottom line was he had to stop representing him, and so someone else represented him from California. And that was the first time he lost."

"No kidding!"

"So they went to the appellate court in the Second Circuit. In the district court, they lost there. We were involved in the documentation there."

"So you were working for...?"

"We were working for the California firm," Fred said, "who was of counsel for a New York firm."

"Representing Gotti?"

Fred nodded. "And then they filed a petition for review at the Supreme Court U.S., which we assisted in, and then that was denied. And then I think Gotti ended up dying a few years ago in prison, with cancer." I checked later and learned that John J. Gotti had indeed died in a federal prison in Missouri, in 2002, of throat cancer.

"That was an interesting case," Fred reflected. "Because you had the transcripts of certain accusations, as far as how people were killed; you know, the hit man..." He shook his head as he remembered. "And the transcripts were so voluminous. It was from a couple of months, so you had thousands of pages of transcripts. And we had to put everything together to be referenced when they did the legal briefs. And then when they did the legal briefs, we put everything in final and got it to the courts."

I wondered whether they'd been paid by the page. On the other hand, it occurred to me that there might be some risk—however small—in working with a firm that wasn't able to keep someone like John Gotti out of prison.

Thanks, but no thanks.

Still, Fred seemed to be doing just fine, and when I asked him whether he was planning to go down to the office after we'd finished our conversation, he said no, he figured it might be a nice day to take his motorcycle out for a spin. "But the cell phone's always on," he assured me. "And that's one point I make with all my people: if someone calls me in reference to a case or a filing, I don't care where I'm at—unless I'm in court where I can't take their call—I want to be called. Because I don't want that person having the opportunity to call someone else."

Not a chance, I thought as I watched Fred ease out of the parking lot in his gleaming black Mercedes SUV.

TONY

Tony Golowski was in one of the white plastic chairs out front as I watched Fred drive off, and I asked him if he'd be willing to be the next victim.

"Sure," he said. "Why not?"

And so back we went, to the booth in the back. Tony's not a big guy, but he's got a big heart. He was wearing his forest-green windbreaker with the Knights of Columbus emblem, along with khaki pants and a pair of clean white sneakers.

"So Golowski," I said, "that's a good Italian name, right?"

He grinned. "I'm half—a half-breed."

"So how long've you been coming to Fred and Pete's?"

"Oh God," he groaned. "Twenty-five, twenty-six years easy. When I first moved out here—1983—that's when I started coming here." The same year that we'd moved here from North Carolina, I thought to myself.

"So Fred was still here," I said.

"Oh yeah," Tony nodded. "Fred was here. I don't remember Pete but I remember Fred. He was always a happy-go-lucky guy, always singing, and he'd come up, 'Hey, my main man!' Stuff like that. Altogether different than Tommy. Tommy's more reserved. So anyway, Fred was here, and then he passed on. And every day, now that I'm retired, I'm here—two or three times a day. It's the place to come, to meet your friends, socialize—you know, have a good time."

"Sure..."

"We break each other's chops..."

I chuckled. "So are you originally from Trenton?"

"Yeah," Tony nodded. "Chambersburg section. Franklin Street. Two blocks from Trenton High. But Trenton's no longer Trenton. It's all beat up now. That's part of progress—that's life, you know." He sounded more philosophical about Trenton's decline than a lot of the other Trenton natives I'd talked to—most of them were bitter, and often angry.

"So what's your favorite thing on the menu here?" I asked him.

That was a no-brainer. "Steak sandwiches," Tony replied instantly. "The ham and egg omelets, they're good, too. And I like the bagels. But it's the people who are here, that's what makes the place—the people."

"No question about it," I said.

"Name of the game," Tony declared. "People you've never met before, you meet them here, and friendships develop. Like Johnny Bella—I've known him since I was sixteen years old; I'm seventy-two now."

"That's the guy you were just talking to out front?"

"Yeah," Tony said. "A lot of people I meet here that I haven't seen in years. And there's a lot of politicians come in here—I've been interviewed twice on TV, stuff like that. Just a nice place to come."

I asked Tony whether he was active in politics himself, and he shook his head. "No," he said. "I just run golf tournaments. I do like to play golf. I'm not good at it, but I like to play. Stuff like that. But politics, no. I used to be a Democratic judge for the election board, but then I got out of that. I always jumped either way. If I liked the person, I didn't care what they were, Democrat or Republican—and that's the way I've always been."

"Do you still follow politics?"

Tony shook his head. "No, just when it's time to vote, that's all. Not like some people who are fanatics," he added with a grimace.

"So Tony," I said, taking a sip of coffee, "what did you do for a living?"

"Worked for the Motor Vehicles Inspection Station," Tony replied proudly. "Inspected cars, did driver's tests, trucks, investigated gas stations... I did that for twenty-seven years. Before that, I worked for Homasote."

"For what?"

"Homasote," Tony repeated. "On Lower Ferry Road? That makes the paperboard?" He was obviously surprised that I hadn't heard of it. "It was a good job. I enjoyed that job. But the dust got me, and I had to move on."

"Are they still there?"

"Oh yeah," Tony said. "This is the hundredth year they've been in business. They've been there a long time and they make a good product. Else you don't last a hundred years, you know."

I nodded. It was good to hear that not every long-time business had packed up and left Trenton.

"And before I worked for Homasote, I worked for the City," Tony added. "I was in an asphalt gang. And I bounced around. But I finally ended up with the State."

I thought about all the hours that I'd spent over the years, anxiously waiting in line to have my car inspected at the inspection station down at Baker's Basin, and wondered whether Tony had ever inspected my car. I always used to worry

that those guys would find something that would cost me a lot to have fixed—
and since I generally drove my cars into the ground, they usually did.

When I asked Tony about his family, he told me that he had one brother,
Joe, eleven years younger. "A sister died in between us," he added with a sigh.
"She died eight days after she was born."

"Is your brother still around?"

"Oh yeah," Tony replied with a smile. "In fact, we went to Atlantic City the
other day. We have Brother Day three times a year and we go out to A.C. And
then we meet for lunch a couple of times a week. We're close, even with the age
difference."

"And you're married, right?"

Tony nodded. "Married, two kids, grandfather. My brother's got two kids,
too. It was all boys until my granddaughter. She was the first girl in fifty-six
years!" His face broke into a big grin.

One of the things I knew about Tony from my earlier conversations with
him was that he'd been active in putting together golf tournaments, so I asked
him to tell me a little bit about that.

"Well," he began, "I started the Anthony J. Golowski Memorial Foundation
in memory of my father when he passed away. First year we made a hundred
and fifty dollars—just the guys in the Cook Athletic Association, which I'm a
lifetime member of. Then we progressed along. In fact, over the twenty-six years
that I did it I think we've given out over $200,000 to charity."

"No kidding!"

"All the money went to charity. Nobody got paid," Tony said proudly.

"Which charities...?"

"We did 'em all: Mayo Clinic, Cancer, St. Rita's Orphanage, the Heart Fund,
Cystic Fibrosis... everybody got a piece. Then I had a heart attack last year, and
I stopped. Too much."

"Sure..."

"And I helped the Knights with theirs, one or two tournaments, but I'm
outta that, too, this year," Tony said. "I'm not doing nothing, because I had a
double bypass, so I'm not going to run no more golf tournaments. Time for
somebody else to get aggravated, you know."

I said it must have been scary having a heart attack, but he said it wasn't like
that. "I went to the hospital and they said, 'Oh, you had a little heart attack.' It
was nothing to me; I just felt a little pain. This year, I was supposed to go in for
a stent and they ended up doing a double bypass—*that* was scary."

"Do you feel better after having the bypass?"

He nodded. "I would say yes. Sore—but I do feel better. I had the bypass in January—January 14th—and the doctor told me, 'You're gonna be sore for quite a while. You're always gonna feel pain.'" Tony shrugged and added that he'd also had surgery for prostate cancer, and that once in a while he'd feel a twinge from that, too—"like something's missing, I guess."

"So you're taking it a little easier now," I said.

"Right now I am, yeah," Tony replied. "But I can't wait to get out and play golf. Even though I'm the world's worst, I still enjoy it, you know what I mean?"

I laughed.

"What is it you like about golf?" I asked him, hoping that he could answer what for me had always been one of life's great mysteries.

"Just being out in the open," Tony said. "It's a game my father told me about as a kid. He caddied and I caddied, and I got involved in it. Then when I retired, I worked for Cherry Valley for ten years, taking care of the driving range and stuff like that, so I had good times there. And then when I got to seventy, I quit. That's it. You know, enough is enough."

"And you're seventy-two now, right?"

"I will be in May," Tony replied, nodding. "Although some days I feel like a hundred and nine."

"It's good you're writing a book," Tony said. "I can't put stuff down on paper. If I could ever write a book, I'd write it about Motor Vehicles. What a book that'd be! Some of the stuff we'd see the customers do or try to pull..."

"What kind of stuff?"

"Ah," Tony groaned. "Like this one guy says, 'My wife only uses the car to take the kids to school,' and the tires are balder than hell and he's got all this heavy construction stuff in the back. Or this one lady comes in dressed like a millionaire and she's got a hole in the back of her car like this;"—he spread his hands across the length of the table—"her kid's standing across the hole, and she says, 'Oh, he won't fall. He knows better.'"

I burst out laughing.

"But it was a good job," Tony declared, and then frowned. "Now, of course, they've screwed everything up. They took too much stuff away from it. Like headlights—which is *important*, you know. They screwed it all up. They'd have people come into the office that didn't know nothing, and they'd say, 'Well, you should have this, you should have that,' and they'd try to speed things up. But you can't speed things up when people come when they feel like it. And they worry about pollution, but they aren't worrying about the headlights blinding people—stuff like that." He shook his head in disgust. "They've screwed that whole system up."

I asked Tony how he felt about the state of the world in general.

"I don't like it one bit," he replied emphatically. "I don't see why the world's in such bad shape."

"What are some of the biggest problems you see out there?" I asked him.

Tony sighed. "I don't know, we're just screwing this world up. I don't like the way things are going. Guys want to marry guys, women want to marry women... Somebody's going to want to marry an animal pretty soon. I mean, you want to live together with people, *live* together—who cares? But I don't want to hear about no *wedding,* you know? That's my opinion, anyway..."

Tony scowled and went on. "I just think the whole *world's* in bad shape—not only us," he said. "Wars, fighting about stupid shit. Like religion: you're never going to change one guy's religion from another. They can't even get along inside their *own* religion. I mean, look at Christianity in Ireland, for example. Five hundred years the Catholics and Protestants were fighting each other. Now you got the Muslims fighting the Muslims—ridiculous!"

I asked Tony whether he was active in his church.

"I go to church every Sunday," he replied. "And I'll usher every once in a while to help out."

"Are you still at OLS?" I asked, referring to Our Lady of Sorrows Church.

"I go to OLS, yeah, and I go to St. Anthony's," Tony said, although he didn't like the fact that the two congregations had been merged. "*That* I didn't like," he declared. "And I didn't like when they turned around and changed McCorristin High School to Trenton Catholic Academy. That was wrong, because the man that built that was Michael McCorristin. And Trenton Catholic left us back in the '50's. And," he added, "I don't like the way some of the priests are now—so lax and everything. Today, nothing's a sin no more. Back when I was a kid, *everything* was a sin."

I chuckled and asked Tony which church he had attended as a kid.

"St. Joachim's," he replied instantly. St. Joachim's was one of the venerable Catholic churches in the Chambersburg section of Trenton, which was then heavily Italian. "I remember Father Paul Butler, the first black priest there," Tony recalled. "Everybody got pissed off that he came, and then when he actually got there, they all loved him—because you could hear him!"

I was curious to know a little more about Tony's childhood and so I asked him about his parents.

Tony smiled. "My father was Polish," he said. "He was born in Trenton, and he was an orphan by the time he was twelve—lived with his sister. He worked for American Steel and Wire for thirty-two years. My mom was Italian, born in Trenton, too. She was the oldest living person on Franklin Street—lived there the longest, from a kid of seven until she was eighty-seven. Misticoni was her name. And my grandparents—Dominic and Margaret—excellent people. They loved me like nobody's business!"

Tony was beaming. "And my father, he was a good guy," he said. "In fact, when he died, all the little kids around the neighborhood, they went out and took a collection—these kids were nine, ten years old—and bought flowers for him."

"No kidding!"

"Everybody loved that man," Tony declared.

"Why?"

"Because he was a nice guy. Never talked bad about nobody. He didn't care what anybody did, as long as you left him and his family alone. And at his funeral, you would have thought the mayor of Trenton had died, there was so many people. We had wall-to-wall people for three and a half hours," Tony said proudly.

"That's fabulous!"

"He was just a nice guy," Tony repeated. "Wouldn't talk bad about anybody."

I was reminded of a man I had worked with for many years who had died recently, and how he, too, had been revered, both during his life and at his death. And he, too, had never "talked bad" about anybody—at least not in the twenty years that I'd known him. It struck me just how rare that particular character trait must be for it to be so widely admired in the very few people who actually lived their lives that way. "Judge not that ye be not judged."

Tony then told me that his favorite movies included *Mama Mia*, *Wiseguys*, and of course *The Godfather*; that he'd been a mess steward in the Army Reserve; that he'd coached baseball at the Cook Athletic Association for fifteen years; and—last but not least—that he was an unabashed meat-eater. I asked him whether his wife was a good cook.

"*Very* good," he replied. "She won an award for her cooking."

"Is that right?"

"My sons are good cooks, too," Tony proclaimed, "and my father could make chicken cacciatore just like the Italians. My grandfather too. Mom made her own clothes and won contests for her cookies, and my grandmother was also a good cook. And my Aunt Mary was an *excellent* cook—her sauce was top shelf. "

"Really!"

"Oh yeah," Tony assured me. "And I used to hunt with my Uncle Gabe—my Aunt Mary's husband. I had a good life growing up. I can't knock it."

"You used to hunt?"

Tony nodded. "Up in the Pocono Mountains. Of course, my wife didn't want me to go hunting; she was afraid I was going to get killed or something."

"Yeah, right..."

"Then who'll cut the grass?" Tony deadpanned.

I lost it.

Addendum: *Tony later told me proudly that about a month after his interview, on June 2, 2009, he finally got his first hole-in-one, at the Mercer Oaks golf course. At the time, he was playing with John Bullaro, Rick Klein and Joe Stica—which meant that he'd had three reliable eye witnesses who could vouch for him in case anybody had any doubts. Not that anybody would, right, Tony?*

ANNE

Friday, May 1, 2009. A rainy day. 9:15, and I'm at the counter. Anne, who's wearing her black Fred and Pete's t-shirt and her big hoop earrings, brings me a cup of coffee and asks me, "What you havin', honey?" I tell her the Swiss—meaning Swiss omelet with a toasted English muffin, which I sometimes refer to as the International Plate. She says it just got busy, and it is busy: Bob Lee and his friend Jim are here at the counter, talking to some guy I don't know; Fred was at the counter when I came in; Marvin was sitting out front, keeping dry under the overhang—just another day in the neighborhood.

I'm going to interview Anne at 10:00—she says she can do it today—and Vicki's here, too, so maybe I can catch her when she gets off at 11:00. We'll see.

Israel's working the grill fast and furious, ladling out quick circles of pale yellow pancake batter, and Kay is the other waitress this morning besides Anne. The TV is off this morning for some reason—not that it matters, since I've never seen anyone ever actually watch it, except once when they showed a replay of somebody striking out A-Rod in the bottom of the ninth. Everybody loved that.

Joe's working the cash register, and Gonzalo, the dishwasher, is coming out of the kitchen with a tray full of clean coffee mugs, wearing a red baseball cap, a faded red t-shirt, a smock, and his usual enigmatic smile.

As Anne brings me my Swiss omelet and I smother it with ketchup, Joe comes over to work the lottery machine, and pretty soon it's chirping like a tree full of birds, spitting out ticket after ticket for the one guy that's standing there waiting.

John Wilwol walks in carrying a dripping umbrella, and takes a seat at the other end of the counter. Tom is here, too, wearing a blue polo shirt with black pants today. Jimmy and Bob are on their way out, but Bob stops to say hi before he leaves. I realize that we've sort of become friends since that first time we got into that conversation last summer and he told me about "Frederico" and about his pulmonary fibrosis.

As I work my way through my breakfast, I watch Kay to see how she works the room. She's at one of the booths pouring the guys there a refill on their decaf, comes back behind the counter, puts the pot back on one of the burners, picks up somebody else's plate from beside the grill, takes it to one of the tables, comes back to get the regular coffee pot, takes it back to the table, comes back and puts the coffee pot back on its burner, comes over to the toaster machine, and starts buttering two big slabs of toast. "You're hustling today," I tell her, and she laughs. I tell her that every time I see her now, I think of "Goodfellas," and she laughs again and says that's really what it used to be like in some of those places she worked in Trenton. "I'll have to see it sometime," I say, and she tells me that they show it all the time on A & E. "You can't miss it." She puts the buttered toast on a plate, sticks a couple of Smuckers strawberry jams beside the toast, and takes it down the counter to John Wilwol. He says something to her that I can't hear, and she bursts into peals of laughter.

Meanwhile, at the other end of the counter, Anne is showing a couple of customers a picture on her cell phone of her grandson Jake holding a puppy. I realize it's the puppy that was killed several months ago—and I remember vividly how devastated she was when it happened.

Now Joe's slicing meat and Vicki's working the lottery machine. An older lady wearing a dungaree jacket and grasping an aluminum cane is buying a wad of tickets, and the machine just keeps churning them out, one after the other.

Theresa comes bopping in and takes a seat at the counter—she must be Anne's relief at 10:00. I tell her hi, and she smiles and waves. She asks Kay what kind of muffins are still left. "Blueberry, corn and banana," Kay tells her, so she chooses banana.

Then the guy with the black cap that says "SECURITY" across the front walks in and takes the seat between Theresa and John. I've talked to him once before and I've asked him whether he'd like to be interviewed for the book, but when Anne told him that I was writing a history of Fred and Pete's, he told me with a grin that he doesn't want to be in a "hysterical" book. But of course now he is anyhow. His name is Tim Desmond.*

Wouldn't you know it? I'd been waiting for months for a chance to interview Anne, but either she was too busy or I was. Ever since my interview with Tom last August, I'd been talking to her about it, trying to find a time when we could sit down and talk. After all, she was a big part of the reason that I was writing the book in the first place. It was her reaction to my earlier book that had first started me thinking about maybe writing a book about Fred and Pete's. And it was her stories—about her life, about her family—that made me realize what a wealth of stories there might be on both sides of the counter at Fred and Pete's.

And now, finally, I had my interview with Anne. But, to my horror, as soon as I got back to my desk later that morning and played back the tape, I discovered that I had accidentally recorded my interview with Vicki, who I interviewed right after Anne, over the first half it. I couldn't believe it!

In a panic, I picked up a pen and started jotting down everything I remembered from the interview while it was still fresh. Thankfully, my memory

---

*   Sadly, Tim passed away on August 5, 2010. He was 70 years young, and a great human being.

seemed to be working a little better than usual on this particular morning, and here's what I wrote:

Born in Kingsport, Tennessee, on Virginia border... Middle child of 5, oldest was a brother who died two years ago... Father half German, half Cherokee, deceased... Mother just died recently, in her 90's... Father was outgoing, but had a drinking problem... Parents both worked at the local newspaper in Kingsport but family moved when Anne was 3.

Moved every year, father managed apartments, last three years of high school in Pennsylvania. Just had their 40th reunion there... Met her old boyfriend Eddie at the reunion... She had broken up with him and married his college room-mate instead ("He swept me off my feet"), but the marriage had only lasted 4 years. Said she apologized to Eddie at the reunion, and said it was very hard. (I remembered her talking about how her re-union was coming up and how nervous she was about it, but I hadn't understood the reason until now.) Eddie told her that he'd waited 12 years for her before getting married himself. Anne said she wonders if she should have gone back to him after her marriage broke up.

Had her twins, Bryan and Jennifer, during the marriage when she was 23... After the marriage broke up she worked flea markets while her kids were still at home... Went into office work once they went to school.

Eventually got into a relationship with a doctor... Moved to Maryland but it didn't work out, so came back and lived with son Bryan in Chambersburg.

Started waitressing through daughter Jennifer... Worked at Golden Dawn Diner for six years, then a restaurant called Eddy's but didn't like it... Was talking to one of the customers who said his friend Tom Armenti was looking for a waitress... Worked out beautifully... That was 11 years ago, a month after Kay.

Bryan was born with diabetes, has had a kidney and pancreatic transplant... But the pancreas didn't work out... Diabetes returned, wound up losing half his foot after walking around all day with a friend in New York City.

But as for the interview itself, Anne and I sat face to face in the back booth, which felt a little strange after so many years on opposite sides of the counter—Anne standing, me sitting. "So what's it like when you get here at five?" I asked her.

She furrowed her brow as she thought about it. "Oh," she said, "there's about three or four guys that are waiting to get in. They wait in their car til we get here, and they'll help me bring in the rolls. I start my... putting the creamers on the tables, doing the butter, slicing the bagels—all that kind of stuff. But by six o'clock," she declared, "every seat at the counter has somebody sitting there."

"No kidding! And is Tom always here when you get here?"

"Oh yeah," she said, her hoop earrings shimmering as she nodded. "Ninety-nine percent of the time. Sometimes Vicki'll open up when he goes down the shore or something. But he's good. Sometimes I'm late—like I'll misplace my keys and I won't get here til ten after five. So I'll call him and tell him, and he's like, 'Don't worry. Get here when you can.' He's a good boss, a real good boss." She sounded sincere—not like she was just saying it in case he actually did read the book when it came out.

"Like when I was having all the trouble with Bryan," she went on. "Let's see: Bryan didn't get the transplant until 2000, so he was going through a lot, being on dialysis and all. And then a year and a half after the operation, he got real, real bad chronic pain in his chest—it's from the scar lesion. It's very typical," she added. "He's on so many different meds. For high blood pressure and everything involved in diabetes..."

I nodded, not really sure what to say. It was amazing to me how someone with so much heartache in her life could be such a source of joy to the people around her. I remembered Marie telling me more than once that Anne was the only reason she kept coming to Fred and Pete's—and she wasn't the only one.

"So now tell me a little bit about Jake," I said, changing the subject. Jake was her daughter Jennifer's son, and I knew that he was the light of Anne's life.

And sure enough, her face brightened like the sun had suddenly come out. "Oh, he's wonderful," she beamed. "Just had his Spring concert last night."

"And he's how old now?"

"Eleven," Anne said proudly. "It was great when he was first born. I got to see him every day. My daughter and her husband and Jake had an apartment downstairs, on Moffat Avenue in Chambersburg, and Bryan and I had the apartment upstairs. Actually, Bryan had the apartment first while I lived with my sister down in Mullica Hill for about a year and a half—this was after I first came back from Maryland—but then when he got sick and had to go on dialysis, I moved up here and took care of him. And then my daughter got pregnant and had the baby, and I would go down and get him in the morning, because I didn't have to go to work until four—that's when I was working at the Golden Dawn..."

"Right..."

"We lived there until he started kindergarten," Anne said. "His father said, 'I don't want him to go to school in New Jersey, and since my parents live in Pennsylvania, I'm going to take him there.' And now he's just excelling in everything," she added with a smile.

"So he lives in Pennsylvania? I didn't realize that," I said.

"Oh yes," Anne replied. "He lives in Levittown with his father. He goes to Walt Disney Elementary School. He plays the violin, he plays the drums, he goes rock-climbing with his dad. They go quadding; they go to Ocean

City, Maryland, every year. He's a good father. He's a real good father. And my daughter is with me helping with Bryan. He's had toes amputated so he needs help, and Jennifer is a great help."

"But you still get to see Jake quite a bit, don't you?"

"Now I do," she chuckled, "because he just made friends with these two little boys right down the street from us. But he's such a sweetheart. He loves me to death."

I asked Anne whether Jake had ever been in Fred and Pete's. She said that he used to come in all the time when she lived right around the corner. "And it was so funny, because when he first started coming here, Tommy's daughter Brooke worked here—and he just *loved* Brooke! He even said to me, 'I'm going to marry Brooke.' He was like three or four years old," she laughed. "But even like a year ago, Jake asked me, 'Does that girl with the dark hair still work at Fred and Pete's?'"

"Is that right?" I laughed. "He still remembers her."

Anne smiled. "Um-hm."

Just then Midge came up with two paper cups of ice water, one for each of us, put them in front of us, then turned and headed straight back to the counter—presumably so that she wouldn't interrupt us. "Thanks, Elaine!" Anne called after her. She was one of the few people at Fred and Pete's who called Midge by her real name.

Midge just waved.

"So Anne, tell me," I said, taking a sip of the water, "what do you think of what's going on in the world these days?"

"Oh my goodness, it's scary what's going these days. Very, very scary."

I asked her how she kept track of it. "Do you read the paper? Do you watch the news on TV?"

"No," she said, shaking her head, 'my son does all that. My son, when he was seven years old, he used to watch the news—with my ex-husband. My ex-husband was very intelligent, used to watch the news all the time. He was just an intelligent man. He would buy sports cars and fix them up and sell them for profit. And I can remember my son playing outside and he would say, 'Mom, tell me when the news is on.' When he was seven years old. My son's very intelligent also."

"No kidding," I murmured.

"He watches the news, I read a little bit of the paper," Anne said. "And it's so scary. Not that I try to hide it or not *know* what's going on—because you have to know what's going on—but it's just scary. I think of my grandson, and what it's going to be like when he grows up..."

"Now when you say it's scary, are you talking about the economy...?"

"The economy, all the diseases and illnesses..." She shook her head again. "You know, the doctors, they have no idea. They try one medication, if that doesn't work, they have to try another medication... I honestly believe a lot of it is germ warfare. I don't *know*," she acknowledged, "but where's it all coming from?"

"Right..."

"And then there's the ozone layer, because the ozone layer is so bad. The rainforests being depleted, you know, all this stuff going on in the atmosphere. I mean, I watch all those shows, and I love them: A and E, the History Channel, Discovery—I love them. And all the crime shows, I love them, too," she chuckled.

I asked her what her favorite show was.

"My favorite show? Oh, *Survivor* right now," she said enthusiastically. "I love that show. People are like, 'Ooh, you watch that?' It's so funny, when it first came on, like eight years ago, my daughter was like, 'Oh Mom, you would be great at that! I'm gonna nominate you to go on *Survivor*.' But I couldn't, because you can't take medication—and I take a thyroid pill. So I missed out," she laughed.

"Well, you're a survivor here," I told her.

"Yeah," she said ruefully, "I'm a survivor here. I've always been a survivor."

Just then Joe walked by, shrugged and gave her a look.

"You be quiet, Joe!" she called after him, laughing.

"And what's your favorite movie?" I asked her.

"Oh," she said, "*The Sound of Music*. I *love* that. And let's see, what other ones do I like? *Dr. Zhivago*—all the old movies."

"The old movies are great," I agreed. "You're the only one I've asked who hasn't said *The Godfather* or *Goodfellas*."

"I've never seen *The Godfather* and I've never seen *Goodfellas*," Anne declared. "I've never seen either of them. But I love movies. I keep track of all the actors and the actresses—who they got married to and who they got divorced from, all that." But she said she'd never watched the Oscars or the Grammies or any of those shows—not even the Miss America Pageant. "I wasn't a nice looking kid when I was younger," she explained. "I think I'm very nice looking now..."

"You are," I agreed.

"...but when I was younger," she continued, "I had these great big brown blotchy freckles and red—I'm talking orange—red-orange hair. It wasn't very pretty. So I was made fun of a lot. I didn't really have boyfriends. And like I never really established a friendship, because we moved every year from sixth grade to eleventh grade. So every time I'd make a friend, we'd move. But then when I got to eleventh grade, I had to repeat it, so I was there three years before I graduated. So I made some friends there."

"Including Eddie," I said.

Anne nodded. "Including Eddie. My little Eddie. Sometimes I think I should call him just to say, 'Hey, let's just meet and have a cup of coffee and just talk.' Because when we were at the class reunion, I apologized to him."

"Did you?"

"Yeah," she replied. "It was something I just wanted to get off my chest. So I just took a deep breath and I apologized to him. But he didn't really even say anything. He just said, 'I just want you to know that I didn't get married for twelve years.'"

"Oh God," I murmured.

For a moment I wondered whether Anne's extraordinary sympathy and compassion for some of the customers who were hurting—like that time when the old carpenter Jake had lost his wife after having been married to her for something like sixty years and Anne was so kind to him—whether that came from her own hurt and loneliness as child and a teenager. And that made me wonder whether it was even *possible* for someone who *hadn't* experienced at least some degree of loneliness and rejection themselves at some point in their lives to ever feel genuine sympathy and compassion for someone else who was hurting. But that probably wasn't a question that Anne could answer.

"So tell me about some of the people here," I said, changing the subject. "Like Marie. Let's start with Marie."

"Oh, little Marie," Anne said fondly. "She used to sit back here and do her numbers all the time, and I would bring her coffee. And then I just sat down one day and started talking to her. And we just found out that we were both giving people and that we liked doing stuff... So we just formed a friendship."

"Well, she says the only reason she comes here is for you," I said.

"That's not true!" Anne laughed, a little embarrassed. "She says that, and I tell her, 'Don't say that.' And she says, 'Oh, if you ever left, I'd never come in here again.' And I tell her, 'Don't say that, Marie. This is a nice place to come. You know people here and you'd miss them...'"

I nodded and remarked that in fact Marie used to come in before Anne had started working here.

"Oh, yeah," Anne said. "She's been here for a while—a long while. But I really like everybody that comes in," she went on, and then added, "except for maybe one or two—and one of *them* doesn't come in any more except on the weekends when I'm not here. So they call him The Weekender."

I laughed.

"But mostly, I like everybody," she continued. "And there's perks with some of them. Like there's one guy—Joe. He used to work at Vespia's, the tire place, and when I first started working here, he was so nice to me. If there was anything wrong with my car and I didn't have the money, he would put it on his account up at Vespia's where he worked and then I would pay off the account. Isn't that wonderful?"

"Sure is."

"And Tommy used to lend me money when I needed money, and I'd pay him back," she said. "Just a lot of perks. The guys, they'd bring me donuts—and then I'd have to eat them," she chuckled. "Or like with my flea market stuff. Every day I go out to my car, and there's something new in my car. And I'm talking full sets of Pfaltzgraff service-for-twelve dishes—the full set!"

I'd never heard of Pfaltzgraff dishes, but it sounded impressive.

"Clothes, jewelry—people just leave stuff," Anne declared in amazement. "Designer clothes! Designer shoes, handbags... Like Kathy brought me a big bag and there were maybe three or four designer handbags in it. That was just yesterday. I mean, God is just so good! He's just *so* good to me!"

"Sounds like it," I said.

"And then I sell in front of my house," she went on. "I've been doing flea markets for thirty years."

"You go to Willingboro, right?" I'd heard her mention the Willingboro flea market many times over the years.

Anne nodded, taking a sip of her ice water. "I used to go to Willingboro Grand Marketplace—only because it was just so cool. I had like an eight by thirteen space, and I just did it so beautifully with all my stuff. It was like having a little store, and that made me feel good. But it wasn't really profitable, because it was new, so not enough people knew about it."

She explained that she used to have a little ledger in which she wrote down what she'd sold and how much it was. Then at the end of the day, she'd add it up, deduct the cost of the gas and the space, and she'd found that it wasn't really all that profitable. "I made like four hundred dollars," she recalled.

"That's not bad," I told her.

"From October til like May," she added ruefully.

"You're kidding! I thought you meant each time!"

She shook her head. "No," she laughed. "Over that whole time."

"So now you're just doing it from your house?"

"I'm just doing it from in front of my house in the summertime," she said. "First weekend of every month. I've got regular customers that come back, and I have people that come to my yard sales. You'll have to come to one some time."

"So that's the other thing you do besides waitressing?" I asked. "The flea markets? And between the two, you're able to make ends meet?"

Anne nodded.

"But it's pretty tough, isn't it?"

"It's *real* tough," she replied earnestly. "I get by by the skin of my teeth. Like this weekend is the town-wide yard sale. I'm like two hundred dollars short on my rent, so I'm thinking, 'Oh! Well, I'll count my eggs before they hatch, and I'll have that two hundred dollars.' But now it's going to rain, and I don't have it. But my landlord's so good. Like I said, God is so good to me. My landlord understands that Bryan is sick and has a problem, and he hasn't raised my rent in six years."

"Wow..."

"But it's fun," Anne declared. "I always like doing the flea-marketing. I love talking to the people. I'll have to show you one of my cards," she added brightly. "When Brooke was working here, she designed the cards and the saying."

"Oh really?" I said. "What does it say?"

"It says, 'Don't kick it to the can, call Anne. She will pick up your useable unwanted treasures.' I passed them out in here, and people just started bringing me stuff—and they still bring it!"

I asked Anne where her compassion came from. She shrugged and said she didn't know. Maybe because she was a Pisces, or maybe because she was a middle child. "And people are kind," she said. "The more you give, the more you get. I don't know, I do it naturally—unless there's someone I don't like. Then I'm nasty and mean."

I cracked up. "In all the time I've been here, I've never seen it," I told her. "I've never seen you be nasty and mean."

"You missed it yesterday," Anne said. "I was nasty and mean yesterday."

I smiled. "Really?"

"We have this new coffee cup," she explained. "Some of the customers don't like the new coffee cups. They like the big heavy coffee cups. So Gonzalo is down at the toaster, and Walter came in, and I was picking through trying to find a *big* cup. So I'm moving the little cups, and Gonzalo and Israel start hollering at me for moving the cups around. I guess I interrupted his design or something. So anyway, I said, '*I* know what I'm doing! *I'm* the waitress here. I know what my customers like. Walter likes the big cup! And you're the dishwasher. You wash the dishes.' So I was mean. That's what I said."

"But can they understand you?" I asked. "I mean, how good is their English?"

"They understand," Anne assured me. "Oh yeah. They've been here so long, they understand. They're not dumb. Gonzalo, he'll act like he doesn't understand you. He'll say, 'Me no speak the English.' And I'm like, 'Yes you do. You know *exactly* what I'm saying.' And then he'll smile—so I know he *does*."

I laughed.

"I've even brought stuff in for *them*," Anne added. "To send home. I'll give them like clothes and jewelry and perfume and stuff." She chuckled and said that Gonzalo made a big point of the fact that he was from Mexico and that Israel was from Guatemala. "It's like a social peer thing. It's kind of funny."

I said it was probably like being from Jersey or Pennsylvania.

"Yeah," she sighed. "Where did I just hear somebody say that Jersey's the arm-pit of the United States? I was like, 'Oh my gosh!' I don't know where I heard that. I think maybe it was on that new show, *The Real Housewives of New Jersey*."

"Oh yeah." I'd seen the promos, but I'd never watched it.

"When I get like I just want to escape, I'll watch *The Real Housewives of New York City*," Anne continued. "Which is unbelievable. This one girl—her husband is a multi-millionaire—it was just her birthday. She went out and bought a designer pocketbook for *sixteen... thousand... dollars*."

"Oh my God..." I murmured.

"For a *pocketbook*!" Anne cried in disbelief. "And I'm just like, 'Oh my Lord...' And this girl, she says, 'I really feel bad about this, with the economy being so bad and all these industries shutting down and laying people off'"—Anne switched to a spoiled-little-rich-girl falsetto—"'but I just *love* this pocketbook!'"

I burst out laughing. "It makes you crazy, doesn't it?"

"It does," Anne agreed, shaking her head in amazement. "And they showed the price tag right on it!"

Addendum: *My interview with Anne reminds me of a short piece that I wrote about my first encounter with Jake Wig, a retired carpenter who used to come in to Fred and Pete's just about every day. I wrote it on January 9, 2007, the day that Anne told me that he'd passed away. I'm inserting it here because, on reading it over, I realize that it's as much about Anne as it is about Jake:*

JAKE

This morning, Annie told me the sad news: Jake had died. She said he died the same day that my van got caught in the flood out in the parking lot. When was that? New Year's Day? So nine days ago. Anyway, she said, apparently that afternoon Jake had told his son that he wasn't feeling well, so his son had taken him out to the car to take him to the doctor, wrapped him in a blanket, and gone back into the house to make sure all the lights had been turned off. When he came back out to the car, Jake was dead. Just like that. And just shy of his ninety-third birthday, Annie added.

It had been a while since I'd last seen Jake. More than a year, because I know he sent me a Christmas card from his new address in Cream Ridge last year, and then another one this year after I'd sent him mine. He'd stopped back at Fred and Pete's off and on since he'd moved away, but never when I was there. Annie would tell me, "Oh, you just missed him." Or she'd tell me the next day, "Oh, he came in yesterday less than ten minutes after you left."

From time to time, I did think about driving out to Cream Ridge to visit him—after all, it was probably only about a half hour drive—but I never got around to it. Not that we were really all that close. Except for that one time when he invited me over to see his house before he sold it, the only place we ever met was at Fred and Pete's. And we never planned it. It was just one of those things where if I came in and saw Jake sitting at the counter, I'd sit next to him, and he'd do the same if I got there first. I'd get my Swiss omelet and coffee, and he'd usually just have his hot chocolate.

I remember that from the very first time I noticed him, which I guess was about a year before he moved away. It was a really busy morning, and Annie was like a crazy woman trying to keep up with all the orders. Jake was sitting two seats down the counter from me—this frail little red-faced guy in a big winter coat who looked like he'd either had a very hard night or a very hard life—and I heard him asking Annie in this broken little voice to bring him a cup of hot chocolate. It struck me at the time, because I'd never heard anybody else order hot chocolate at Fred and Pete's, and so I didn't think they'd have it. But Annie said OK. Only then, instead of hot chocolate, she brought him a cup of coffee.

As soon as he realized it was coffee, he tried to get her attention. "Chocolate!" he called out, feebly. "Chocolate! Chocolate!" Over and over. But the place was in an uproar, and Annie was so busy with all the other orders, trying to cover the tables as well as the counter, that she didn't hear him, and I could see that he was getting more and more worked up. So when she came back behind the counter to pour more coffee for the guys in the booths, I got her attention and told her what had happened.

"Oh, Jake," she said, turning to face him. "I am so sorry. I know you said you wanted hot chocolate. I just wasn't thinking."

That's how I found out his name.

Anyhow, Annie stopped what she was doing, and fixed Jake his hot chocolate, which basically just meant pouring the mix out of a little foil packet into some hot water and stirring it up.

"So how've you been, Jake?" she asked him gently, as she set the steaming cup in front of him.

"Not so good," he muttered.

"Sorry to hear that," she said. "You been sick?"

"I can't stop thinking about her," Jake said, and suddenly he was in tears. "I miss her so much, Annie."

I turned away, feeling like an intruder.

"I got some pictures," he told her in a broken voice.

"Of your wife?" Annie said.

"I just got them back from WalMart last night," Jake said. "They're from the week before she died."

I turned back and saw Annie slowly thumbing through the photographs. "Oh," she murmured as she paused at one of the pictures, "what a beautiful smile! Did she always have such a beautiful smile?"

Jake nodded, the tears still streaming down his thin red cheeks.

"How many years were you two married?" Annie asked.

"Sixty-seven."

"Sixty-seven years! Oh, my God!" she cried. "My husband and I didn't last ten years together before we split up. Sixty-seven years!"

"She was everything to me," Jake said, so softly that I almost couldn't hear him.

"Well, you know that she's still looking after you," Annie said soothingly. "Right this very minute, she's up there looking down at you with that same beautiful smile, just like in this picture. You can feel that, can't you?"

Jake looked up at Annie with a small, brave smile. "I guess I can," he said.

I didn't say anything to Jake that first day, but I saw him there again maybe a week later, and somehow—I don't remember how, exactly—I started up a conversation with him. And it turned out that, among other things, he was a musician: a guitarist and a singer. His favorite music, he said, was the old standards, songs like "Stardust," and he especially loved the old cowboy songs by groups like the Sons of the Pioneers, who were big back in the 1930's. He told me how he used to be quite a yodeler, something that he'd picked up from listening to the old cowboy singers.

Along with yodeling, Jake also loved to talk—not just about music, but about fishing and gardening, about his family, about his long career as a carpenter and a builder, and about his days growing up in Trenton back when it had still been a great place to grow up. Mostly, I just listened. Every so often, he would mention something about his wife, and his eyes would tear up. But gradually, as the months wore on, he seemed to have come through the worst of his grief, and he started to look and sound less fragile.

One day, I asked Jake if he ever played his guitar anymore. He said he had tried to, but he couldn't get his arm around it the way he used to. "It's because I hurt my shoulder when she died," he said vacantly, his face clouding over. "I was holding her in my arms, you see, and I wouldn't let her go."

But then a few weeks later he told me that he'd tried a smaller guitar, and that he'd managed to play it for almost an hour before his shoulder started hurting again.

"You should make a recording," I told him.

Jake grunted.

"For your kids," I said. "And for your grandkids and your great-grandkids. It would be a great thing for them to have."

I kept after him about it for months, telling him how easy it was to make a CD and how little it cost for studio time nowadays, and how his son—who was an excellent pianist and who had made a CD himself—might be able to help him. "Maybe you guys could play on it together," I suggested.

Jake always told me that he'd think about it, but he still hadn't done anything about it by the time he moved out to Cream Ridge. So I figured that was the end of that. But I did say something in my Christmas card to him this past December about how I hoped that he was still playing.

And in his card back to me, Jake wrote, "I made a CD."

I told Annie about it this morning, and she said she'd get in touch with the family to try to get one, and that if she could, she would get one for me, too.

I hope she can.

VICKI

It's almost 11:00 when Anne and I finish the interview, so I decide to wait a few more minutes for Vicki to finish her shift. She comes over when she's done and joins me in the back booth. She's wearing her usual black pants and black shirt, her hair cut short and her eyes squinting, as if she's trying to see something far off in the distance.

"OK, Vicki," I began. "I really appreciate your taking the time to do this. I know you've been on your feet all day and you must be tired."

"No problem," she replied.

"So you know Noreen going way back, right?" I said, figuring that was as good a place to start as any.

"Since we were twelve." Vicki's very soft-spoken, and I had lean forward to hear her over the usual background racket.

"Since you were twelve," I repeated. "And are you from Trenton originally?"

She nodded. "Ewing, yeah. Born and raised in Ewing. I'm still in the same house."

"Still in same house?" I said, incredulous.

"Yep. Fifty-seven years."

"Fifty-seven years? But you're not fifty-seven years old!"

"Yeah, I am," she said, flashing a quick grin.

"So were you and Noreen in the same class?" I asked her.

Vicki shook her head. "We went to totally different schools. I went to the Catholic school; she went to the public schools. It was through mutual friends. Through mutual friends a bunch of us girls went to a dance at Incarnation School, and coming down Olden Avenue—on the side of Olden Avenue where the church is—my street cuts off from Olden Avenue. The rest of the girls, they wanted to walk down Parkway, all the way around, and I said, 'Well, I'm just going to walk down here, because this is my street. Why should I walk all the way around?' But they didn't want to do that, and so Noreen says, 'Well, I ain't gonna let you walk all by yourself.' So that's how it happened."

"Isn't that something!" I cried.

Vicki nodded. "We just met that night. Me and her walked home, and it started from there."

"That's really neat," I said. "Because that's sort of the way she is."

"Yep," Vicki agreed. "Always looking after somebody else. It turned out she lived a couple of blocks over from me, and we just started to meet up."

"And then later you both wound up working at the phone company," I said, recalling what Noreen had told me. "How did that happen?"

Vicki thought for a moment. "Noreen, actually, she finished her sophomore year in Ewing. And then all of a sudden, her family came home one day and said, 'We've bought a house in Hamilton.' They did not tell her or her older sister. Her brother was going off in the service..."

"Oh, man..." I murmured. It sounded as if Vicki was still upset about it all these years later.

"And so that's how it came out to be," she continued. "They bought this house over here on Wilson, so she had to finish her two years of high school at Steinert. She was really upset about that, of course. Didn't know anybody—all that. So I'm like eight months older than her, but before I got my license I had my older sister drop me off here in the summer and we'd hang out—because she didn't know anybody over here. And then I got my license..."

"So you could come over on your own."

"Right," Vicki said, nodding. "And I had two sisters working for the phone company, and so we worked there in the summer of our junior year. Then April of our senior year we came back and started part-time, and as soon as we graduated, we went full-time."

"And you were there a long time, right?"

"Yep. Thirty-four years. I was assistant manager for switching. We surveilled the offices to make sure there was no blockage—make sure there was a dial tone on time," she explained. "And I also supplied the data for engineering to the central offices. So we did engineering and surveillance of the switching machines."

"OK," I said, not really understanding a word of what she had told me. "And you did that until you retired?"

Vicki nodded.

"And when did you retire?" I asked.

"I retired November 2003, when they offered a package." She chuckled. "I couldn't refuse it."

"When you say you couldn't refuse it..."

"It was a very good package," she declared, smiling broadly. "Plus I was traveling up to Irvington every day."

"And you didn't want to do that any more?"

"Well, it didn't make sense, you know. I spent more time and all the money on gas—especially with the way gas prices have gone up," she added. "I'm glad I did it."

"So is that when you started here?" I asked her.

"Here to the deli, you mean? That was 2005," Vicki replied. "Brooke got a full-time job, so she was going. And Kent was going with another job... So Tom didn't really *have* anybody. So me and Noreen said, 'Well, we'll have to learn, but we'll help out as much as we can.' Because he was stuck. Come to find out, I just helped out until it came into full-time," she said, and started laughing. "Six days a week."

"Six days a week?" I exclaimed. "So how many hours is that?"

"Usually I do about five or seven. But then sometimes it's eight," she added. "Or sometimes twelve."

"So you're putting in more than thirty hours a week."

"Yep," Vicki said. "I never worked weekends in my life with the company; never worked a holiday. Now I work weekends and holidays all the time," she laughed.

"Great retirement, huh?" I said.

She kept laughing.

I asked Vicki if she liked working at Fred and Pete's.

"Oh, it's not bad," she said. "At the phone company I never worked with the public. It was all inside the company. But it's all right for part-time." She grinned. "I use it for my casino money."

I laughed. "Is that right?"

"Besides," she said, "I couldn't stay home. Even my grand-nephews, when I retired, they said, 'What are you gonna do? You're gonna go nuts!' So this came along and now..."

"And now you can go nuts here—and get paid for it!"

Vicki shrugged. "Pretty much."

I asked her what her job was, and she said that basically she worked up front. "Up front you take care of the checks, and cutting the lunch meat, doing the salads, and doing the catering orders. And the lottery," she added. "And of course whenever they get stuck back here, you clear the tables off or pour the coffee or whatever. Just like sometimes the younger kids'll come up front and take the checks when *we* get busy, you know."

"Everybody pitches in," I said.

"Everybody. Like Anne'll run up and answer the phone. The only thing they don't do is cut the meat—or the lottery," Vicki said. "Then they just tell 'em, 'You'll have to wait.' So basically, that's it. Oh, and I do deliveries," she added, meaning that she handled the deliveries from the various suppliers to Fred and Pete's—the bread guy, the meat guy, the soft-drink guy—all that.

"So what's the best part of the job for you?" I asked her.

"Meeting all the wacky people," she replied without skipping a beat.

"Who are some of the wacky ones?" I laughed.

"The older ones," Vicki said. "Some of them, they're not with it, and then they make it your fault because it was wrong. And some of them are very arrogant, you know. They're old and set in their ways, and they don't have patience. It's them first and it's their way—especially at the lottery machine."

I laughed. "And you say this is the *best* part of the job?"

"It's really the whole place," she explained. "It's not a business as most businesses are today. This is a family-run business that welcomes everybody, OK? If you don't have the money to pay, come back later. Now what store would do that?"

"Yeah, right..." For a moment, I tried to imagine trying something like that at one of the nearby fast-food franchises.

"Or like a guy came in the other day," Vicki continued. "Said he just came from the hospital—rushing his mother to the hospital. He's right out front and he's out of gas. He's gotta get home to get his wallet and get back to his mother, and he wanted to borrow five dollars. He said he'd leave his cell phone for collateral. Five dollars. You know, if he comes back, he comes back."

"Did you know him?" I asked.

"No."

"And did he come back?"

"Not yet," she said. "I wasn't here yesterday, though. But there's people like that that you'll meet out front, and they'll be like, 'I need two dollars for the bus,' you know, that kinda stuff. But like even in here, we don't take credit cards, so they'll say, 'I'll come back with it.' And most of them do. In fact, I haven't seen anybody who hasn't yet."

"Is that right?"

Vicki nodded. "In fact, there was one lady who didn't realize we didn't take credit cards, so she said she'd be back. Well, guess what? A year later, her *mother* comes in. It turns out she was from out of town and she'd totally forgotten about it. But then every time she'd come up to visit her mother, she'd remember—but then she'd forget to get here. So this time, her mother came in and said, 'My daughter is so-and-so. She's from another state and she owes you for a potato salad from more than a year ago.'" Vicki chuckled as she remembered. "Since then, she'd had a baby and everything, but her mother came in and paid for it."

"She paid for the potato salad?"

Vicki shook her head. "Tom was there," she recalled. "He said, 'If you came back a year later to pay for it, you deserve to get it for nothing.' And so he wouldn't let her pay for it."

"He wouldn't take the money?"

"Nope. Since they came back a year later to pay for it—they were that honest—he said they deserved to have it for free. So you see what I mean?" Vicki said. "You'll never get that in any of these other places."

No argument there.

"Or like we don't collect pennies," Vicki continued. "If it's $2.53, we'll take $2.50. A lot of places, everything's to the T. But he just tries to make it easy for everybody."

"Sure..."

"A lot of seniors," Vicki reflected, "they don't really have any place to go hang. Like all the guys hanging out front—it's something for them to do. They get up in the morning, and it's like, 'I'm gonna go to the deli, I'm gonna have my coffee, I'm gonna meet so-and-so there, I'll have a little conversation.' There ain't no places like that any more."

"That's right..."

"The only time he kicks them out of the booth is when it starts to get busy. Most places, you couldn't have one person just sitting in a booth. But people sit here all day long. Then there's the crowd that comes in for breakfast, comes in for lunch, and then they come back again for dinner. But these are like single men that have no families or no place to go. So they come here and see Mr. Smith or Mike here or Harry here, and they'll have dinner together—instead of always sitting home alone."

I nodded.

"He's tried to keep it reasonable. *We're* the ones that raised the prices," Vicki declared. "I said, 'Tom, you've got to raise them a little bit'—because his costs were going up, you know? But he looks at it and says, 'I think that's a little too high.'"

I wasn't sure who she meant. "When you say 'We'..."

"The waitresses," Vicki said. "Like he never charged for tomatoes. He's never charged for all that extra stuff—and he *still* won't do it. We bring in menus from all over the place to show him. He says, 'Yeah, I know, I know...'" She sighed. "He tries to keep it down—but it's costing *him* more."

"But I guess he's doing all right," I said.

"It's the catering," Vicki declared, shaking her head. "If it wasn't for the catering, we wouldn't make it." She said that the deli business was down from what it used to be, and so was the lottery. "Everybody's got one now," she said. "Used to be, the line was out the door."

I asked her if she ever bought a ticket herself.

"Yeah," she replied. "I buy 'em every day."

"Do you ever hit?"

"Yeah."

"What's your biggest score so far?" I asked her.

"Seven hundred and fifty dollars," Vicki replied. "It was the Pick-Four. I play it three times."

"So you think you got your money back now?"

"No," she said. "Not by a long shot."

I burst out laughing, and so did she. "But it's something to look forward to," she told me as she caught her breath.

I asked Vicki if she ever went to Atlantic City.

"Yep," she said. "And we go to Philadelphia Park, because it's closer." Philadelphia Park was a big casino in Bensalem, Pennsylvania, less than half an hour away. "We go to Philadelphia Park a lot. Usually once a week, or at least once every two weeks."

"Who's 'we'?"

"Noreen, her sisters, Tom's son..."

"So you've got a whole group."

"Yeah," she said. "If one don't go, at least three of us'll go."

I asked Vicki if they went to the same casino every time, and she told me that when they went to Atlantic City, they'd go to different casinos. "But Philadelphia Park is just too close," she said with a grin. "It's very convenient."

"Is that right?" I said. "You mean it's too easy to lose your money?"

She laughed. "Too easy to lose your money. If it was further, you'd think twice about going. You know, like we could be sitting over at Tom's house in the summer, sitting on the patio having dinner, and somebody'll say, 'We should take a ride, it's nice.' And all of a sudden, the dishes are gone and everybody's up and gone! Because it's so close. You wouldn't do that if it was Atlantic City."

"So it looks like you and Noreen still have lunch together most days," I commented. "A lot of times, I'll see you guys sitting over that table when I come in for lunch."

Vicki shrugged. "She comes in here usually every day," she said. "Then afterwards we might run to BJ's, or we'll go to the outlets or whatever."

"So you guys have been lifelong friends, and you still are," I said.

"Oh yeah. I was the maid of honor at their wedding, and I'm Kent's godmother," she said proudly.

"That's terrific!" I exclaimed. "So do you remember when Noreen met Tom?"

"Oh yeah," Vicki replied. "In here."

"Tell me about it." I'd heard the story from both Tom and Noreen, but now I wanted to hear Vicki's version.

"We worked on Route One in Princeton at the time," she recalled, "right down from the Princetonian Diner. And we came here for lunch once in a while.

Tom used to work up front, and so one time I went up to pay the check. She had already walked out the door, and he said to me, 'What's her name?' So I said, 'Noreen'—which is an unusual name."

"Right..."

"And he says, 'Oh, OK.' Well, her sister-in-law used to come in here, too, to buy lunch meat and stuff, and he knew that she was her sister-in-law. And so he says to her, 'Your sister-in-law Lorraine...' And she says, 'I don't have any sister-in-law Lorraine.' And he goes, 'Yeah, your sister-in-law *Lorraine.*' And she says, 'I don't *have* a sister-in-law Lorraine.' And he goes, 'Yeah, you do. She comes in here with Vicki.' So she says, 'You mean *Noreen!*'"

"So he didn't realize..."

"And then he blames me til this day that I said Lorraine," Vicki chuckled. "I says, 'Tom, I think I know her *name*, you know.'"

I cracked up.

"So that's how that got started," she went on. "And then they started talking and he asked her out."

"And the rest is history," I said.

Vicki smiled broadly. "The rest is history."

While we'd been talking, Noreen had come in and taken a seat at their usual table under the clock, and now Brooke and Kent had joined her. It was 11:40, just about time for lunch, so Vicki went over and took a seat with them at the table.

Feeling kind of hungry myself, I decided to stay for lunch and took a seat at the counter. Kay fixed me a really good cappy sandwich on soft rye with plenty of mustard—cappy is capicola, a spiced Italian ham, that, according to Kay, they cut fresh for every sandwich—and then, while I was eating, Midge came over and so I asked her how her dachshund George was doing.

"Fine," she said brightly. "I gave him eight hundred kisses before I came in to work today. And then the week after next, he's going to my mom's for a week, and he gets lots of kisses from her. Plus, she's got a stroller for him."

"A stroller?" I said. "For a dog?"

"He doesn't know he's a dog," Midge explained. "And he gets tired when he has to walk a long distance. So we put him in the stroller."

"Well," I said, trying to keep a straight face, "don't ever let him get in front of a mirror, or he'll find out he's a dog."

"Oh," she said breezily, "he's already been in front of a mirror. He thinks he looks like me. We've got the same nose."

Now what in the world do you say to that?

TOM PYLE

Monday, May 4, 2009. It's another rainy morning. You can smell the bacon and pork roll cooking on the grill, and somebody's burned another bagel in the toaster oven. As soon I sit down at the counter, Tom Armenti comes up to me and says, "You gotta interview this guy. He's a regular here." He points to a man in sitting alone in one of the booths and says his name is Tommy Pyle. "But they call him 'Suits,'" he adds. I ask him why, but Tom just grins and says, "He'll tell you."

It occurs to me that so far, I've known all the people I've interviewed for the book, at least a little bit. But I've never talked to Tommy Pyle before, never even said hello, so it feels a little strange to go up and ask him, out of the blue, whether he'd be willing to be interviewed.

Still, if Tom thinks he's worth talking to, it's probably worth a shot. So I go up and introduce myself and ask the guy if I could interview him after I've had my breakfast. He looks up from the sports page of today's Trentonian, smiles and says sure, he'd be happy to talk to me. Seems like a nice enough guy, I think, as I go back to the counter for my Swiss omelet and English muffin.

After I'd finished my breakfast and paid the check, I brought my coffee cup with me to the booth where Tom Pyle was sitting and introduced myself again. "My name is Paul," I said as I slipped into the seat across from him.

He smiled, reached out and shook my hand. "Tom Pyle," he replied briskly. His thinning brown hair was slicked back and he was wearing a white turtleneck with neatly pressed brown pants—more stylish than most of the clientele at Fred and Pete's.

"So how long have you been coming here?" I asked him.

"Oh," he said, "since my twenties. I'm sixty-four now. I was coming here when his father had it."

"Tell me about his father," I said, mostly as a way to get the conversation started. It seemed that everybody had liked Fred Armenti.

"Oh, Freddy was a jokester," Tom recalled with a wave of his hand. He used his hands a lot when he talked. "Freddy liked gambling. A friendly guy. But that was towards the beginning, and then Tommy took over. I know Tommy a lot better than I knew his dad. Because when I knew Freddy, he was already starting to get sick. And then since Tommy took over, I've been coming over regular— I'm here fifteen, twenty times a week."

"Is that right?"

"I eat breakfast and dinner here," Tom explained. "So two times a day, times seven days..."

I asked him why he came so often.

"Well, I like the people," he said genially. "This is like a family to me. Because I lost all my family..." For a moment, he choked up and it looked like he might be blinking back tears. "I lost my brother and my mother, my father... And so it's just me and the two dogs."

"Oh man..."

"So these people are like my family," he repeated. "Some of them, we go out to dinner sometimes... I go to the track with some of the guys in here that I'm friends with... We go to Phillies games. And like I've known Midge, the waitress, since she was in her late twenties..." He paused and looked me in the eye. "Because you see, I walk. I don't have a license because of my panic disorder."

Panic disorder? Tom Armenti hadn't mentioned that. I asked Tom how far away he lived.

"Shady Lane," he replied. "About six, seven minutes from here. It's very comfortable. And I like the people here. It's a very friendly place."

"Even Tommy?" I joked.

"Tommy?" He smiled. "Tommy's my *man*! If he needs a little help on a delivery, I'll go with him. If it's a bad area, he takes me. And I know the kids. I knew Brooke and Kenny when they were four, five years old."

I asked him why Tom Armenti took him along when he went to a bad area.

"Well, to watch the truck, I guess," Tom responded. "So they don't run off with the truck. I mean with two people, they'll think twice. And as long as you're feeding the minority people and doing stuff for them," he added, "in my opinion they don't bother you."

I asked Tom where he'd grown up.

"In North Trenton," he replied. "I grew up on Chase Street. Then we moved to Paul Avenue, Evans Avenue—that's where my mother's mother was from."

"Tell me about your family," I said. "Any brothers or sisters?"

"Just the one brother," Tom answered. "He died at fifty. He had a bar over on Broad Street—Adams Tavern—for like seventeen, eighteen years. And then one day, he got the flu and they told me he was going in the hospital. We didn't think nothing of it. He spent four months in there, and he died from renal failure. Everything shut down."

"Oh my God!"

"Him and my mother died ten months apart," he added. "She was eighty. She died in October and he died in August. Ten months apart. And so now all of a sudden I've got the house to worry about, I've got all his problems with the bar, and then I started to get a little sick myself. I was getting panic disorder."

"Have you had that a long time," I asked, "or did it start then?"

"It started then, and it eased off," Tom replied. "But every now and then I can feel one coming on, and I've got to take my medication. It'll just come out of the clear blue sky. Anything that'll upset me and start me thinking. Like I can't think about the past," he said anxiously.

I realized that I'd have to tread lightly.

Tom took a breath. "I've always had two or three dogs," he remarked. "And they seemed to take..." He stopped mid-sentence and looked down at the table, as if he wasn't sure what he wanted to say.

"What kind of dogs?" I asked him softly.

"Pit bulls," he replied. "I had four. One would die and I would replace it, because usually one can't survive without another dog—even though they like to battle. You have to be very careful, because they do like to fight," he explained. "They're not trained to fight, but they *like* that. That's their m.o."

"Do you have them for protection, or do you...?"

"I just like dogs," Tom declared. "Although I did have a cat once, that they did a little thing about on TV. You know Larry, the guy that comes in here with the glasses on?"

I didn't.

"Well, they did something on my cat," Tom said proudly. "She was thirty-one, almost thirty-two. She was on Channel 6, the *Trentonian* covered her..."

"Because she was so old?"

Tom nodded. "Yeah, she was supposed to get in the *Guinness Book of Records*, but the oldest cat was from England, and they didn't want to come down and certify this one because they didn't want to relinquish..." He shook his head.

"What was her name?"

"Her name was Angel," Tom replied. "My mother found her in the cemetery with three more. She was thirty-one years and two months."

"Wow!" I said. "That's amazing."

"And she would lay on the couch with the two pit bulls," he continued. "They wouldn't bother her. She would lay right in between, and if they fussed up on her, she would paw them. And towards the end of her life, she would go out in my yard and walk right along with them."

"No kidding!"

"She was an amazing cat," Tom affirmed. "In thirty-one years, she was only to the vet twice."

I asked him how long ago he'd lost her.

"Maybe four or five years ago; I think it was August," he responded. "She'd come up with a floppy paw—either she'd had a stroke or she did something..." His voice trailed off and then picked up again. "She died and I buried her right in the yard. I put up a little thing like a statue."

I asked him whether he'd gotten another cat, but he said no, that she'd actually been his mother's cat. "I really ain't too crazy about cats," he admitted. "But she was a rare breed of cat. She just wanted water and her food. I guess it was in the diet, because she wouldn't eat nothing else."

I took a sip of my coffee, which was stone cold by this time, and asked Tom whether he was still working.

"No," he said. "I'm retired. I worked with the County in the road department. Working construction—you know, roads, blacktop, anything. I spent twenty-nine years there, and now I get a pension and I get Social Security."

"And that's enough?"

Tom frowned. "Well... I just about survive with that. But where am I gonna get a job at sixty-four? Christ, they're not even hiring *kids* today." He shook his head. "But I try to eat healthy in here, I try to work out a little bit..."

I asked him what he liked to eat here at Fred and Pete's.

"Well, in the morning," he said, "I'm one of the rare guys here who'll have egg whites and tuna."

"Egg whites and tuna?"

"With rye toast," Tom added. "My philosophy is—and my mother's was the same thing—when the owners eat in their own place, the place is great."

I chuckled. I remembered a sign over the door of a Mexican restaurant where I'd once eaten in Galveston, Texas, that said: "So good even the owner eats here."

"And he makes good dinners, too," Tom added. "I'll get the turkey, I'll get the pot roast; if he's got chicken, I'll get the chicken dinner. And the macaronis— if I could eat them, I'd eat them every day, but I got watch or my sugar'll go out of whack."

"You've got diabetes?"

"Well, I'm borderline," Tom replied. "Even with all the working out I do, it runs in the family. My mother had it, my brother, and everybody on my mother's side. Everybody on the Italian side's got it."

"So your mother was Italian; how about your father?" I asked, although I had a pretty good idea from Tom's last name.

"My father was Irish," he replied, confirming my hunch. "He worked with the state, too, for years. When we were younger, he was a huckster—you know, years ago, when they sold fruit out of the trucks and all? I did that with him when I was nine, ten years old. We went all over. He had a grey truck, and we went into the projects on Prospect Street. It was a good little thing on the weekends and at night. Then he worked for like twenty years for the state, and then *he* died young. He was only sixty-three. My brother and me was still in our twenties."

"So that's one of the reasons you watch your health," I murmured.

Tom nodded. "My father died at sixty-three, my brother at fifty, and my mother ten months later when she was eighty," he said heavily. "That was a shocker, having the two of them die so close. I didn't get done paying for one funeral when I got another one ten months later. Them two deaths took a lot of starch out of me."

"I can imagine..."

"Because I was about a hundred and eighty pounds then," he said. "I was altogether different than I am now." He must have been—he looked liked like he couldn't weigh much more than a hundred and fifty now, as near as I could tell.

I asked him whether he'd been close to his brother.

"Oh yeah," Tom replied. "Any time there was any trouble at the bar, he'd give me a call and I was up there. Because he had a rough joint," he explained. "And he had a dog in there. Because where he was on South Broad Street, the area was deteriorating. Broad and Hudson, right near Tom Petro's, the weight-lifting joint."

I told him that I knew the area because I was in band that played at Sweeney's, right up the street from there.

Tom knew right where it was. "You probably passed my brother's place," he said. "And he used to have bands, too. He had Paul Plumeri there for about a month. They were mobbed."

"So were you down there a lot?" I asked him.

"Yeah, on occasions," Tom replied. "Or like when he'd have a shindig for Halloween or Christmas. He was the type of guy—my mother would make meals, and if he had something going, he would sell it. And if there was any left over, he would give it to the people. I mean the people that would come in off the street that were down and out or homeless, maybe they were drug... They knew him, because he was the only guy in that area that didn't get robbed or mugged—because they were doing that back then."

"But he was good to them?"

Tom nodded. "He used to give them food. 'You want a sandwich? Here. You wanna use the bathroom?' So they respected him over there. He was respected by them people—people that were on their last legs. And he just about made a living over there for about seventeen years. Then I got it, I took it over—I lasted three weeks."

"Oh, you took it over?"

"For three weeks," Tom replied glumly. "But I couldn't... You know, 'Gimme a beer, you mother-effer...' That kind of stuff." He shook his head and frowned. "I just couldn't do it."

"No kidding..." Not exactly Fred and Pete's, I thought.

"But it took me three years to sell it," Tom recalled with a sigh. "I did finally sell it to two brothers, and I don't know what happened, but they never opened up. They didn't sell a single beer."

"But you got your money," I said.

"I got rid of it," Tom corrected me. "But whatever I sold it for, everybody else made more than me. Because he owed three years in back taxes, he had a lien on it... I'm surprised the City didn't come in and take it." He sighed again, shaking his head. "But they probably didn't know what to do with it either."

Tom looked a little despondent as he thought about his brother, and remembering what he had told me about not wanting to think about the past, I decided it was time to change the subject. "You mentioned that sometimes you go with Tommy on his catering runs," I said. "What's that like?"

His face brightened. "Well, when Tommy gives them a time, that's when he's gonna be there," he declared. "If he says 12:30, he'll be there at 12:30. Not 12:31—12:30. He's right there. And the people like him. They want him to come back, because it's the best—the best there is in Mercerville, if you ask me. Probably if he had a little more help, he might go into it bigger than it is. But I guess it's tough to get help these days. But he keeps on going. He loves it."

I nodded.

"I mean, nobody likes to work," Tom went on, "but this is his baby. He wouldn't trade this in if you offered him something else, I don't think. Maybe down the line, once he gets tired of it. But this is his baby. I mean people will talk to me and they want to know if there's another place like this anywhere around, like in Vegas or New York. Would you find a place like this, with this kind of camaraderie you got here? I mean, you'd be laughing, and they got nicknames for people... Like they call me 'Suits.'"

"Suits?" I said. "Why do they call you Suits?"

"Well, years ago, a guy in here gave me the name," Tom explained. "Because I used to go out on the weekend to listen to music, and I always had a suit on. So this guy Gary gave me the name 'Suits,' and it stuck with me."

"Well, it suits you," I said, but Tom ignored the bad joke.

"Sometimes, I can't wait to get here," he told me. "Especially during baseball season. People talk baseball..."

"You sound like you're a Phillies fan," I remarked.

"Oh yeah," he replied, beaming. "Been that way since I was a kid. Some of the people here like the Yankees or the Mets, or even the Red Sox. But a lot of the people here like the Phillies."

I asked Tom whether he'd ever played when he was growing up.

"I played Babe Ruth ball, and I did a little amateur boxing when I was sixteen, eighteen years old," he recalled. "In fact, I still train now. I still got the stuff down in my cellar. I work with the weights—though not as heavy as I used to. And I still punch the bags a couple of days a week, the heavy bag and the speed bag..."

"Did you ever fight?"

"Yeah, I was in the Gloves in the '60's," Tom replied. "I enjoyed that training. I was a hundred forty-seven back then, and I'm only up to a hundred and sixty now. So I didn't put on too much weight on in all those years."

"Must be all that egg white and tuna," I chuckled.

Tom shrugged. "Yeah, well, I had a stricter diet before, but it looked like I wasn't eating enough meat. I mean, if I ate a hamburger once every seven months, it was a lot. Now I'm starting to get variety. I'll have a pork roll, I'll have bacon and eggs, I'll have pot roast. But basically I lived on chicken and turkey for four or five years. Chicken, turkey, and egg whites. Everybody laughs when I get the tuna. 'What? You get tuna in the morning?' they say. I get a little scoop, though. And then, for a change of pace, maybe every three, four days, I'll get a pork roll with the egg whites. But I stay with the egg whites," he assured me, a look of determination in his eye.

The lunch crowd was starting to come in and the noise level was picking up. "So were you in the service, Tom?" I asked him.

"No," he said, "I was with the city fire department for a couple of years, and that protected me from being in the service. When I was like twenty-one to twenty-two, twenty-three, I was with the City. I was making like fifty-two hundred back then, and I was temporary, pending the civil service exam. They were really strapped for firemen back then. Nobody was taking it, and nobody was passing the test. So I did that for about a year and a half, but then I figured I'm an active guy and I was getting kind of bored just sitting around."

"You spend most of your time waiting, don't you?"

Tom nodded. "You're cleaning the house, maybe you got KP, washing the dishes, or you might be making the beds. And then when you go out on the truck, you're hanging off it, not sitting in a covered jump seat like they do today. But it was an experience at twenty-one to do that. And then I went with the County all them years. At least I got a pension out of that."

I asked Tom to tell me a little more about his job with the County."What exactly did you do?"

"Oh, you know, black-top, paving roads, cleaning inlets, leaves," he replied. "If you got on the thing where you pick up leaves, you would go maybe one whole section—like Ewing Township. Everybody put their leaves out front and you had to clean them, even if they were this high," he said, reaching up over his head with both hands. "But we had a blower, and we'd suck 'em up with the blower."

"Right..." I'd seen the truck come through our neighborhood and was always amazed at the volume of leaves it could handle.

"And then if you got on the patch truck, it'd be a driver and two guys, and you'd be all over the county," Tom explained. "They had seven or eight different jobs you could go on, so you weren't stuck with just one job. They would switch off. Which I liked."

I asked Tom what his favorite movie was, and like a lot of his fellow customers, he liked gangster movies—specifically *Goodfellas* and *A Bronx Tale*. "I like anything that's real," he said earnestly. "I don't like anything that's fake, you know, where it could happen but it won't happen. I like stuff that's reality—that really could happen. I mean, them movies, or like *The Godfather*, that stuff really happened. In the fifties, sixties, that stuff was *real*."

"Was it going on in Trenton?" I asked.

Tom hesitated. "I assume... Back in the fifties, probably a little bit," he said. "Not like in New York or Philly, but it probably was a little bit like that. Most of your guys in that... field... was probably from North Trenton, where we were brought up. Tommy, me... most of these people that come here was brought up in North Trenton." He pointed to a guy in another booth. "That one's from North Trenton," he said. "This is actually a North Trenton hang-out that moved into Hamilton."

"Do you ever go back to North Trenton now?" I asked him.

"Just ride through," Tom replied. "Like I used to live on Parkway Avenue, and I'll go by the church that I used to go to when I was a kid—St. James. And it's not..." He frowned down at the table. "It's really bad," he said glumly.

I asked him what he thought had happened to Trenton.

"I guess it was the people coming in," Tom answered. "The minorities that's come in, I mean... But you gotta give them... I mean, you just can't cut the people off, or you'll be..." He tried to find the right words. "You gotta try to help. You just can't take them off, because now you've got serious problems. Like people say, 'How can you give them welfare?' Well, you can't take them off. Jesus Christ," he cried, "they'll come up here and they'll be killing people up here that they think have money! So you *gotta* help them kind of people," he said, taking a deep breath.

He paused and glanced around at the people who had come in for lunch. "I guess as people who lived in North Trenton and the Burg," he continued thoughtfully, "as their jobs come up with money, they got out and come out here. They figured it was safe to raise their kids up in this area. And so they let that area in Trenton go to *them*. Now you've got, what, six or seven killings down there already this year. Or was it fifteen? I saw the number, and it's a lot. But basically, they're killing their own people. If you go up there and look for trouble, you might get hurt, but you ain't supposed to be up there. But basically they're doing damage to their own people," he repeated. "They're not affecting me or you."

Tom then told me about an incident that he himself had been involved with in Trenton about ten years ago.

"I was traveling to pick up my brother's last month's rent from the bar in the bad area," he began, "and for me to get up there, I had to take a bus from JoJo's"—a local restaurant right off Five Points, about a block and a half from Fred and Pete's. "It would drop me off at Trenton High. Now, I'm walking at about eight, nine o'clock, I'm dressed up, I got a couple of bucks in my pocket, and I gotta collect the money. And instead of putting it in my buddy's car, I happened to take it in the place I'd been going, River City. I used to hang in there."

The River City Cafe, I later found out, is an Italian restaurant down in Chambersburg, near Chambers and Liberty, and I surmised that the "it" that Tom happened to take into the River City Cafe was probably a gun.

"I had dinner," Tom continued, "and then I don't know what happened. I bumped somebody with it, and I don't know if they felt it, but an hour later, here comes fifteen cops. They surrounded the place. They had their hats backwards and they come right up to me. 'Tom,' they said, 'you got a gun.' Now I'm startled! And I said, 'Who the hell...?' But they come in and got it, they had the back door covered... I don't know *who* they thought I was..."

"Sounds like somebody must have called them and said, 'There's a guy in there with a gun,'" I interjected. "You said the cops knew who you were?"

"They knew my name," Tom replied. "And so they cuffed me—that's after all that trouble with my brother, and my dog had just passed away a week before," he added mournfully. "So I figured, 'Jeez, I might be in big trouble here.' Because I didn't know if the gun was stolen. It was my brother's at the bar. Anyway, they booked me and they fingerprinted me, they took pictures and everything."

"Ooh boy," I murmured.

"*But*," Tom declared energetically, "they didn't read me my rights. They didn't read me my Miranda rights. And then they said, 'You must've had this before. You must've carried this for a while.' But they wouldn't tell me who did it. They just said, 'Whoever called it in even knew the color of your socks.'"

He paused and gave me a meaningful look, but I was having a little trouble following the story.

"And they wanted to see my shoes," he recalled. "Because I used to wear nice Italian shoes. And so they all come around and look at my shoes and say, 'What you pay for them?' You know, they made like it was a joke." He scowled; then added, "But to me, it sounded like it was a girl."

"That called it in, you mean?"

Tom nodded. "I would assume. I accused a couple of people, and they come to my house and said no, it wasn't them. But it could've been the girl that I was going out with at the time, because her boyfriend was in there singing at the time. It wouldn't have been the owner," he reflected, "because they didn't want heat brought down on them. So it had to be somebody that either had it in for me for some reason, or somebody... I don't know," he said, shaking his head.

I wondered about the singer whose girlfriend he'd been going out with, but I kept that to myself. "So what happened?" I asked.

"I had to do six months community service, which I did in a church as an usher," Tom replied. "And I had to pay like two, three thousand to my lawyer. And so that was the end of my going out days. Because I figured that if I went back there, they might be laying for me with another trumped-up charge. So now I'll go out every now and then, like I'll go out to dinner with somebody, but I won't drink. I was a one- or two-drink man when I went out, but that was it. I liked to mingle in with the people, and I loved the entertainment."

I asked Tom what kind of entertainment he liked.

"I like the music," he said fondly. "I like oldies, like from the fifties and sixties. And I like a little jazz if it's got a saxophone in it." His favorites included the Temptations, the Skyliners, Frankie Lymon and the Teenagers, the Cadillacs, the Duprees, Frankie Avalon... "And the guy they got a play about... you know, *Jersey Boys*."

"Oh, Frankie Valli," I said. "The Four Seasons."

Tom nodded enthusiastically. "So if there wasn't no music in the place, basically I would leave. Because I really don't like DJ, but that's what it is now. My cousin Joey that comes in here, he plays with a band. He'll fill in with the guitar. You'll see him sitting in the booth with me every now and then. He's got blonde hair and plays the bass guitar."

Israel was cooking onions and peppers on the grill and the smell was starting to make me hungry again. I took the last few sips of my coffee.

"I'm glad you're doing this," Tom said thoughtfully. "This might get in the *Trentonian* or the *Trenton Times*, a book like this."

"Well, it's a special place," I said.

He nodded. "I don't know where else you'd find a place like this, or where else you could go to get this mingling with these people. Even the help—the help's friendly. And they're funny. Like Midge, I've known Midge since she was a kid. And I know Annie from the Golden Dawn when she worked there. Kay, she goes way back. And all the kids they've had, going way back. And now they got Theresa—she's probably one of their best workers. And then you got Meghan that works a couple of days and Sundays."

"She works the dinner shift, right?" I said.

"She'll be here; she works Friday nights," Tom replied. "She's gonna be a teacher. She's a nice kid. Some of these kids started here at fifteen, sixteen years old, and this got them their start in life. This got them their working start, the mingling with people. Because you're meeting all kinds of people. You're meeting older people, you're meeting middle class people, people with different backgrounds—and they listen, and they laugh."

I asked Tom whether he'd made friends here at Fred and Pete's with people he hadn't known before.

"Oh yeah. Most of the people I know here I didn't know before I come here. Like there's a couple up front I met a couple of years ago, Joe and Betty," he said, gesturing toward one of the booths by the refrigerator cases. "They've been great to me. They were concerned when I had problems with my house."

"What kind of problems?"

"They wouldn't lower my mortgage—Countrywide," Tom responded. "I finally got it lowered, or I was gonna lose it. They knocked the payments down to where I could just about survive, so now I got a little bit of money to buy food and pay for the cable and my dog food for the dogs. But the people here were all concerned, and they helped me, you know. Like Joe and Betty, they gave me a number to call if my prescriptions got too high. And they'd tell me, 'Hang in there, Tom. Everything's gonna work out.' That kind of thing."

It clearly meant a lot to him.

"And you'll see me dressed up on Sunday in here," he continued, "because I go to church every Sunday—Our Lady of Sorrows. I was usher there for two, three years. But if it wasn't for this..." Tom swept his right arm before him as if he were embracing everyone in the place. "Because I'll spend like two hours dinner time here, and possibly three at breakfast. So at least I'm out of the house five hours. After breakfast I'll go back home, I'll work around the house, get my workout in, I'll fool with the dogs a little bit—and then it's back to dinner. Then I'll go back home, and it's time for a little TV."

I asked him what he watched on TV.

"Just baseball," Tom replied. "Baseball, and I got a couple of shows I like to watch. Like *CSI Miami*, that kind of thing—like I told you, I like anything that I think could really happen in real life. I like the animal show with the dogs, where they confiscate when you're cruel to animals. And I like baseball players. I'm not prejudiced that they're making a fortune, but I really like Chase Utley and his wife because that's what they do: they save battered dogs. I think they just adopted one a couple of years ago—not a bulldog, a pug. Because his wife's into that, and he got into it, too. So that's pretty good, where you take a millionaire ball player, and him and his wife are interested in saving dogs that are abused."

"Sure..."

"I respect people like that, I don't care if they're making *twenty* million a year," Tom went on passionately. "When you do *that*, it means you like people. My mother always told me, 'If you like animals, you like people. You'll get along with anybody.' I mean, I can sit down and talk to you, to a guy off the street, anybody—and hold a good conversation with them."

No question about it, I thought. "You know, one thing I noticed," I told him, "is that everybody that's walked by here while we've been talking, they've all said, 'Hi, Tom.' They all know you. And they all like you."

Tom nodded. "And I like this place," he said. "If it wasn't for this place, I don't know what I would do."

As if on cue, a young guy in a camouflage jacket stopped and said hello to Tom on his way back to the men's room. When he'd gone, Tom turned to me and said, "I feel sorry for some of these kids coming up now."

I asked him why.

"Because," he replied earnestly, "when your father and my father was around, you could buy a house for four, five thousand. These kids'll need a hundred thousand to get a house—just for the down-payment!" He shook his head. "I mean, my grandmother had ten kids, and my mother and father had two. Today, you're lucky if people want to have *one*, with the economics what they are. It's tough to survive!"

"It's true," I agreed. "You pay more for a down payment today than you used to pay for the house itself."

"People only have one kid because they can't *afford* two or three," Tom declared vehemently. "Because there's no jobs paying no money today. Christ, you've got to have a college background to get a forty thousand dollar job. I know some guys that did college that are doing construction work! Because they couldn't find nothing in their field. There's nothing around today." He slumped back in his seat exhausted, as if he'd just gone two rounds with a pro.

I asked him whether he thought things would get any better.

"I hope this guy's gonna try to do it, this Obama," Tom replied. "I mean, I gotta give this guy a chance. He's trying to stimulate the lower class working people, but I don't know. He got in such a jam with this economy... So I don't know if he's gonna be able to do it in four years. I mean, my house was worth three-fifty three or four years ago; they come in and offered me two-thirty.

Two-thirty for a rancher with a hundred and fifty foot yard. I got a Little League yard. And they said two-thirty—maybe! Maybe two-*ten*. I *owe* more than that!"

"It's tough," I agreed.

Tom leaned forward, his elbows planted firmly on the table. "If you sell your house for two-thirty and you owe two-fifty, they don't even wipe the difference off!" he declared angrily, looking me in the eye. "That extra twenty? Ninety percent of the time, they want that, too. So you can't win. You can't win today," he repeated, shaking his head despondently. "You can't win."

The young guy in the camouflage jacket came by again and nodded to Tom on his way back to his table.

"Well, it's thankful this place has kept me sane," Tom sighed. "'Cause it's always laughs over here. You see them guys arguing outside, or over here in the booth—that gets your juices flowing. That means you'll forget any kind of problem. I come here for nine months, and I didn't know what day I was gonna be evacuated from the house. And I come here, and I still could laugh."

"Right..."

"Because of the people," Tom explained. "I'd say, 'Maybe next week I'll be out here with a backpack on.' And I would make *them* laugh." He paused as remembered the moment, and a smile lit up his face. "It actually rejuvenates you," he said quietly, and I could see in his eyes that it did.

Tom and I shake hands at the end of our conversation, and he tells me again that he hopes the book gets into the Trentonian. "It'd be something positive for a change," he says, and tells me he's enjoyed the conversation.

As I start toward the door, Tim Desmond, wearing his black "Security" cap as usual, stops me and asks if the book is going to be as long as War and Peace. I tell him that it might have been, if he'd agreed to let me interview him. He laughs.

Marie is sitting a few seats down the counter from Tim, so I say hello and ask her if she has a date yet for when she's going to move out to Chicago. She says she hasn't sold her house yet, but she thinks she will soon. I wish her luck, but tell her that we'll all miss her when she moves. "I'll miss you, too, hon," she says.

"See ya!" Anne calls as I head out the door into the early afternoon. "See you tomorrow!" I call back. Out in the parking lot it's still raining.

OUT FRONT

A rainy Tuesday morning, May 5, 2009, out in front with the guys in the chairs:

"You take the fish off the hook…"
"I gotta catch him first."
"This guy's a fisherman here. You wanna go fishing today?"
"He's scared to touch those little worms. He's never seen nothing that big…"

"You hear that Gino had a problem with his heart? He says they fixed him up. So I says to him, 'What'd they do?' And he says they gave him Angelo Plastic."
"Angelo Plastic?"
"That's what he said. He said they put in a couple of stunts."

"Jimmy said he's losing money in the market. He said, 'My 301-k is down.'"
"That right?"
"Well, he said it was down."
"Yeah, it went from 401 to 301."

"Well, I gotta go buy some tomato plants."
"I got pumpkin plants. You want 'em?"
"No."
"They're on my kitchen counter. You can have 'em."
"When do you plant 'em? The 15th?"
"No. If it wasn't raining all the time, I'd a had 'em in already. And if it gets cold, I'd cover 'em up at night."
"I got parsley still sitting on the front porch. In a flower pot."
"Yeah, but I want tomatoes."
"I'd like to try that slicing thing you see on television. Looked like it worked pretty good. Nineteen dollars."

"You don't get the hangers."

"No, but you get the slicer."

"Yeah, you really need that tomato slicer."

"You put 'em on your salad?"

"Nah, I don't eat salad."

"Hey, where's Charley going?"

"He's going to work."

"Work? I thought he was retired."

"I went to work when I retired."

"Charley was laid off, he didn't retire."

"He got laid off?"

"Yeah."

"I didn't know."

"Well, I have to depart, guys."

"Where you going, Jack?"

"I can't take it no more..."

"First you gotta find your car."

"I know, I know... It's out here somewheres."

"When you go across the tracks, where the Acme used to be..."

"You gotta cross them."

"That's what I say."

"It's about a block from the Yardville Hotel."

"Before you get to the light, about half a mile."

"The tracks are the other side of the Acme. They don't cross there. They're a ways down, toward Trenton."

"You gotta go towards the Yardville Hotel, right where the bank is."

"Right. And then there's the driveway for the Acme."

"No."

"No?"

"No, the railroad tracks run right next to the gas station."

"Gas station? What gas station? Tell me the name of the gas station. There is no gas station where I'm talking about. There's the Roma Bank, going towards the Yardville Hotel."

"That was before. You go right across to what used to be K-Tex or K-Rod."

"That's the other side! I'm talking about... You know where Iccara is?"

"Yeah..."

"And that barber shop?"

"That's across the tracks..."

"There's no tracks there!"

"I said the tracks are more towards Trenton from the light than towards the Yardville Hotel."

"You're right."

"Well, he said I was wrong before. When I explained it to him, he said I was wrong."

"I'm talking about when you're coming from Trenton."

"I'm talking about from Roma Bank. Say you were at where Roma Bank's on your right and you're at the light. You turn right to go to the tracks."

"You're right. The tracks are on your right."

"Yeah, that's right."

"You have to get out of North Trenton..."

"The tracks are close to Iccara, yeah. By the light."

"What light?"

"Where Roma is!"

"Aw, you're..."

"Wait! If you're in the parking lot at Iccara, and you turn right..."

"And now here's another question. At the gas station that the tracks are near..."

"If you're at Iccara, you have to pass Roma."

"You pass Roma and the entrance to the Acme, then the railroad tracks, then the gas station..."

"Remind me never to ask him for directions."

"But we're talking about Iccara."

"You mean I-CA-ra's?"

"That's the American pronunciation. The Italian is IH-cara's. It's the name of a town in Italy."

"Iccara dickera dock?"

"The owner says it's IH-cara's. The town he's from in Italy. So he should know."

"What is it? A restaurant?"

"Yeah. It used to be a gas station."

"So how do you get there?"

"You gotta go through the red light, you gotta pass Roma, you pass the entrance to Acme, then you got the railroad track, then the gas station."

"I don't understand if you're coming from Allentown."

"I'm coming from Iccara! Why would I be coming from Allentown?"

"That's what I said!"

"Look, let me ask you a simple question... Do you turn left or right?"

"Left or right of what? I'm coming from Iccara. I said I'm at Iccara and the tracks are PAST the red light. Aren't they?"

"But he's coming from Allentown."

"Three times I said from Iccara I gotta pass the Roma Bank, the Acme, then the tracks. Tell me, if I'm at Iccara, which way do I have to go to get to Roma Bank?"

"Which one? Which Roma bank? The one over here...?"

"The one in Toledo! They got one in Toledo they just opened up."

"OK, but if I'm at Fred and Pete's..."

"You are."

"Yeah, but if I'm at Fred and Pete's, which side of the road is it on? The left or the right? That's what you were asking me. I said I'm at Iccara. You said is it on the left or on the right."

"If I'm at Fred and Pete's facing the kitchen..."

"If you're in Fred and Pete's and you're facing the kitchen, it ain't left or right: it's all around you. You're in the center of it."

"So how do you get to Iccara from Fred and Pete's?"

"You go down Whitehorse-Hamilton Road..."

"No, you go down Yardville-Hamilton... That's Yardville-Hamilton. Now when you go out there, you get to Broad Street. Now where are the tracks?"

"On the right."

"Right. You go over them, but they go round the buildings and around the Acme. You turn at Roma, you go past Yardville Bank's parking lot, you hit the railroad tracks, then you get to the gas station. And if you come to that same light and you wanna go to Iccara, you gotta go left."

"Wait a minute, wait a minute... I got it figured out. If they knocked Iccara down, you can't find your way home from Yardville!"

I'm laughing so hard, I'm in tears.

Despite the rainy weather and the fact that I have real work to do, I decide that I have to go and see for myself. So I drive down Route 33 and make a left at Hamilton Square-Yardville Road to see whether I can find Iccara. I drive past Veteran's Park, across the Interstate, on into Yardville, until I cross the railroad tracks and stop for the red light. Sure enough, I can see the Acme on my right and the Roma Bank on the corner. So now the question is: do I turn right or left?

I decide to turn right, and drive past the Acme, followed by Picerno's, a gas station with a sign that says "Exotic Car Rentals;" Clayton Admixture Technologies, a manufacturing place of some kind; a Gasco gas station; The Pizza Kitchen; Frank's Barber Shop; Bagels and Beyond; The Baseball Card Locker; Kim's Broad Street Bark, Pet Store and Grooming—but no sign of Iccara. I drive a little further, past a worn-out little strip mall called Dover Park Plaza, past a 7-11, past Yardville Heights Elementary School, but still no Iccara.

So maybe I should have turned left at the light.

I pull into a side-street, make a U-turn, and double back, past the Acme and the Roma Bank, through the Hamilton Square-Yardville Road intersection, and, sure enough, there it is, on my left: Iccara!

Mission accomplished!

It's a simple enough place, with a neon sign and a few cars parked out front. It even looks like it's open, but it's still early for lunch, so I decide to head back. Maybe Susie and I can try it for dinner some time.

But the bottom line is: if you want to get to Iccara and you're coming from Fred and Pete's, you go down Hamilton Square-Yardville Road to Yardville, you cross the railroad tracks, and then you take a LEFT at the light, and Iccara will be on your left.

You can't miss it.

WHERE YOU ARE STANDING NOW

I know that I should go home now and get to work, but before I do that, there's one other place I want to see, if I can find it: the memorial for Viet Nam vets that Dave Stout had told me about during his interview. Earlier that morning, I'd run into Dave in Fred and Pete's and I'd asked him where exactly it was. Given that it was a veterans' memorial, I'd assumed it was in Veteran's Park, but Dave told me, no, it was in Mercer County Park, just off Old Trenton Road.

Fortunately, thanks to Dave's directions, the memorial turns out to be a lot easier to find than Iccara. It's right off one of the main park roads, and I park my car in the empty lot across the road. There's not a soul in sight. A light rain is still falling, and a chill passes through me as I zip up my jacket and cross the road.

The memorial is situated in a fairly large grove, surrounded by a wall of thick dark pine trees that seem to screen out most of the traffic noise from Old Trenton Road. There's a tall flag pole in the center of the grove, and a bronze plaque that reads: "We, the members of Viet Nam Veterans United, Inc., dedicate this memorial to our fallen brothers who did not come home from the Viet Nam War. They have made the ultimate sacrifice for their country and government. We will never forget them, for they were our relatives and neighbors who were part of our lives. May God bless them and their families. September 22, 1991."

There's a garden around the plaque, with delicate Japanese maples and small pines, all very well kept up, and surrounding the garden, a large circle of headstones. On each headstone is a pair of boots, and each has a name inscribed on it: Robert J. Burroughs, USA 1967. Joseph McCants, USA 1969. Robert C. Healy, Jr. USMC 1968. Cecil F. Dixon, USA 1967. Frederick A. Pine, USA 1968. Thomas E. Francis, USA 1967. John S. Zymanski, USMC 1967. William T. Jacobus, USA 1968. Ronald E. Van Barriger, USA 1968. David T. Bryant, USMC 1967. Jonathan E. Sykes, USMC 1968. Thomas R. Grover, USA 1969.

Leon J. Kramer, USA 1963. David Carol, USA 1967. Walter S. Simpson, USA 1968...

And then behind me, more stones, more names: John D. Donovan, USA 1968. Carl Parton, USA 1969. Dennis J. Brophy, USA 1966. Ronald Robbins, USA 1969. Norman Everett, USA 1970. Clifford R. Stout, USA 1966 (any relation to Dave?). Francis J. Juranic, Jr., USMC 1968. Willy Dowling, Jr., USA 1967. Vincent C. Mauro, Jr., USA 1971. John S. Berg, USAF 1967. Jerry Sylvia, USMC 1969. Ronald Delorenzo, USMC 1969. David T. Graham, USMC 1965. Howard W. Johnson, Jr., USA 1967. William S. Smoyer, USMC 1968.

Those are all on the outside ring. Then there are more on the inside ring: Douglas R. Dickerson, Jr, USMC 1967. Frederick A. Billingham, Jr., USMC 1968. John D. Ossmann, USMC 1967. Warren Lively, Jr., USA 1970. Richard D. Shepherd, USA 1967. Erwin J. Haarwaldt, USA 1967. James E. Thompson, USMC 1966. Robert W. Worthington, USA 1970. Herbert M. Beaumont, USMC 1969. Robert Korona III, USA 1967. Anthony Dicesare, Jr., USMC 1967. Raymond E. Stone, USA 1967. Joseph L. Hicks, USMC 1967.

And then three stones, with a lot of names on each one. Oh my God... Lee E. Marsh, Jr., USMC 1970. Robert L. Ball, USMC 1968. Carl R. Steffen, USMC 1965...

And there's a large stone monument that says: "The Viet Nam Service Medal is about one thing... Home. Here. Where you are standing now. It is about the fear that we carried in Viet Nam and the fear that carried us home. It is about what we lost in Viet Nam. Our buddy, our brother, our sister, our father—our very innocence. And how death made home so different. Once upon a time, the Viet Nam Service Medal was a representation of the flag and the country we died to defend. That country no longer lives. Today, as you stand here, the Viet Nam Service Medal stands for our resolve to never forget the past, so that we can continue to learn to live in peace at home."

Richard C. Drewes, USA 1968. Harry E. Wagner, USMC 1967. Arnold C. Hayward, USA 1969. Preston H. Turner, Jr., USMC 1967. David J. Decker, USA 1966. Robert B. Reed, USMC 1967. Bruce R. Backes, USA 1968. David J. Scharibone, USMC 1967. John J. Nemchik, Jr., USMC 1967. Calvin E. Thompson, Jr., USA 1969.

Then another stone with a lot more names: David E, Dean, Donald Ronka, Richard Carl, Willie Crawford, Lawrence W. Rasch, Richard W. Chesney, Richard T. Leopardi, Harold W. Kroske, Jr., Robert J. Piazza III, Henry W. Cunningham, Charles W. Paul, Charles S. Mercer, Alexander Fore, Donald E. Harper, Timothy Z. Borden, Richard E. Stephan, Sherman Chapman, Jr., William F. Aaronson, Daniel J. Piotrowski, George C. Schoettner, Charles A. Southard III, Lester Johnson, Jr., Terry Ketter, John M. Bass, Paul L. Vernon, William T. Dunn, James D. Burness, Joseph R. Dinolfi, Joseph R. Bangham,

James R. Fortson, William T. L. Stewart, Jr., Lawrence W. Sellnow, Jr., Joseph F. Frascella.

There are fresh flowers at some of the stones, and a lot of small flags planted in the ground, drooping in the rain. So many names! The names of sons, husbands, brothers—guys who by all rights should have been sitting at the counter at Fred and Pete's with the rest of us, paging through the *Trentonian* and arguing about the Yankees and the Phillies and about how to get to Iccara.

All those names—and this is just Mercer County. I walk quietly back to my car, utterly overwhelmed.

EARLY BIRDS

Wednesday, May 6, 2009. *The next morning, for some unaccountable reason, I wake up at 3:30 and can't get back to sleep. So at 4:30 I decide that this might be a good day to find out whether it's really true, as the sign says and as Tom himself told me, that Fred and Pete's opens at 5 a.m. And so at 4:47, I'm in the parking lot, quietly watching from my car. The blacktop glistens from the night's rain, although it isn't actually raining at the moment, and the damp air gives me a chill that I can't seem to shake.*

There's one other car already there, and I remember that Tom told me that there were a couple of guys who always got there before him, waiting for him to open up. Hard to believe unless they were getting off the night shift some place. The sidewalk in front of the stores is lit by buzzing fluorescent lights and the red and white electric Ace Hardware sign glares brightly in the darkness. It's completely dark inside Fred and Pete's, and the white chairs out front look almost ghostly in the fluorescent glow.

Another car pulls into the lot and quietly parks behind me; like me, the driver shuts off his motor and stays in his car. An occasional solitary car drives by on Route 33, its tires hissing on the slick wet pavement; an empty city bus rumbles off toward Trenton. Minutes later, a black mini-van pulls up in front of The Reading Center on the far side of the Rite-Aide, and a guy in a dungaree jacket gets out and starts unloading bundles of newspapers from the back.

At 4:59, another car, an aging white sedan, parks across the aisle from my car and turns off its lights—again, no one gets out. Everyone's waiting.

Finally, at 5:05, the Fred and Pete's van pulls into the lot, moving fast. I can see Tom behind the wheel. He jerks to a stop, climbs out, and trots up to Fred and Pete's and unlocks the door. Now the white car door opens and I see that it's Anne. She follows Tom into the store, carrying a cardboard box.

Almost immediately, the guy who's been waiting in the car behind me gets out—a big man in a checked work shirt—so I get out too, tell him good morning, and walk into Fred and Pete's behind him.

I take a seat at the counter. "Hey, Annie," I say, "how're you doing this morning?"

"You here to interview somebody?" she asks me as she's ripping open the cardboard box she brought in with her.

I tell her no, I'm just here to see the place open up. *"I've never been here at opening,"* I say.

"Oh my goodness," she says.

"So how're you doing?" I ask.

"Oh, I'm hanging in there," she replies in a tired voice.

Tom's busy lighting up the grill. Then he turns around. *"Paulie!"* he says. *"What are you doing here?"*

I tell him I had to come see for myself. *"I couldn't believe you guys actually opened up at 5 o'clock."*

He grunts. *"Of course I was three minutes late. That never happens. I watched that Yankees game last night. They lost."*

Anne's getting all the coffee pots ready. She still has her coat on. The guy who walked in with me is sitting a few seats down from me reading the Trentonian. I tell him good morning again, but he doesn't respond.

"Don't talk to him," Anne warns me. *"He'll bite your head off. At least until he gets his coffee."*

Fortunately, it doesn't take long for the coffee to be ready. As Anne pours me a cup, a woman walks in. *"Hey, Annie!"* Anne calls to her. The woman comes up to the counter. *"Annie, this is Paul,"* Anne says. *"He's writing a book. About Fred and Pete's Deli."*

"That right?" the woman says.

I nod. *"You come here every morning about this time?"* I ask her.

"Every morning, yeah," she says. *"I work at Robert Wood."*

"At the hospital?"

"Yeah."

"What do you do over there?"

"Housekeeping," she says.

"Ask her how many years," Anne says to me.

"How many years?" I ask.

"Thirty-eight years," the woman says.

"Wow," I say. *"That's a lot of getting up early."*

A man walks in. *"Hey, Jerry!"* Anne calls to him. He grunts something in response and the woman Annie joins him in one of the booths. *"You guys waiting for the bagels or you want some eggies while you're waiting?"* Anne asks them.

I pick up the morning's Trentonian from the counter, on which Anne has already scrawled "House," signifying that it's the house copy. The big headline reads: TRENTON SCORES, and beside it is a picture of a model in provocative lingerie and a subhead that proclaims: "Lingerie League Kicks Off At City Arena (page 3)." I resist the urge to turn to page 3, and then I notice something that I'd never noticed before: just below the masthead, it says, in smaller letters, "A Pulitzer Prize Winning Newspaper."

They've got to be kidding.

"Anne," I call to her, "did you know that the Trentonian is a Pulitzer Prize Winning Newspaper? That's what it says."

She comes over and I show it to her. "I never saw that before," she says, shaking her head in disbelief. "That's a misprint. Hey Bob," she calls to the big guy who'd come in with me, "did you know that the Trentonian got the Pulitzer prize?"

Much to my surprise, he did. "Yeah," he says. "That was Emil Slaboda. He was a writer."

"Was that a long time ago?" I ask Bob.

"Yeah," he says. "I think it was Slaboda that got it."

(Later on, I check online, and sure enough, Emil Slaboda, who was the Trentonian's managing editor at the time and was fondly known as "the Bull," along with F. Gilman Spencer, the paper's executive editor, received the Pulitzer in 1974 for their editorials attacking the rampant corruption in New Jersey's state government.)

"How about that?" Anne muses thoughtfully, and then goes back to taking the little ultra-pasteurized creamers out of a cardboard box and scooping them into the brightly colored plastic bowls along the counter.

Having started a conversation with Bob, I decide to continue. I ask him how long he's been coming to Fred and Pete's.

"Here?" he says. "Since they opened."

"That's a long time," I observe.

Bob grunts. He's probably not all that much in the mood for conversation at 5:15 in the morning, but I press on. "You working or retired?" I ask him.

"Retired."

"So you don't really have to get up this early," I say.

"I'm up early every morning," Bob replies gruffly. "Three o'clock, four o'clock. I'm usually here about five when they open the doors. I carry all the stuff in because the waitress won't," he adds, loud enough for Anne to hear.

Anne chuckles. "He's got a sweetie at home, you know," she tells me. "A youngster."

"I wanted you," Bob says to her, "but you played hard to get, so..."

"So who's sorry now?" I said.

"Not me!" Anne laughed.

"Walter!" Anne cries as another customer walks in and takes a seat at the far end of counter. Walter, who is probably about Bob's age, is wearing dungaree shorts, a wine-colored t-shirt, and a blue net baseball cap. He also wears glasses and has a set of keys hanging from his belt. Anne brings him his coffee right away.

Tom comes out of the kitchen, drying his hands with a towel. "That's Annie's favorite," he tells me. "You have order your food before Walter comes in or you'll never get it—not once she starts talking to Walter."

"So Tommy," Bob says, "when did your dad open up here?"

"Next week'll be forty-six years," Tom replies. "May 23, 1963."

"I came over in '63," Annie chimes in from the booth where she and Jerry are still eating their breakfast. "I'm originally from Bermuda, and I came over in '63."

Tom nods. "When I was in high school, nothing was here," he says. "Then the A & P went up and they put this in the middle."

"Dave Stout told me this used to be a horse farm," I say. "And I said to Dave, 'Well, that explains it.'"

"You mean all the horseshit," Tom says dryly.

Everyone cracks up.

I finish my first cup of coffee, which tastes especially good this morning, and after Anne refills my cup, I move down the counter to talk to Walter. I introduce myself and tell him I'm writing a book about Fred and Pete's.

Walter laughs. "You're kidding!"

But I tell him, no, I'm serious, because, after all, this place won't be around forever.

Walter nods his head in agreement. "This place is an icon," he says. "I've been coming here twenty-five, thirty years."

"That's a long time," I say. "How much has it changed since then?"

He shrugs. "Not a whole lot."

I ask him whether he always comes in this early, and he says that now that he's retired, he comes in whenever he feels like it. He tells me that he was a custodian for the West Windsor schools when he retired, but before that, he worked for Garden Foods. "I worked twenty-seven years with them," he says. "In fact, I used to deliver here."

"No kidding!" I exclaim. "What kind of stuff did you deliver here?"

"Canned goods, mostly," Walter replies. "In fact, we used to be his coffee distributor. That's back when they were using Yuban—that's real good coffee. Now of course it's Maxwell House," he adds with a note of resignation in his voice, although I notice that his cup's already empty.

"So what's brought you back here all these years?" I ask him.

"The people. I know a lot of people here," he replies. "Besides, I'm an early riser, so where else am I gonna go? I can just sit here and read my paper."

"Do you always have the same thing for breakfast?"

Walter points at his coffee cup. "That's it," he says proudly.

"That's it? Just coffee?"

"I can't eat anything this early," he says. "I have to wait a few hours. Maybe I'll come back like around ten o'clock and have something to eat."

I ask Walter if he grew up here in Mercerville, and he tells me, no, he grew up in Ewing until his parents moved to Hamilton, and now he lives on a side street near Pullen's gas station.

"That's where I get my gas," I tell him.

He shrugs, apparently unimpressed. "I don't get my gas there," he says. "I just live near there."

I return to my original seat at the counter and leaf through the Trentonian. WITNESS CLAMS UP IN GANG SLAY TRIAL, a headline on page 3 reads, just below the Lingerie League story. The dateline is Trenton: "A judge declared a prosecution witness in contempt of court and had him locked up yesterday after he refused to testify at the trial of the Latin King accused of ordering the murder of the gang queen who knew too much..."

Hard to believe this stuff is real. This isn't Goodfellas or The Godfather. It's reality. And it's happening just a few miles down the road. I could get in my car, drive down Hamilton Avenue or Greenwood or East State, and in less than ten minutes I'd be right in the middle of where this kind of stuff happens all the time. Where people have to live with this kind of craziness day in and day out. Jesus.

"Hi guys!" A bright-faced young woman in a blue Rite-Aid shirt strides up to the counter and gives all of us a radiant smile—almost too radiant for this hour of the morning.

"Good morning, Lucy," Bob says, smiling back at her.

Then I recognize her. She's Theresa's mother; she manages the Rite-Aid next door. I'd seen her in here before, talking to Theresa.

"How are you?" she says to Bob, then adds, "How are you, Anne?"

"Hanging in there," Anne says wearily.

"I know what you mean," Lucy says. "Today's gonna be a long day for me. I shouldn't say that, though, because Theresa has a long day, too." She orders a cup of coffee to go from Anne. "So is the sun gonna come out one of these days?" she asks all of us.

"If it does, it's gonna be today," I say.

"Figures," she laughs. "Tomorrow's my day off."

Tom comes out of the kitchen again, and I ask him which of the two guys sitting to my left I should interview: Bob or the guy sitting next to him.

He shrugs. "Both of them," he says. "Bob's been coming here for ever, and Joe's been here a long time, too."

Bob looks away like he's not interested, so I ask Joe, a stocky dark-haired guy dressed in blue shorts and a grey sweatshirt. "Joe, how about you? Would you be willing to be interviewed?" I ask.

"Joe used to work here," Bob says.

Tom nods in agreement. "Yeah, Joe was employed for a while."

"As a cook?" another guy asks.

"Delivery," Tom says.

"And he didn't get lost?" Bob asks.

"Seriously," I say to Joe. "Would you be willing to talk to me for a few minutes? We can go to one of the booths in the back."

"Sure," Joe says, as he gets up and follows me to the usual booth, the second one from the restrooms in the back. We both bring our coffee with us.

"Second best smelling booth in the house," I say.

"That one's the best," Joe laughs as he slides into his seat, nodding toward the one right by the men's room door. He has an easy smile.

JOE GRESKO

I began by telling Joe about the book, and mentioned that I'd been coming to Fred and Pete's for quite a few years now.

"Have you?" he said, sounding surprised.

"Yeah," I said, "but I come later."

"Oh, OK," Joe said. "We're the early crowd," he declared proudly. "We're the five o'clock crowd."

I nodded. "Tom told me there was a five o'clock crowd, but I didn't believe it. Then this morning I woke up early and I decided to come see for myself."

"Well, it used to be better than this, though," Joe said. "Five o'clock he used to have at least fifteen people in here."

I asked Joe his last name and he said it was Gresko. "G-R-E-S-K-O," he said to make sure I got it right.

"So how long have you been coming here?" I asked.

"Oh, I don't know..."

"Were you here when Fred was here?"

"No," Joe replied, and then corrected himself. "Well, he was here, but I didn't come in that much. After he died I was here when Tom's mother was here. We were very close," he said feelingly. "And then when she died..." He shook his head.

"So how did you know her?" I asked.

"Just from here," Joe said. "But I became good friends with her. I used to help her out at her house. As far as I care, she was a tremendous person. If she really knew you, you could've teased her—but if she didn't know you, you couldn't tease her. And she was a cleaning fanatic."

"A cleaning fanatic?"

"She always made sure everything was clean," Joe explained. "Else he got hollered at."

I laughed.

"She used to take things home to clean 'em and then she'd bring 'em back," Joe continued fondly. "Like the salt and pepper shakers, she used to take 'em out, empty 'em, clean 'em and put 'em back. As far as I care, she was a tremendous person."

"That's great." I was glad to know a little more about Tom's mother and the role that she'd played in the early days. "So now tell me a little bit about yourself," I said. "Did you grow up around here?"

"In Trenton," Joe replied. "I lived on Cass Street, near the state prison. Then I moved out here to the township I guess about thirty years ago, when I got married. Then I was an iron worker, and then I started coming in here. I was a sheet metal worker first, and I started hanging here. Then I became an iron worker after I got divorced—I changed my trade. Then I started coming in here every day."

"You always come at five?"

Joe nodded. "Five o'clock ninety percent of the time. Sometimes at night. Quarter to five we was sitting out there waiting for him, and a lot of times he used to *be* here at quarter to five."

"You mean Tom?"

"Yeah," Joe said. "And then I was starting to help him a lot—you know, going out with him on catering jobs, stuff like that. And we became real good friends. We were like family. I used to go out and eat with them all the time, him and his wife. His kids. They're just tremendous people," he added, and it was clear that his admiration for Tom and his family was straight from the heart.

"So are you retired now, or are you still working?" I asked him.

"I'm on total disability," Joe replied unabashedly. "I had two knee operations. I replaced both my knees."

"Jeez," I said. "Was it work-related?"

Joe nodded. "That's what they say. And then I had seven stents put in."

"Seven?" I was impressed. "That might be some kind of record in here. There's a lot of guys walking around with stents, but seven?"

Joe chuckled. "They just fixed two of them not long ago. And I broke my femur in three places last year."

"How'd you manage that?"

"In the ocean."

"In the ocean?"

"In the ocean," Joe repeated. "Got caught in the undertow. I went in and I couldn't get out. I planted myself, but it just knocked me down. I guess the knees are so strong that it went up and cracked the top part of it."

"Wow, that's really something," I said, shaking my head. "So what were you doing out there? Fishing?"

"Swimming," Joe said. "And then after that they used to always call me—'Do you need anything? Can we bring you anything?' Because I was in a wheelchair for four months. So they used to come all the time. If I needed something, Annie used to bring it."

"Is that right?"

Joe smiled. "Oh yeah. You know, when Annie started here, she was a really good person. And she still is. Anyone gets hurt, she always asks, 'Do you need anything? I'll bring it.' So I used to order stuff, and they'd bring it over. You know, lunch meats, stuff like that."

I sipped my coffee. "So talk to me a little bit about your work when you were an iron worker. What were you doing?"

"Structural steel," Joe replied. "Buildings you'd put up. I worked in Atlantic City on some of the casinos. Then I got involved more in fence work. Like I did the train station with their fence. I did a lot of fence down at Great Adventure. Replaced all the old fence with a new one."

"That's a big job," I murmured. I knew Great Adventure was a huge amusement park about forty-five minutes east of Mercerville, although I'd never been there. "And why'd you go from sheet metal to iron work?" I asked him. "Was it better money?"

Joe shook his head. "Not on account of the money, but I hated being cooped up inside. With sheet metal, when the building's up and the walls are up, then you're in," he explained. "I wanted to be on the outside. I liked doing it. And I met different people. The contractors were a lot different. And like I said, I got to work at Great Adventure. I loved working at Great Adventure. I mean, I had the run of the whole place. They let me do whatever I wanted."

I asked Joe whether he had any family—any kids—and he said he had two kids. "My son's nineteen and my daughter's twenty-two. In fact, they used to come in here when they were little. They used to help Tommy and Noreen clean up. We used to shut down on a Sunday and clean the whole place."

"Is that right?" I was impressed. "Do they still come here?"

"Once in a while," Joe replied. "My daughter graduates the seventeenth of this month from college. She goes to Hofstra out on Long Island. My son lives with me, so he comes in with me now and then. But he don't get up this early."

I chuckled.

"He's working for a contractor," Joe went on. "Not that I want him to do that, but for now he's doing it. He wants to go back to school and become a teacher."

"So Joe, what do you do the rest of the day when you're not here?" I asked him.

"I go over to a friend of mine who owns a car lot," Joe replied, "and I go hang there. A couple of hours, three or four hours—that gives me something to do. Then I go back home and that's it."

"You watch TV?"

"A little bit. Not much. Then I go back out, I help my aunt."

"Your aunt...?"

"My aunt's eighty-eight years old," Joe explained. "So I go help her. Like this Friday I have to go pick up her nephew from Saint Joe's College, 'cause I got the truck so I'll bring him back home... And that's it!"

I asked him whether he'd been in the service, and he said he'd been in the National Guard for fourteen years.

"Wow," I said, "that's a long stretch."

"Yeah," Joe nodded. "I wanted to stay for twenty, but... I just couldn't make it. And I loved it. It was a good thing."

"And how about here?" I asked. "You made a lot of friends here?"

"Oh yeah!"

"Like who?"

"Like Annie, Bobby Barber..."

Just then Anne came up with a fresh pot of coffee and refilled our cups. "Don't believe anything he says," she told me.

"Tommy Walsh—he's not here today," Joe continued. "And Jerry... Even some of the people later in the day. I'll come in and pick up a sandwich sometimes. You know, some of those guys. All of them. You meet everybody."

"Sure..."

"Now, namewise, I'm very hard with names," he said apologetically. "But I know a lot of people here—a *lot* of people."

I asked Joe if there was anyone in particular he remembered from the old days.

"Oh yeah," he said. "Me and Tommy, one winter we were going to do a catering job, I went outside in the back, and all of a sudden I saw a guy lying on the ground. So I tell Tommy, and Tommy goes, 'Look, the guy's dead.'"

"Oh Jeez..."

"We call the cops, so the cops come, and the cop says, 'I wonder if the guy drove.' And Tommy goes, 'Yeah, his car's right there.' And the cop says, 'Oh, we'd better go check that out.' I mean, the cops are so in another world that me and Tommy are laughing. So we come back in, and the cop goes, 'You two can't leave yet.' And Tommy says, 'What are you—nuts? I got a catering job. I gotta leave! You know where I'm at—come back and see me.' You know, I thought that was funny in one way," Joe said, shaking his head as he remembered it all.

"This was right here?"

"Right here," Joe replied. "Right in the back here. Tommy knew the guy. An old man. He slipped on the ice. I mean, *that* wasn't funny..." He picked up his coffee cup, still shaking his head.

"So what do you usually get for breakfast here?" I asked him, changing the subject.

"Most of the time pork roll and eggs."

"On a hard roll?"

"Nah, on a platter. With potatoes. And Friday I come in for the fish. I used to make the fish in the back."

"Oh you did?" I'd been in on a Friday evening once for the fish and chips and the place had been mobbed.

"Yeah, I used to help him out every now and then," Joe said. "And I used to help him out on the catering runs. Some of the runs, when they ordered all that stuff, you'd have to make sure all the trays were in, light up the Sterno... We used to go all over the place—Hightstown, Allentown, one of them was down past Columbus."

"Wow, that's a long way."

"And now I think he's going farther yet," Joe continued. "Because he has good food. He cooks good and he gives you more than enough. You tell him fifty people and he'll make sure there's enough for sixty-five. That's just the way he is—and you can't beat the prices. The people all love this food, no matter where you go. I mean, I went to one house this one time, and I ring the doorbell, the lady opens up the door, she has her *negligee* on! She says, 'Oh yeah, bring the food right on in here.' I'm looking, and I'm like, 'Bring the food right in *here*? Lady, you ain't even *dressed* yet!'"

We both laugh so hard that finally Anne calls over and asks us if we need her to bring us some water.

Addendum: Some time later, I mention to Dave Stout that I've interviewed Joe Gresko. "Who?" he says. "Joe Gresko," I repeat. "Don't know him," Dave says. And sure enough, it turns out that even though both of them have been coming to Fred and Pete's just about every day for the past several decades, they're on different "shifts" at Fred and Pete's—Joe on the 5 a.m. shift and Dave on the 8 a.m. shift, more or less. And so, in all these years of sitting at the same counter every morning, their paths have never crossed.

HEIDI

Tuesday, May 12, 2009. Dave Stout and I are having breakfast in one of the booths and I ask him how the antique business is going. "Not too good," he says. I ask him if it's the economy, and he says, "Partly. But mostly it's the young people. They're not interested in antiques." Then, abruptly, he changes the subject, as if young people are too depressing to think about on such a nice day. "If you're in Detroit," he says, "and you go directly south, what's the first foreign country you hit?" He grins, but I know the answer because I've been to Detroit. "Canada," I say. He shakes his head and says, "You're the first person I've ever asked who knew the answer." So after breakfast, we go out front and Dave asks the guys in the white chairs. "Canada," one of them says. I think it was Nick. Dave looks positively crestfallen. "I gotta get me a new trivia question," he mutters.

Then he brightens and asks me if I'd have time to interview his eighty-eight-year-old mother-in-law, Heidi Krall. He's told me about her before. She'd been a professional opera singer who used to sing at the Met in New York, and now she lived here in the Township and came in to Fred and Pete's every once in a while.

"Today?" I say. "Sure, why not?"

So Dave calls her on his cell phone, and she says that we should come on over in about half an hour. Dave tells me to meet him in half an hour at the entrance to Pulte Homes, which he says is the gated retirement community where she lives over on Hamilton Square-White Horse Road, up past the Shop-Rite. "Wait for me there, and I'll lead you in," he says, telling me that he has to stop by the house first.

I get there before Dave, and the sign says: PULTE HOMES: TRADITIONS AT HAMILTON CROSSING. A COMMUNITY FOR ACTIVE ADULTS FIFTY-FIVE AND BETTER. It occurs to me that I'm already fifty-seven, but I'm not so sure that I'm two years better than I was at fifty-five.

A few minutes later, Dave pulls up in his white Chevy truck and waves, so I follow him in, down Sparrow Drive and up Falcon Court. The houses are all pretty much the same, but they're well-maintained and all the lawns are freshly clipped. Heidi's front walk is lined with deep purple irises, gently nodding in the morning breeze. As soon as

Dave knocks on the door, we're greeted with a burst of shrill barking from what I imagine must be a very small dog.

"That's Chichi," Dave says, fondling the small white dog as Heidi lets us in. "She can run twenty-eight miles an hour, because I tried to follow her one time in my car, and that's how fast she was going."

"She'd beat a race horse out of the gate," Heidi adds. Heidi is in terrific shape. Her skin is flawless, like fine porcelain, her posture is impeccable, and she's wearing pink lipstick that goes perfectly with her powder-blue blouse and pants outfit.

I tell Dave to ask Heidi his Detroit question, so he does.

"Canada?" she says without missing a beat.

"How'd you know that?" Dave asks her, sounding dejected. "Everybody always says Mexico. And now today you're the third one to get it right. Maybe it's because you're from the Cleveland area," he adds, consoling himself.

Heidi's home is conservatively furnished, with very thick carpeting that muffles our footsteps and many pictures of foxes and horses adorning the walls. The one piece that clearly stands out is a leaping wooden horse, about the size of a mid-sized dog, mounted on the wall with large brass brackets. I've never seen anything quite like it. The three of us sit down at the big dining room table, and I start the interview.

"So Heidi," I began, "how long have you been going to Fred and Pete's?"

"Since I moved out here," she replied. "A few years."

"Did Dave take you over there?"

"Yeah," she chuckled, "that's the only way I knew about it. I still go over there. I like their breakfasts, and I hate to eat alone. I mean, if I'm here, I'm with the dog most of the time—she's my company. She's the only dog I've ever had that I decided I wasn't going to train. I was going to let her grow up whichever way she would be."

"She's got a very sweet personality," I said.

"She's very intelligent," Heidi declared warmly. "She anticipates everything I'm going to do. No matter where I am in the house, if I look up, she's watching me."

Rubbing Chichi's head—which she (Chichi) seemed to enjoy—I asked Heidi what she usually had for breakfast at Fred and Pete's.

"I usually have two eggs looking at you," Heidi replied, "and toast with butter on the side, and some jam. And coffee," she added. "I think their coffee's good."

"So do I," I said, and I asked her if she bought the scratch-offs.

She grinned. "Oh, I like those, but I don't win anything on the darn things."

"And I understand you know Cash," I said, remembering that Dave had told me how much she liked the big Ukrainian who mostly worked weekends nowadays.

"Yes," Heidi said, "He's a sharp fellow—smart. I like him very much. I used to bake cookies and take them over to him. Macaroons."

"Coconut macaroons," Dave chimed in. "Every doctor has a can full."

"I think that's going to end, though," Heidi said. "My own doctor's retiring and going to Florida, and I gave him a big box of them. One day he was wearing one of those little hats—you know, the skull caps—and I said, 'Are you too Kosher to eat macaroons?' And he said, 'I'm not that good a boy.'" She laughed. "So I take them and he loves them. But I think that's going to end now. I get more tired all the time."

I asked Heidi where she was from originally.

"Toledo," she replied.

"The one in Ohio?"

She nodded grimly. "I was there through high school. It's a place everyone leaves as soon as they can—if they've got any sense."

"But you went back to the Hall of Fame there," Dave said.

"Oh yeah," she admitted. "They featured me and gave me an honor, putting me in the Hall of Fame or something."

"So you went to high school there? Then what did you do?" I asked.

"Then I went to Cleveland," Heidi said. "I went to work at the Alpine Village in Cleveland. That was a theater restaurant that seated about five hundred people; it was right across from the Palace Theater on Euclid Avenue. It was run by a Bavarian—I think he was from the Tyrol. He and his two brothers ran the place. A lot of people came there and it was very successful."

She told me that she sang Swiss folk songs there; both her parents had in fact been Swiss, and although she herself was born in the United States, she said that she still had Swiss citizenship if she wanted to claim it.

"And what was the talent that you had there that you're not telling him?" Dave broke in with a grin.

"The talent...?" Heidi didn't understand. "I told him I sang Swiss folk songs."

"You yodeled," Dave said.

"Yeah," she said, a little sheepishly. "I did."

"And when did you start singing?" I asked her, as eager as she seemed to be not to dwell on her yodeling days.

"I was twenty-three years old," Heidi replied, "and there was a tenor who used to direct the shows there, at the Alpine Village. So they started using me in those. Then one of the customers who used to come in—his name was J. A. Bohan; he was head of Carling's Ale in Cleveland—the tenor talked him into giving me a fellowship. He called all his friends around there, and I got a fellowship to the Institute of Music. It was in an old mansion out on Euclid Avenue, and I studied there for three years."

"Was that the first training you'd had?" I asked.

Heidi nodded. "I studied with this one teacher, and then I went to Tanglewood in '46. And from there... Well, I had a daughter in '45. My husband came home from the war, and..." She paused and shook her head. "I guess we were victims of the war, you know. People were separated... We were together maybe one year and then he had to go to the war, and he was over there three years... We were both young, and you know, people change in three years at that age."

"Right..."

"So we both... decided to break it up," Heidi said, her strong voice faltering as she remembered. "But I can remember that when he got mustered out of the Army, I didn't hear from him for a long time—this was after Susie was born." Susie, I realized, was Dave's wife. "And I thought, 'I wonder what's going on?' So I called where he was to be mustered out, and they told me, 'Oh, he was mustered out two weeks ago!'"

"Oh my gosh!" I gasped, but Heidi laughed.

"I was really angry about that," she recalled, still chuckling, "so I called the home of his mother and dad, and I asked for him. So they put him on the phone and I said, 'Well, you can just stay there. I'll make it alone.'"

"So that was the end of it?"

Heidi nodded. "I got a divorce," she said. "Susie was only two months old, and so from there I went on. She was my real inspiration to have a career."

"You mean because you had to support her?"

"That's right," Heidi replied resolutely, "although my mother lived with me and helped a lot, taking care of her. And when I moved to New York, I got a job singing in the chorus in *Oklahoma*."

"When was that?" I asked.

Heidi thought for a moment. "After Tanglewood," she replied. "It was either the end of '46 or the beginning of '47." She added that Leonard Bernstein had been at Tanglewood when she was there. "He was the resident 'wunderkind' at Tanglewood at that time," she recalled, shaking her head.

She got the *Oklahoma* job through Everett and Sylvia, a Hispanic couple she'd met at Tanglewood. As "non-whites," Everett and Sylvia weren't allowed to live on the grounds at Tanglewood, so Heidi let them use her "beat-up old car," and they became close friends for life, even after Everett went to Sweden, where he could "pass for white," and married a Swedish woman.

"I had to have a job," Heidi recalled, "because I needed an income. Well, Sylvia taught piano to the brother of Richard Rodgers"—Richard Rodgers as in *Oklahoma*, *The Sound of Music*, and *South Pacific*!—"and so she asked him"—meaning Richard Rodgers' brother—"to give her a letter for me, and so that's how I got introduced and got the job!"

"So you had a letter to Richard Rodgers?" I asked.

"Yes," she said, "and Oscar Hammerstein. The thing is, I was in the chorus there, but I didn't care. Because I'd never had a false feeling of pride or anything. I needed the money and the job, and so I took it. And through that—through a show-girl in that show—I got an apartment."

"Where was that?"

"Right on the edge of Hell's Kitchen," Heidi said proudly. "It was at 300 West 49th Street—on the corner of 49th and 8th Avenue. It was an old building," she added. "I don't know if it's still there or not. It was right across the street from the old Madison Square Garden."

She asked me if I'd ever been there, and I told her that long ago, as a kid, I'd gone to see the Ringling Brothers Circus at the old Madison Square Garden.

"We used to watch the circus come in with all the elephants," Heidi remembered. "We saw that every Spring. And we had a boxer," she added. "We called him Sparky."

"When you say 'we,' was that just you and Susie?" I asked.

"My mother was there, too," Heidi replied. "My father had died. Anyway, we lived there until I got in the Met in '53. I won the audition on the air. I got that because the girl who was scheduled was sick."

I asked her whether she remembered what she sang for her audition.

"Oh yeah," she said as if it were only yesterday. "I sang the aria from *Tosca* and the aria from *Trovatore*."

"When did you actually start singing opera?" I asked her, since it was a pretty big leap from the chorus of *Oklahoma* to Puccini and Verdi arias.

"Well, I started in '46 with Boris Goldovsky in Tanglewood," she replied. Goldovsky had been a famous Russian opera conductor who for many years had had his own opera company and who had become known to millions through his commentary on the weekly Saturday afternoon radio broadcasts of the Metropolitan Opera.

"And what was your first part?" I asked. "Do you remember that?"

"Yeah," Heidi said nonchalantly. "Santuzza in *Cavalleria*."

"Really!" I was impressed. If I remembered right, Santuzza was the female lead in Mascagni's classic opera *Cavaleria Rusticana*. I had a recording of Zinka Milanov, the famous Croatian soprano, singing the part.

"Boris was a booster," Heidi recalled. "He was always a dear friend, because he originally came from Cleveland also."

"So what happened after the audition?" I asked.

"Well, I won it," she said. "So they called me in—it was March 10th—to audition on the stage. And then they offered me a contract, and on Good Friday of that year, they asked me to come in and do a part in *Parsifal*—one of the flower girls."

"So was that your first performance on the Met stage?"

"Yeah," Heidi replied, "but then I supposedly made my debut that Fall. It was in *Carmen*. I did the Frascita"—one of Carmen's friends—"and then I was pushed up to Michaela"—one of the top parts in the renowned Bizet opera. "I did all of the *Carmens* with Rise Stevens," Heidi added. "She was a very dear friend and colleague, and she used to boost me a lot. She and Richard Tucker."

Rise Stevens, I later learned, had for many years been the Met's leading mezzo-soprano whose performances as the gypsy Carmen had been widely acclaimed throughout the opera world. And Richard Tucker, the world famous Brooklyn-born American tenor, was a name I already knew from several of the classic Verdi opera recordings I owned.

"You know, nobody can do it alone," Heidi remarked. As she talked, Chichi had quietly nuzzled up to her, panting rapidly, and Heidi stroked the little dog soothingly behind the ears. "It's the people who are around you—and it's fate, I guess," she added wistfully.

"And a lot of hard work," I said.

Heidi looked up. "Oh yes," she agreed. "You have to be dedicated, like with anything you do. So anyway, one thing led to another, and I got big management with Columbia Artists. Then I was asked to go up to the Yale drama school to do an opera—*Dido and Aeneas*"—a beautiful early opera by the English composer Henry Purcell. Heidi laughed to herself as she remembered the experience. "It didn't pay anything, but it was prestige, you know. And I figured anything I could do on the stage, I'd learn from."

Then in 1955, she said, she signed a contract to sing in London and Berlin. "I sang at the opera in Berlin," she recalled, "and in London I sang at the Royal Albert Hall in their pops concert."

Not exactly your typical Fred and Pete's customer, I thought to myself. "So what was all of this like, for a Buckeye from Ohio to be singing at the Met and the Royal Albert Hall?" I asked her.

Heidi thought for a moment before answering. "Well, you know, I never had any idea that I wasn't going to make it. It wasn't chutzpah or anything like that," she quickly explained. "It's just that I had a goal, and I was going for it."

"Sure..."

"I can remember that with Sir Malcolm Sargent"—the eminent British conductor and composer—"we had a run-through, and I was *very* near-sighted in those days—I couldn't see three feet ahead of me. Well, I went in there and rehearsed a run-through, and he had a smooth chick with him in there, sitting next to him—he was a bird, really. Anyhow, I just saw their outlines there at the piano, and we went through everything. Then later I put my glasses on, and there he was, with a great big boa constrictor wrapped around the girl's neck. It was huge!"

"Oh my gosh...!" I stammered. Dave was laughing.

"And I acted like I saw it every day," Heidi continued, and then she started laughing, too. "Maybe they thought I was nuts—I don't know. But I didn't panic, because I knew that was what they wanted me to do. Anyhow, then I was invited back there to sing with the BBC. I did a full opera with the BBC—we did *Otello*"—one of Verdi's last and greatest operas—"and I did the Desdemona..."

"That's a beautiful part," I murmured.

Heidi smiled. "Yeah," she said. "It was in color. And then my husband came over—followed me over."

"Oh, so you had remarried by this time?"

"Well, over there I got remarried," Heidi replied. "He followed me over to Europe—said he was going to look at horses—but he never got to Ireland, I don't think." She chuckled softly. "We got married there, in Marylebone"—a particularly well-to-do section of London. "His name was John D. Preece. No 't' in it: just P-R-E-E-C-E. He was from Nebraska."

"And he followed you to Europe?"

"Yeah."

"Not bad," I said.

"Well, I wasn't particularly looking to get married," Heidi explained. "You know, I was rolling along, and I was doing OK."

I asked her whether she had taken Susie with her on that trip, but she said, no, Susie had stayed with her mother.

"She went to Germany with you, though," Dave interjected.

"Yeah, I took them over to Switzerland," Heidi said. "They stayed with relatives over there. And then Susie got injured over there, which was scary. She fell off of a carousel and tore a kidney—but we got through that," she added, still greatly relieved after all these years.

"So Heidi," I said, "what was your favorite opera?"

She thought for a moment. "You know, it's the one you're doing at the time," she replied. "It really is. I love Wagnerian music—and it's not the singing that I particularly like. I just think the orchestration is so fabulous. You don't even have to see the singers or hear them, you know, because the music is so beautiful. I think *Boheme* and some of the other lighter Puccini operas are good for people to hear for the first time, and I like *Otello* very much."

I nodded; so did I.

"And then I did a lot of concert work after I got with Columbia," Heidi went on. "German lieder, arias, English composers—things like that."

Dave asked her when she'd gone on the radio. "Like Friday night at the Met, remember that?" he said.

"Oh, ABC had a summer night program," Heidi recalled. "I was on that."

"You sang on the last one, didn't you?" Dave said.

"On the Firestone program, yeah. I sang on there frequently," Heidi said. "But that was because Rise Stevens and Richard Tucker pushed for me. They asked for me, actually. Isn't that great?"

"Sure is," I said.

"Every time I open the paper, I'm afraid I'm going to see that Rise passed away," Heidi sighed. "She must be ninety-five or ninety-seven. She's gotta be up there. But I never hear anything about her. She was really a classy woman. And her husband was very nice, too," she added. "I liked him a lot."

I asked Heidi who had been some of the great singers that she had sung with over the course of her career.

"Well, the first one you would probably remember was Renaldi—oh, what was her first name?" Heidi cried, frustrated that she couldn't remember.

I knew who she meant, but couldn't remember either.

"It's only been fifty years," Dave chuckled.

But Heidi didn't give up. "Renata..."

"Tebaldi?" I guessed.

"Tebaldi—that's it," Heidi agreed. "I sang all the *Bohemes* with her," she recalled fondly. "We made a lot. They recorded all those broadcasts for Voice of America, so all those are available."

"But we couldn't get a machine that could play them, remember?" Dave said. "Because they were these really big records," he explained to me.

"They are big," Heidi agreed. "But there are a lot of them, and different companies have pirated them, so they are for sale. But I feel like every time they're transposed onto another record, it loses some of the original quality."

"That's true," I said. "But now tell me about Eisenhower. Dave said I should ask you about Eisenhower."

"Oh," Heidi laughed, "that was the first professional job I had after I had studied in Cleveland." She turned to Dave. "There's a picture on the table back there that you can show him, David. It's tarnished but you'll get the idea," she said, turning back to me. "He came as the featured guest, and they asked me to sing. So I sang an aria for him, and then they took me up to meet him. He signed a menu and said, 'Thank you.' I didn't ask for it—he just signed one and said, 'Thank you, that was beautiful singing.' But you know, someone stole that..."

"Oh no, you're kidding...!"

"And I know who did it," Heidi said. "And in a nice way, I said, 'I can't find my autographed piece from Eisenhower.' And she said, 'Oh well, you probably had three or four of them anyhow.'"

"What a shame!" I cried. "But that's a wonderful picture of the general shaking hands with you."

"Yeah," she said, "but I really was P.O.'d at her. I never trusted her again."

Dave handed me another picture. "Here's her Coca-Cola advertisement," he beamed, clearly very proud of his mother-in-law.

"Gosh!" I said. "You were almost as beautiful then as you are now," I told her. And in fact, in the picture she put Lana Turner to shame.

Heidi chuckled. "It's nice of you to say so," she said demurely. "That was backstage at the old Met. You see, the stagehands got free Cokes, so for *that* Coca-Cola wanted this... Atlanta was the place where the Coke CEO lived, and they were *very* big for the Met when we went there. They gave parties and everything..."

"You might want to sell this picture back to them," Dave suggested.

Heidi laughed. "I never even drink Coke," she said.

"So you enjoyed singing," I said.

"Oh yeah," Heidi replied enthusiastically. "It was a wonderful outlet for me. It was like therapy."

"Especially at the farm," Dave said. "You could hear her a quarter of a mile down the drive."

I asked Heidi whether she still sang at all.

"Just around here—with her," she said, fondly rubbing Chichi's head.

"We'll have to get you to Fred and Pete's for a recital," I said.

Dave cracked up.

"Oh, I wouldn't sing publicly any more at all," she chuckled. She said that she'd wound up her career around 1970. "I remember I did *Boheme* with the Trenton orchestra—it was a benefit. That was the last time I sang, I think."

"That's marvelous," I declared. "What a wonderful career!"

"You know what her strong point now is?" Dave said. "She's the best cook you can ever imagine."

Heidi smiled. "Well, my mom, when she was about seventeen, her family sent her to Geneva, and she was taught to cook with style. And I just learned it from her."

I asked her what her specialty was, besides macaroons.

"Red cabbage," she said proudly, and she nodded toward the kitchen. "I've got a big pot of it out there now. But I don't cook much for myself any more; I just nosh."

"She likes to cook for groups," Dave explained.

"It's hard to cook for one," Heidi said. "And I eat mostly vegetables and fruit anyhow—and toast. I don't like to eat meat any more. I have a hard time swallowing it because I think of the animals. I just can't. I'll never eat veal. I like the taste of lamb, but I don't buy it any more. But I do still eat eggs."

"As long as they're looking up at you," I said.

"Yeah."

"Now Heidi," I continued, "you said you stopped singing around 1970. That's almost forty years ago. So what have you been doing for the last forty years—besides hanging out at Fred and Pete's?"

"Well, you know, it seems like yesterday," she said, shaking her head in amazement at the thought that it had, in fact, been almost forty years.

"You're a great card player," Dave told her, and turned to me. "Especially bridge. Don't ever challenge her to bridge."

"Oh yeah," Heidi said. "When my husband died, we lived on a farm in Newtown over in Pennsylvania. He got lymphoma, and he died in '94. After he died, I was there about a year, and then I moved out. That was the year there was so much ice, you know, so I was snow-bound out there."

After that, she said, she'd lived in Pennington for a couple of years, and then she'd bought this place. "I like it over here much better. I wanted to be closer to Susie anyhow—and now she can send David over," she chuckled.

But she didn't play cards any more, she said, because there was no one out here to play with. "I don't have patience to be a teacher," she explained. "I just don't. And it's very frustrating when you play with people that get the good cards and don't know what to do with them," she added with a laugh.

"Do you ever listen to music any more?" I asked her.

"I do," Heidi said.

"Do you ever listen to the recordings of yourself from back then?"

"No," she said, "but I listen to the Russian music. Shostakovitch and Tchaikovsky—I love the *Sixth Symphony* of Tchaikovsky. He had a troubled life, and you can hear that in his music. I think it's beautiful, although some people look down on it. I like Wagner, too," she added. "But I like the Russian composers very much."

"How about Stravinsky?"

Heidi grimaced. "No, I don't like his music."

I laughed. "Somehow, I didn't think you would. You prefer the more romantic style, don't you?"

She nodded. "I don't like the atonal stuff. Mathematically, it may be very clever, but I think music should be beautiful. Really, the only American composer I really liked was Gershwin. I loved his music. And Irving Berlin, he was clever. But they wrote different types of stuff. Bernstein was clever, but I think he copied a lot."

Suddenly Dave's cell phone went off with a burst of loud music that startled both Heidi and me. He ducked out to the kitchen and was having what sounded like a pretty animated conversation about an upcoming auction. Meanwhile, Heidi told me how she didn't think much of Gian Carlo Menotti, the Italian-American composer best known for his Christmas operetta, *Amahl and the Night Visitors*, which I had always enjoyed seeing with the kids when they were growing up. "I don't know whether he died or not," she said, "but he looked very evil when he got old."

I laughed. "Did you know any other composers besides Menotti and Bernstein?"

No, she said, but she'd known plenty of conductors. "I sang with all of them," she recalled. "My favorite was Bruno Walter. I loved him." She smiled. "I sang in all the performances that he conducted in his last run at the Met."

"What made him such a great conductor?" I asked.

"Talent," Heidi replied. "And he was very spiritual. He conducted with such... I don't know what the word would be for him. Tenderness? Warmth? They loved him; the orchestra loved him. And I loved singing with him, because somehow he conducted the way you wanted to sing it—even though I'm sure it was really because you were following what *he* wanted," she laughed. "But he was a wonderful conductor. And a nice man. He had tragedy in his life, too."

We sat quietly for a minute as Heidi continued stroking Chichi. Dave was still going at it on the phone, making arrangements of some kind.

"And who were some of your favorite singers over the course of your career?" I asked her after a while.

"Well, Rise Stevens and Dick Tucker," Heidi replied. "They were the foremost—and not just because they helped me, but because they were great artists. Oh, and Pinza, of course"—Ezio Pinza, the great Italian basso—"he was one in a million!"

"Is that right?" I had several recordings of his that I really liked, so I was relieved to hear that he, at least, was not evil.

"He was gone from the Met when I got there—he was in *South Pacific* at that time—but he had such a beautiful sound. And Leonard Warren had a beautiful sound," Heidi added. "He had a gorgeous sound if you closed your eyes, although he was a stiff performer." Warren, I later learned, had been a highly acclaimed baritone at the Met for many years. "But so many performers can't say no to a performance, you know," Heidi lamented. "They keep going, and they ruin their voices. Today, they don't last more than a year or two."

It sounded a lot like what some of the Fred and Pete's guys in the white chairs were saying about today's baseball players. I asked Heidi whether she ever listened to the singers who were out there now.

"Well, I've never heard Fleming in the flesh," she replied, meaning Rene Fleming, the soprano superstar, "but they say she's very good. I don't know. I don't listen to many of them any more."

I asked Heidi whether she ever listened to other kinds of music, and she told me that she liked the blues, and she liked jazz, especially swing. "I go back to that era," she said. "Harry James—I used to love the trumpet he played. Oh, it was beautiful. And Nat King Cole. I've got all his recordings. *He* was a class act."

"That was a nice recording of him and his daughter," Dave said, coming back in from the kitchen. "You know, after he'd passed away."

"They were a very loving family," Heidi agreed. "But there was sure a lot of crap—if you'll excuse the expression—with the racial thing," she added bitterly.

"Yeah," Dave said.

"Oh, and Jackie Onassis gave me roses once when I did a concert in Hyannis," Heidi suddenly remembered. "And I didn't know that she did that until I read the review several weeks or months later."

"You're kidding!" I laughed.

"Because I was so near-sighted, I couldn't see," Heidi explained. "But I got cataracts on my eyes and had implants, and now I can see everything."

Dave mentioned that he'd been looking through some of the old German editions of *Life* magazine that he had back at his house. "Your write-up is in there, too," he told Heidi.

"Oh yeah," she said, as if it were no big deal. "Well, I got write-ups from all over."

"So Heidi," I said, "as you look back over your career, is there anything that you're particularly proud of?"

She thought for a moment before answering. "Yeah," she said resolutely. "I didn't sleep with anybody to get anything."

Dave and I both burst out laughing. "She's got a sense of humor," Dave said fondly, shaking his head.

"I'd do my gigs, and I'd go home to my mother and my daughter. And from there, the door was closed and it was private. It was family," Heidi said, her strength and defiance still unshakable after all these years.

"And I imagine that might have set you apart," I said.

"Yeah," she said mildly, and Dave chuckled.

Then there was the story of how Heidi wound up on the front page of the *New York Times*. Dave had brought out another box full of pictures from Heidi's career, and as she started going through them, she suddenly remembered the night Zinka Milanov fainted onstage at the Met while singing the Verdi *Requiem*.

"She faints, just before the big aria," Heidi recalled.

"Oh my gosh," I said.

"Well, I was in the house," Heidi continued, "watching it on stage left, up in the box, which is the furthest place away from the stage. I had to come all around the horse-shoe and then I had to step over her body"—meaning Milanov's—"to get on stage. She was laying there on the floor of the stage."

"You're kidding!" I cried. "So you were out there in the audience and you just decided you'd step in and rescue her?"

"Well, I had to," Heidi explained. "I was cover."

"Oh, you were?"

"I was dressed in a travel dress," she said. "A black wool travel dress—I was supposed to fly out to Toronto or Montreal that night to do a concert."

"But instead you wound up on the front page of the paper," I said.

"Yeah," Heidi replied, still thumbing through all the press clippings and photographs with Chichi panting on her lap. "The *New York Times*. I think I've still got that one around here somewhere."

"Wow," I said, "what a life you've had!"

Heidi broke into a big smile. "I've had a *great* life," she said, and there was no question that she meant it.

AND NOW THIS

May 26, 2009. It's kind of a gloomy, rainy Tuesday morning, and Jim Fennelli is at the counter when I come in. He asks me if I've heard about Johnny Woo. "Heard what?" I say. Jim says John got hurt and wound up in the hospital. Broke his leg or something. Theresa, who's working the counter, says no, it was his pelvis. He broke it when he was mowing the lawn or something.

When I come back in around lunch-time for a pastrami sandwich, Tom is there and he says, no, it wasn't a lawn-mower, it was a Weed-Wacker, and that he's out of the hospital and over at Care One, a rehab center just down the road from the hospital. I tell Tom that I may stop in to see John and I ask him what John usually has for lunch. "Nothing," Tom says. "He don't each lunch, just breakfast and dinner. For breakfast he has poached eggs and bacon, and for dinner he has whatever the special is." Then Tom says, "If you see him, ask him if he wants me to bring him by some dinner tonight."

I decide that I will go to see him, and I find Care One easily enough. There's a big banner over the entrance that says NO DEFICIENCIES IN 2008. Very inspiring. I find John up on the second floor, in room 237, and he has a visitor—a guy with a pony tail and a Harley shirt who's obviously quite a bit younger than John. We shake hands. It turns out he's John's cousin Richard; their grandmothers were sisters, he explains. He seems like a nice guy, and he's obviously concerned about John. He asks me if I'll stay with John for a minute while he goes out and talks to the therapist.

I can see that John's in pain. He says it hurts to move, and the physical therapy really hurts. He confirms that it's his pelvis that's broken and that it was a Weed-Wacker, not a lawn-mower. He was backing up while he was using it and tripped over the raised edge of the sidewalk behind him. I tell him, "Forty years you were up on a roof without a single accident, and now this—with a Weed-Wacker!" He kind of chuckles, although even that seems to hurt.

(A few days later, Tom tells me that a couple of the guys went over to Care One to see John, but when they told the receptionist that they were there to see Johnny Woo, she told

them they didn't have anybody there by that name. None of them knew his real name, so the receptionist couldn't tell them what room he was in. They left without seeing him.)

June 10, 2009. *John Wilwol has been in Care One rehab facility for about two weeks now, after several days in the hospital. I've been visiting him every couple of days, bringing him the Trentonian. His cousin Richard also visits John regularly. Today when I was at Fred and Pete's for dinner, Theresa was my waitress. I asked her if she missed John. She said yeah, but she'd been over to see him. I said, "I bet he was glad to see you," and she said, "Yeah, but he was even happier to see Meghan. He's in love with her."*

June 12, 2009. *I stopped in for a ham sandwich today, and Meghan was working the counter. It was about 2 pm and the place was practically deserted so I had a chance to talk to her about John. She said she misses him, and said she called him yesterday but there was no answer. He tried calling back later but didn't reach her. I told her that I planned to go see him after I finished my sandwich and that I was going to bring him a cannoli from next door. She said to tell him that she missed him. I picked up the cannoli and a Trentonian and brought them to John, who was sitting up in bed when I got there. His cousin Richard was visiting him—this is the third time we've been there at the same time. John seemed to be feeling a little better today, and said they'd just done an X-ray of his left leg, which is still causing him a good deal of pain.*

Addendum: *Not too long afterwards, John went home. He couldn't drive yet, so once in a while I'd pick him up and take him over to Fred and Pete's, where Meghan and Theresa greeted him like a conquering hero returning from the wars. After another couple of months, he was fully recovered and back to his old routine—although he swears he takes it easy with that Weed Wacker now.*

PUT THAT IN YOUR BOOK

Thursday, July 16, 2009. I head over to Fred and Pete's to have breakfast with Dave Merritt, the drummer in our band, to talk about how things are going at his store. I get there at about 9:00 and I don't see Dave's van in the lot yet, but I do see a shiny black Mercedes sports car, parked right up in front, so I know Fred Wright must be there. And sure enough, there he is, in one of the white plastic chairs, shooting the breeze with Richie and some of the other guys. I say hello and take a seat in one of the plastic chairs myself so I can keep an eye out for Dave.

Richie's telling the guys how he might have a chance to play baseball in a seniors tournament out in Colorado, but he doesn't know whether he wants to do it. Plus he's not sure how his wife would feel about him being gone.

Fred starts laughing. "Did I tell you about the time I was gone for a week on a business trip? I come back Friday evening with my suitcase and my wife comes down the stairs. She sees me with the suitcase and she says, 'Where are you going?'" Fred's laughing so hard now that the other guys are laughing, too. "She thought I was just leaving. Here I've been gone a whole week," he explains, "and she didn't even know it. Put that in your book," he tells me, laughing so hard he almost has tears in his eyes.

So I did.

HE'S LATE

Monday, November 2, 2009. It's a cold, overcast November morning—All Souls Day. I stop in for breakfast and ask Anne how her trip to West Virginia went, even though it was a week ago. She says it was great—and the fall colors were just amazing! "Even hot pink!" she tells me. Marvin Block, who was born the Bronx, comes in and is feeling pretty good because the Yankees are only one game from clinching the Series. He was at his place in the Poconos this weekend and says the colors were amazing there, too. "But there's so many hunters out in the woods!" he says. "Even on Sunday!"

Then Bob Lee comes in and sits on the other side of me. He's not looking too good. He's got his oxygen with him and I figure that maybe it's his pulmonary fibrosis acting up. I ask him how he's doing, and he tells me quietly that his wife died last week. "You hadn't heard?" he asks me. Stunned, I tell him, no, I was in California working. I tell him how sorry I am. He looks me in the eye and says that he's never, in all his life, felt pain like this. Never. He looks stricken. I can't begin to imagine how he must feel.

Then he looks up, pulls himself together and says, "Wonder where Jimmy is?" Jim Fennelli is his best friend at Fred and Pete's. And sure enough, like clockwork, Jim comes in. "He's late," Bob tells me. "He's usually here by five after nine." I look up at the clock: it's 9:07.

JOE AND ISRAEL

Tuesday, June 29, 2010. Another hot summer day, overcast. It's the kind of stifling heat that makes it hard to breathe. We've been expecting rain for about a week but it never comes, apart from a few random sprinkles. The ground is like a rock and the plants in the back yard are dying.

Not at Fred and Pete's, though. For some reason, the place is jumping, even though it's 4:30 in the afternoon. It's just Meghan waiting on the tables now, although Joe is helping out some. Tommy Pyle and John Wilwol are sitting together in the same booth where they usually sit, their table littered with empty juice bottles and half-empty cups —looks like they've been there a while. And Israel and Gonzalo are both still here, gazing up at the TV where they're replaying some of the Spain-Portugal World Cup game from earlier this afternoon. The ceiling fans are going full blast, so you really don't feel the heat in here, and the ice machine is cranking away. I ask Meghan for a big cup of ice water, and when she brings it, I ask her if she can take a few minutes after her shift for me to interview her. But she says today's not a good day because she has to drop Joe off at his place right after work and then she has to be somewhere at 6:30.

After a plate of meatloaf, corn and mashed potatoes (one of tonight's dinner specials), I go up to the counter to pay my check ($5.35), and when Joe takes my money, I start talking to him. He's wearing the standard-issue black Fred and Pete's t-shirt and jeans, and has a towel hanging out of his back pocket. He's forever going back and forth, back and forth behind the counter—kind of like that "gotta make the donuts" guy in the old Dunkin Donuts commercial. I ask him if he'd be willing to be interviewed. "Nah," he says, "I might say something nasty about somebody." I assure him that if he does, I won't use it. He shrugs.

"So how long have you been working here now?" I ask him.

"A little bit over a year," Joe says. "Hard to believe it's been that long."

"What were you doing before?"

"I worked with my father," he replies. "Before that—you know the Hurry Back Inn?"

"Leonard's Hurry Back Inn?" I say, remembering the place over on Klockner where we used to take the kids for breakfast once in a while when they were growing up.

"I worked there for about twenty years," Joe says.

"No kidding!"

"But then after about ten years I got tired of it, so I quit. I didn't know if my dad would hire me or not, but I went home and asked him and he said yeah."

"What did your dad do?" I ask him.

"He had a shoe repair shop in Princeton," Joe says, smiling. "So I worked there for ten years. But I never got out of the restaurant." He lets out a rueful laugh. "They wouldn't let me quit."

"So you were working both jobs?"

Joe nods. "Then my dad retires, and he got screwed bad. He was retired, but he didn't even last three days. He was in the hospital; three weeks later he died."

"Oh my God..."

"He didn't even get a week off," Joe says bitterly. "He had cancer and they didn't know nothing about it. Even though he went to the doctor constantly, they didn't know nothing about it. He had a sore back; thought he'd just pulled a muscle, either working in the yard or back in the shop..."

I ask Joe if he remembers Marie who used to come in here. I tell him the same thing happened to her husband. He had a heart condition that he used to go to the doctor for all the time, but the doctor never noticed that he had cancer until it was too late.

"Same with my dad," Joe says. "He had polyps taken out six months before. You'd think if there was polyps, they'd look for that, wouldn't you?"

"Was it colon cancer?"

"It was all over," Joe says. "That's why his back was sore. The cancer was going into the bones. By the time they got him, he was third stage or something. So I'm glad he went fast. I got a friend of mine who's father was hanging on for like a year and a half." He shakes his head and sighs.

"So your dad didn't get his retirement," I say.

"Just three days," Joe says. "By the third day he was in the hospital."

I ask Joe what his last name is.

"Persicketti—with a K," he says. "Some of them spell it with an H. It got screwed up when they came over."

"Happened to a lot of people," I say.

A big beefy guy in a dungaree jacket wants to buy a lottery ticket, so Joe goes over and prints it out on the machine for him, but he comes back to the counter without skipping a beat. "They say sometimes cancer can come on just like that," he tells me. "Some forms of cancer can be very aggressive—that's what they told me."

"Well, maybe," I say. "So did you grow up in Trenton?"

Joe shakes his head. "Hamilton," he says. "I went to Steinert."

Just like Tom Armenti and Justice Samuel Alito, I think to myself. Then some more people come in to buy lottery tickets—probably on their way home from work—and Joe has to take care of them. The interview is over.

But I don't leave yet.

Israel's turned the grill off by now, and most of the people that are going to come in for dinner already have their dinners, or they've already had them, like me. So this might be a good time to try to interview Israel. His English isn't great, and my Spanish is non-existent, but it seems a little weird to write a book about Fred and Pete's without talking to the guy who fixes the food. I figure it's worth a shot.

"I want to talk to you, because you're the cook, and without you, there'd be no food," I tell him. "Without you, everybody'd be hungry."

I'm not sure he understands, but he smiles and nods. Yes, he says, he's willing to be interviewed. I follow him into the kitchen—the inner sanctum at Fred and Pete's that I've never set foot in before. It's much bigger than I expected, and it smells like beef stew and detergent. Gonzalo is standing in the back, by the sink, and he grins at me. I have the impression that he speaks even less English than Israel.

"So, Israel," I say, "the first thing I need is your last name."

"Me?" he says. "You need to know my name?"

"Your last name."

He spells it for me. "C-H-A-V-E-Z."

"Like the guy in Venezuela?"

He smiles and nods.

"And you're from Guatemala, right?" I ask him, and he nods again. "Where in Guatemala?"

Israel looks around, finds a grimy yellow pad and a pencil lying beside the stove and writes it down for me: ESCUINTLA. It's in the southern part of Guatemala, he says. (And sure enough, when I get home and look it up in my world atlas, there it is, big enough to be on the map, and located about halfway between Guatemala City, the capital, and the Pacific coast.)

"So how long have you been in this country?" I ask him.

"Here?" he says. "In this country?"

"Yeah."

He says something I don't understand. "Twenty years?" I guess.

Israel shakes his head. "Eighteen."

"And how long here at Fred and Pete's?"

"Nine years," he says.

"And you have four kids, right?"

Israel nods and smiles. He tells me they're 23, 21, 19 and 17 years old.

"And you work here every day, right?" I ask.

"Seven days," he says. I know it's true, because I see him in here every day. In fact, Israel and Tom Armenti are the only ones whom I've seen working here every day of the week—although I know that Israel doesn't start until 6:30 in the morning, an hour and a half after Tom.

"How do you like working here?"

Israel shrugs. "It's OK," he says. "My job is my job, you know."

It reminds me of what Tom told me when I asked him how he and Israel communicated: a hamburger's a hamburger.

"And you send money home, right?" I say. We've talked about this before.

"I send money home, yes," Israel says.

I ask him whether he thinks he'll ever go back to Guatemala to live, or whether he wants to bring his family up here to the States.

"I go back," Israel declares. "But my family comes here for vacation, you know. Maybe this year my son, maybe next time my daughter."

"They come up here for vacation?"

"Yes," he says, smiling, "but they can't all come here together. It's too much. Because they come here and they want to spend money, you know."

I ask Israel what he did before Fred and Pete's.

"Cook," he says. "Many places. It's a long story."

"But this one's OK?"

He shrugs again. "Sure," he says. "Once you pick it up, you know what to do."

"And a new job is hard to learn?"

He nods.

I ask Israel where he lives.

"Hamilton Avenue and Olden Avenue," he answers. "Where they cross."

"And how do you get here?"

"Bus," he says. "Much cheaper."

"Than a car, you mean?"

"Yes."

I say that it must be hard to be away from his family for so long. He says it is, but it's better now with the computer.

"You have a computer?" I say, a little surprised.

Israel nods. He e-mails them all the time, he says. His 21-year-old son is in college, he says, studying to be a lawyer, and his 19-year-old daughter starts college next year.

"What about the 23-year-old?" I ask.

"My daughter? No, she got married," Israel replies, chuckling.

I ask Israel how much schooling he himself got, and he says only two years, when he was seven and eight years old. After that, he had to work. Then later, when he went into the Guatemalan army, he got a little more education. I ask him where he learned to cook, here or Guatemala.

"Here in America," he says. "I started as dishwasher for six months, but I see the cook make more money."

"But you've always been a cook here at Fred and Pete's?"

"Yes. Always."

"Well, you do a good job," I tell him. "Everybody says they love the food. And you always make me a good Swiss omelet."

"You always the same," he laughs. "Every day the same."

Meghan sticks her head in the doorway with an order for a couple of dinners, so I let Israel get back to work. But before I leave, I decide to take a closer look around the kitchen.

There's a big Garland stove with ten burners and with a bunch of different pots going on it, and an Imperial deep-fat fryer for the French fries that I get sometimes when it's cold out and I order a hot turkey sandwich. There's also a battle-scarred microwave oven, a shiny stainless steel refrigerator that looks big enough to hold a whole side of beef if necessary, and a giant floor fan that's keeping the place cool, even in this heat.

There are cans everywhere: everything from soup to Sterno to pineapple juice. Dozens of big coffee machines and plastic coolers stacked on the shelves along the wall—must be for all the catering runs. Big jars of cinnamon, garlic powder, paprika, rosemary, basil. Not to mention shelves of containers of mustard, tartar sauce, fish and chips batter, spaghetti, green beans, potatoes, pickles—you name it. Plus boxes and boxes of paper plates, paper napkins, plastic spoons. For a moment, I'm reminded of Dave Stout telling me about all those thousands of cups of coffee he's gotten here over the years, always with a plastic spoon in it, even though he always drinks his coffee black. I consider asking Israel how much it costs for a box of 500 plastic spoons, but then I figure (a) he probably doesn't know, and (b) even if he does, I'm not sure that Tom would really want to know how much he's spent over all these years on plastic spoons that Dave Stout has never used.

After another minute, I'm done looking around. "Gracias," I say to Israel, with a nod to Gonzalo.

"De nada," Israel says graciously.

"Vaya con Dios," I add, pretty much exhausting my Spanish.

"De nada," Israel says again, and turns back to big Garland stove, his black cap tilted back and his red Fred and Pete's t-shirt soaked with another day's worth of steam and sweat.

When I come back out of the kitchen into the dining area, John Wilwol is helping Meghan clear the tables, and Meghan's dad, Guy Norton, is in the middle of a spirited conversation with Tommy Pyle about Little League baseball, telling him how ridiculous some of the parents are.

"It's really bad when you sit in the stands and you see some of the parents laugh when some kid on the other team strikes out," Guy says indignantly. "They make fun of them—and these kids are twelve years old! I mean, it's not like you're watching the Mets and it's some guy who's making thirteen million a year. These are twelve-year-old *kids*," he repeats, shaking his head.

Tommy barely nods. It's been a long afternoon.

"I mean, I was over at Paxton Avenue," Guy continues energetically, "and this kid's up at bat, and the parents are yelling, 'Miss it! Miss it! Miss it!' And the poor kid's only twelve years *old*!"

"Makes you wonder which ones are the kids," I murmur.

Guy looks up at me, probably not really sure who I am but glad to have someone who shares his indignation. "At one of the games," he says, "a lady drove an hour from Wall Township just to put fliers on everybody's car because she thought Bordentown was using an illegal player. She drove all the way up from Wall Township!" he repeats emphatically. "I mean, Wall Township's down at the *shore*!"

Tommy grunts, and I get the feeling that maybe this isn't the first time they've had this conversation.

As I head toward the door on my way out, Joe is back at the counter straightening up the racks of scratch-offs. I decide to ask him one more question before I go. "So, Joe," I say, "how'd you wind up working here?"

Joe turns and leans on the counter. "After my dad retired and passed away, I took about a year off," he says. "And then I just started looking for a job. So I was walking around, and I came up here. Most of these places, no one was hiring. But for some reason I looked over here and saw Fred and Pete's and figured I'd try it."

"Had you ever heard of Fred and Pete's?"

"Oh yeah," Joe says, "I used to come here when I was a kid. My father was here on Sundays for twenty, thirty years."

"So you knew about the place," I say.

"Oh yeah, I remembered coming here when I was a kid, and I'd get lunch meat here sometimes when they were open at night."

"So you just walked in and said, 'Hey Tom, you need somebody?'"

"Yeah, pretty much," Joe says. "He took my name down—scribbled it on a piece of paper—but I didn't expect anything. And then a week later, I got a phone call."

"And so here you are."

"Yeah, here I am." Joe shrugs. "Life goes on."

GARY

Wednesday, July 21, 2010. I'd seen Gary Amico in the same booth just about every morning since I'd started coming to Fred and Pete's, sometimes alone reading the newspaper, sometimes with a crowd of other guys—often with an extra table added on to accommodate the group. I'd also seen him one night over at the new DeLorenzo's Tomato Pies a couple of miles down Route 33 in Robbinsville, working behind the counter. Gary's a short, quiet, serious-looking guy, and Anne had once told me that he owned the original DeLorenzo's Tomato Pies down on Hudson Street in the Chambersburg section of Trenton, a legendary institution in this part of the world. That night when I spotted him behind the counter at the new DeLorenzo's, he'd nodded when he saw me—probably recognized me from Fred and Pete's—and that's when I decided to ask him if he'd be willing to be interviewed for the book. He said OK. This particular morning, he was dressed in a purple polo shirt and grey shorts, his gray hair neatly combed.

"So Gary," I said, sitting across from him in his usual booth, "how long have you been coming here to Fred and Pete's?"

Gary thought for a moment, wanting to get it right. "Fifteen years, I guess," he replied, his voice surprisingly deep.

"And how'd you wind up coming here?"

"Because it's a place where people from my old neighborhood generated to when the neighborhood changed," he replied. "So it was to renew and keep relationships that I've had all my life."

"And where'd you grow up?"

"North Trenton, on Princeton Avenue," Gary said laconically. "Now it's Martin Luther King Boulevard."

I asked him whether he had any brothers or sisters.

"I have a brother who comes here also," Gary replied. "A younger brother— six years. We were a working class family—factory workers."

"Where'd your dad work?"

"General Electric."

"And where'd you go to high school?"

"Trenton High."

"So when did you move out here?" I asked him.

"The last twenty years," Gary said. "After I got married, I lived in the City; then I moved to Hamilton Township. Natural progression."

I nodded, taking a sip of my coffee. "So Gary, tell me a little bit about your business," I said.

"Well," he said, "it's my in-laws and my wife—my father-in-law started the business in 1947. It's in Trenton. It's called Tomato Pies. DeLorenzo's Tomato Pies."

"On Hudson Street," I said.

Gary nodded. "On Hudson Street. And it's a good recipe. Been there forever. Stayed consistent. Business is decent right now. Thursday, Friday, Saturday, Sunday, four til nine. And now my son's opened a place over in Robbinsville on Route 33—DeLorenzo's Tomato Pies."

I asked him what the secret was. "What makes your tomato pies so much better than the others?"

Gary shrugged. "Expensive ingredients—the flour's expensive, the tomatoes are real good, expensive oil, and hands-on care for the product."

"I've seen you working up there at the new place," I said. "Are you keeping an eye out to make sure everybody's doing it right?"

Gary shook his head. "If he needs somebody to help, I'll go in for an hour or so," he said.

I asked him how long he'd worked at the Hudson Street place, and he said he was still working there. "Forty years," he added. "Forty years."

"Forty years?" I was impressed. "And it's one of the best places in the country, from what I hear."

Gary seemed a little embarrassed. "Well," he allowed, "it has a good reputation. A well-deserved rating in Zagat and a number of other places, but, you know..."

I told him I'd eaten at some of the best pizza places in New York, Chicago, and other cities around the country, but none were as good as DeLorenzo's.

"Well, it's found a niche," Gary said modestly. It was clear that he was not the kind of guy to get carried away with other people's hype.

"So Gary," I said, "speaking of niches, what exactly is the difference between pizza and tomato pies?"

I figured that he must have been asked that same question at least ten thousand times in the forty years that he'd been in the business, but he was surprisingly patient with me. "Traditionally," he explained, "when they make pizza, it's sauce, toppings, and cheese. But here in Trenton, for some reason, the cheese went on first—the toppings and tomatoes last, the emphasis being on the tomatoes. So, tomato pies, OK?"

I nodded. "Makes sense."

"That's a reasonable definition," Gary said. "I'm sure other people would... But that's exactly what it is. Tomato pie is Trenton. Joe's Tomato Pies, Papa's... There's lots of them."

I asked Gary how, given all the changes that had occurred over the last forty years, he'd managed to maintain the quality of his tomato pies.

He shrugged. "Well, you try to stay exactly the same," he replied. "Don't try to change anything. But of course the place in Trenton is slowly getting old, breaking down... It's a little harder than it was, but..."

"You still have the customers coming in down there?"

Gary sighed. "Not really, no," he said. "My sons are closer to business. But we kept a lot of the Pennsylvania business. It's a hike to go out there"—meaning from Pennsylvania to Robbinsville—"and they don't read the *Trentonian*," he added. "If you read the *Trentonian*, you ain't coming around."

"I guess that's right," I said. It seemed that almost every day, the headlines announced another knifing or shooting or gang-related murder on the city's streets.

"People feel threatened," Gary said, "which is why we have a cop every night."

"Oh, you do?"

"Yes," he said grimly. "Unfortunately, it's the price of doing business. But it's a big hit. People like it. They feel secure. He'll walk you to your car, he stands out, he shows the flag—you know what I mean?"

"Sure."

"And if there *are* bad guys thinking about doing something, they'll figure, 'They got a cop there,' and so they'll go somewhere else. So it works," Gary concluded. "But it's expensive," he added. "So for now, it's month to month..." He shrugged. "Who knows when we're gonna close? Eventually, probably."

"Talk to me a little bit about your crew here," I said, changing the subject. "They're all from North Trenton?"

"Yeah," Gary said. "My brother Joe, my cousins, a couple of second cousins. There's two Manny Tramontanas—so we call them Tall Manny and Little Manny."

"And they're cousins?"

"Yeah, they're first cousins; they're my second cousins," Gary explained. "So basically, that's it. The guys come in and out, you know. There's a guy named Steve Trapani; and another cousin, Carmen Vitellaro..." He spelled their names for me, so that they'd be right in the book.

"So what is it you like about this place?" I asked him.

"It's the people," Gary declared, patiently stating the obvious. "It's the relationships you form here—and keeping the relationships that I've always had. Everything else is secondary."

"So you form new relationships here, too?"

"With the people at the different tables," Gary explained. "You gotta get to know people. You know, there's a lot of kidding around. And basically, it's an hour in and an hour out"—meaning an hour inside Fred and Pete's and another hour outside on the sidewalk out front by the white chairs. "And then this table here, for some reason, is very argumentative," he added with a dry laugh. "Me and my brother are probably the only liberals—the rest of them are very right wing."

I was amazed. "You're a liberal?" Even most liberals didn't have the guts to call themselves that any more; they called themselves "progressives," or maybe "moderates."

"I'm the lone liberal, with my brother," Gary chuckled. "And the rest are probably very right wing."

"How did that happen?" I asked. "How did you wind up being a liberal? That's unusual for North Trenton."

"We were always for the underdog," Gary replied. "My father was in the labor union. I come from a union household, and I stayed with it. These guys were all in it, but I stayed with it and these guys went to the right."

"So you talk about that," I said.

"Well, yeah," Gary chuckled, "but I wind up on the other side all the time."

"So is there any point in arguing?"

"No," he said dryly. "There's no point."

I cracked up.

"Over there, they argue sports," Gary went on, gesturing toward the table under clock. "And there's another crew..." He paused. "We got names for them," he said. "That one over there, there's three or four coaches that sit there—that's Coaches' Corner. And down here," he said, nodding toward one of the booths, "that's ESPN—they've got all the experts. And then this table's The Arguers— we just argue. Ask Tom." He turned and called to Tom Armenti, who was behind the counter at that moment. "Tom, how many times you get complaints about us arguing outside?"

"All the time," Tom deadpanned, without missing a beat.

Gary chuckled. "All the time," he repeated proudly.

Curious to hear his perspective, I asked Gary what he thought about the state of the country these days.

Gary considered the question before answering. "Well," he said thought-fully, "he set out with an agenda, and he's carried it out. Health care, he did. Financial reform, he did. Ratcheted up the war in Afghanistan—he campaigned on that. So the first two years, he did what he said. It cost him in the polls—he lost the middle—and the second two years he's going to be re-elected, I think. He won't close the borders," he added. "Nobody wants to close the borders—they're afraid of the backlash. So I don't think anything's gonna be done about the borders."

"Right..."

"Of course, if he doesn't have the economy turned around by election time, well, he'll get beaten," Gary acknowledged. "But right now, I don't see any match-up. There's nobody out there that can beat him one on one. Romney's probably their best shot, but what the polls show is dissent. And so other guys that otherwise would not run are gonna say, 'What the hell, I got a shot. Anybody could beat him. Why not me? Guys like Eric Cantor, Haley Barber—different guys that you wouldn't think would be candidates, they're gonna say, 'I'll take a shot. Maybe I'll get some money and I'll run.' But two years from now, I don't know."

It was about as astute a political analysis as any I'd ever heard or read. "You follow this stuff pretty closely," I said. "Not a lot of people know who Eric Cantor is."

"Well, I'm a little bit of a political junkie," Gary chuckled. "I watch MSNBC..."

"You also read the *Post*," I said, spotting today's edition of Rupert Murdoch's conservative New York daily among the papers piled in front of him.

"I like a little trash every once in a while," he grinned.

I asked Gary what else he liked to do when he wasn't working.

"When I'm not making pizza?" he asked. "I go to Atlantic City. I like to go out, have a drink. I try to say it's not over."

"For sure it's not over!" I cried. "How old are you?"

"Sixty-seven."

"Sixty-seven? Hell, it's just starting!" I said. "I mean, you look like you're in good shape, good health..."

Gary smiled thoughtfully. "You know what Jewish people say? 'Hope for the best, expect the worst.' That's a little bit of philosophy that I live by. 'Hope for the best, expect the worst.'"

I asked him if he got that from his father.

"You mean that attitude?" he said. "No, it evolved. It just sounded good to me when I heard it."

JOHN BELLA

As soon as Gary and I wrap up and I move to the counter to get my breakfast, Little Manny joins him in the booth—almost as if he'd been waiting in the wings for me to leave—and within minutes, the rest of the crew comes in and they've added on another table to accommodate them all. So far, they don't seem to be arguing about anything—yet.

After I finish my breakfast, I take a seat in one of the white plastic chairs out front. It's already hotter than blazes and there's no breeze whatsoever, just the acrid smell of fresh asphalt wafting up from the intersection where PSE & G has been digging things up again. I'm sitting next to John Bella, who's decked out in a particularly sporty palm tree-studded tropical shirt this morning. He's probably one of the most laid-back people I've met at Fred and Pete's, and he's one of those guys who truly seems to appreciate the humor in life.

I tell him that I've just interviewed Gary and ask him whether he's willing to be interviewed, too. "Sure," he says. "Why not? When do you want to do it?" How about now, I say. "Right now?" he says, a little surprised. He shrugs. "Sure, why not?" So we go back inside and sit in the back booth, far enough away from Gary's table that hopefully he won't be totally drowned out on the tape.

"So how long have you been coming here, John?" I asked him, to start things off.

"Years," he replied. "Years and years."

"So were you coming here when Tom's dad was running the place?"

"Oh yeah," John said. "We had a good time. He used to sing—opera, that kind of thing."

"So how'd you first come here? How'd you find this place?"

"Well, I live in the area," John said, "and so I just started hanging around here."

"Did you grow up around here?"

"No," he said, "I grew up in Trenton. I was born in Trenton, grew up on Hamilton Avenue. 241 Hamilton, between Hudson and Clinton."

I asked John whether he used to go DeLorenzo's on Hudson—Gary's place—for the tomato pies.

He nodded. "On Hudson, yeah. And we'd go to Papa's, and Joe's Tomato Pies on Clinton Street. I went to St. Joachim's, played basketball every Friday night, and after the games, we used to go there."

John told me that he had one brother, seven years older, and that his father had died when he was a sophomore at Trenton Catholic. His father, who died at age 52, had owned his own gas station where they lived at 241 Hamilton, and then had gone to work at Delaval as a machinist. "That's when he passed away," John recalled gruffly. "A blood clot from an ulcer operation."

"Was your brother already gone by that time?" I asked.

"No, he was still home," John replied. "Because he was the sole supporter."

"He must've been about twenty-one years old," I said.

"Yeah."

"Jeez, that must have been a tough time for you guys," I remarked.

John nodded. "It was, but we got by." He didn't seem to want to say anything more about it.

"Tell me a little bit about your mother," I said.

John shrugged. "A housewife, you know. Worked as a young girl at the cigar factory. She passed away when she was seventy-six."

"And were both your parents Italian?"

"Oh yeah," John replied. "My father came over to this country when he was about two years old, and my mother was born in Troy, New York. My mother's parents lived on Division Street—192 Division Street. My father's parents I didn't know. They passed away before I was born."

I asked John what he did after he graduated from Trenton Catholic.

"I went to to work for the *Trenton Times* as a copy boy," he said. "I did that for about six months, but then my brother got drafted, so I got a job at General Motors. I was nineteen."

"This was over in Ewing?"

"Yeah. In the Turnsted Division. They did all the hardware," John explained. "At nineteen, I couldn't run a machine—you had to be twenty-one. So I was a trucker, moving the goods around to the different machines, and then I got into being a salvage repairman. Then when I became twenty-one, I ran a machine. I was a bender operator."

In all, John said he spent five and a half years at General Motors, supporting his mother while his brother was in the service. "And when my brother got out in 1956, then *I* got drafted. So I went in the service for two years."

"So where did you wind up going?" I asked. "Did you stay in the States?"

"No, I went out of the country—to Fort Polk, Louisiana," he chuckled.

I laughed.

"For twenty months," John added mournfully. "In fact, New Orleans was the only thing that kept me alive."

I asked him where Fort Polk was, and he said it was about two hundred and fifty miles from New Orleans. "But we used to travel that every weekend, just to get away."

"I can believe it!" I laughed.

John groaned and recalled, "The only thing around Fort Polk was Leesville and DeRidder." According to my road atlas, Leesville, Louisiana, has a population of 6,753 and DeRidder has 9,808 residents—so there was probably not a whole lot of night life in either place.

"Was this Army?" I asked him.

John nodded. "First Armored Division."

"And you got out as soon your time was up?"

"Oh man," he said, "the minute I was done... And believe me, they kept me right up to that minute—eleven o'clock, I'll never forget it."

After his discharge, John came straight back to Trenton, back to the General Motors plant in Ewing, and soon afterwards he met his future wife Shirley—a hairdresser—on the beach at Seaside Heights on the Jersey shore. "We got married on June 27, 1959," John recalled with a smile, "about a year after I got out of the service."

He stayed with General Motors another two years before he quit and, like his wife, he became a hairdresser. "We had the Capri Salon of Beauty here on Route 33," he said proudly. "For forty-two years."

"No kidding!" I cried. I'd driven past it many times. "So how did you learn to become a hairdresser?"

"I went to school," John replied. "At first, I didn't know how I was gonna like it. My mother said, 'You know, the kind of person you are, you're gonna like that.' And I thought, Well, I can always get a job at a factory if it doesn't work out. So, I went to school, eight hours a day..."

"Wow..."

Just then, Fred Wright walked by our table on his way to the men's room and made an unprintable wisecrack. John and I both burst out laughing. "Don't print that," John told me when he caught his breath. Then he said, loud enough so that Fred could hear him before he closed the men's room door, "Now where were we before we were so *rudely* interrupted?"

I reminded him.

"Oh right—eight hours a day for six months," John continued. "At the Lawrence Academy on Route One. Then I went to New York a couple of months more, maybe once a week, and then we leased a shop. There was three of us, and we got busy, so we hired another person. And then, after three years, we bought a hunk of land and we built our own shop."

"That was the one here on Route 33?" I asked.

John nodded. "The Capri Salon of Beauty."

"That's a big jump," I said. "From the assembly line in Ewing to the Capri Salon of Beauty. Did you like it?"

John shrugged. "Sure," he said. "I *had* to like it. I was in the middle of the stream—sink or swim, you know." He'd borrowed from his in-laws to buy the land and had taken out a full mortgage from the First National Bank to build and equip the shop. "My wife and I got along good working together, we had a beautiful shop—and we had beautiful customers," he added.

"So when you started, were you doing bee-hives, that kind of thing?" I asked.

"Oh yeah," John chuckled softly. "Bee-hives, French Twists, you name it..." He shook his head. "And so here I am," he concluded with a rueful smile, glancing around at all his fellow customers. The volume at Gary's table had definitely picked up since we'd started talking, and you could smell the pork roll sizzling on the grill.

"Sounds like you did all right," I said.

John shrugged. "Eh, pretty good, you know. The stock market didn't do us any good, though."

"Didn't do any of us any good," I murmured.

"But here I am," John said again. "We've got two sons—beautiful sons. One just turned fifty last Thursday."

"No kidding!" I exclaimed. "So how old *are* you?"

"I'll be seventy-eight."

I wouldn't have guessed it. I asked John what else he did with his time these days when he wasn't at Fred and Pete's, and he said that he'd worked part-time at Trent Box over on Yardville-Hamilton Square Road for about six years after he'd retired. "Then I got laid off for maybe a year when business dropped off from the recession," he said. "Now I work there maybe one day a week, maybe two..."

"So you're still working?"

"Yeah," he said. "Like I worked last week for one day. I'm a spare tire, you know."

Better that than a flat, I thought to myself. "So what else do you like to do in your spare time?" I asked him.

"Hunt," he replied.

"Is that right?" I said, a little surprised. "Where do you hunt?"

"Down in the Jersey Pines," he replied. "Deer hunting. I belong to the North Trenton Sportsmen Club. It's a good club. I've belonged to that since 1958—since I got out of the service."

"Are you a good shot?"

"Nah," John chuckled, shaking his head. "I don't practice. I just go out there, and if I hit 'em, I hit 'em. Most likely I miss. But when I go, I enjoy it."

Like Gary and a lot of the other people I'd interviewed, I asked John his thoughts on the state of the world.

"Ah," he said, "it's moving too fast. And there's too much vulgarity—on TV, in the newspapers..."

"Not to mention in the white chairs out front," I interjected.

"Oh yeah." John shook his head. "I holler at 'em," he growled. "Freddy calls me Father John. But you know, there's *women* that walk by there. They don't want to hear that garbage."

I asked John how his sons were doing. He said that his younger was doing all right, but his older son had been laid off when the company he'd worked for, which made glass shower stalls and other upscale bathroom products, had been closed and relocated to Canada. "He was the boss," John added.

"Boy, that's not easy," I said. "Not when you're in your fifties."

It turned out that John's one grandchild—a seven-year-old girl named Anna Maria—was his older son's daughter, and John told me that she was already one heck of an ice-skater. He was clearly very proud of her. "Friday she's skating in Delaware," he said. "And in August she'll be in Atlantic City. At seven years old."

"So are you going to go see her in Atlantic City?"

John beamed. "Oh yeah!"

We were ready to finish up. "Well, John, thank you," I said, reaching across the table to shake his hand. "That didn't hurt too much, did it? Not too painful?" He'd been a little hesitant about being interviewed when I'd first asked him.

"Nah," he said. "Just use a fictitious name."

I laughed. "That's B-E-L-L-A, right?"

"Yeah, Bella," he chuckled. "Like beautiful, you know? How could you forget that?"

BEST ALL-AROUND PLAYER IN
THE HISTORY OF THE GAME

Thursday, July 29, 2010. I conducted a little poll today at Fred and Pete's in connection with my work, and asked Tom Armenti and nineteen of his customers who, in their opinion, was the single best all-around baseball player in the history of the game. Willie Mays got five votes; Joe DiMaggio, Babe Ruth and Ted Williams each got three votes; Lou Gehrig got two votes, and Derek Jeter, Mickey Mantle, Stan Musial and Jackie Robinson each got one vote.

In other words, there was no consensus—which was the point I wanted to make with my survey (Willie Mays may have gotten the most votes in part because he once played for the Trenton Giants, and several of the guys had actually seen him play in Trenton). But most of the guys had fun with it. Some answered right off the bat (so to speak), while others took it very seriously and really thought it through before giving me their answer.

Dave Stout, for instance, really went back and forth before finally picking Jeter because of all that he had done for the image of the game. And Guy Norton, after running through all kinds of statistics, finally picked Jackie Robinson for playing as well as he did despite all those people booing him and throwing things at him when he was out on the field. "Real grace under pressure," he said. There was some block voting— for instance, all three votes for the Babe came from Gary's booth.

Later, when I went up to the counter to pay for my breakfast and I mentioned to one of the guys from Gary's booth that Tom Armenti had picked Ted Williams, he said to Tom (who was working the register) that all Ted Williams ever did was spit. "Yeah, I know," Tom replied over his shoulder. "I gave him extra points for that."

STEPHANIE

Friday, July 30, 2010. Stephanie Caldwell, whose honey-brown hair is pulled back in a ponytail and who's wearing a maroon Fred and Pete's t-shirt, blue running shorts and sneakers, is a middle-school teacher. During the school year, she just works at Fred and Pete's on weekends, but during the summer she's also here on weekdays. Anne has mentioned to me that Stephanie would like to be interviewed for the book, so today I ask Stephanie whether she'd have a few minutes to talk to me. "Sure," she says with a big smile, and she asks Anne to cover for her for a few minutes while we talk in one of the booths.

"So you've been working here how long, Steph?" I began.

"Twelve years," Stephanie replied.

"You remember your first day?"

"I remember feeling awkward my first day," she recalled, "because I didn't think I was ever going to be able to get it."

I asked her how she got the job in the first place.

"Joe Nalbone," she said without hesitation. "Joe Nalbone is a customer here and his daughter and I are best friends. He was basically like my step-father. And he's been coming in since the place opened. I was looking for a job—I was eighteen at the time, I had to pay for my car—so he said, 'Why don't you come over to Fred and Pete's, and I'll get you a job there?'"

"Had you been here before?"

Stephanie shook her head. "I'd never been here before. Never even knew the place existed. But he got me the job here, and I remember working night-times when I first started—this was when we used to be open til eight o'clock at night. We had two girls at night serving dinners, we had pizza on Fridays, and it was super, super busy. And so I remember being really overwhelmed, and I'd say that for the first two weeks I was thinking, I'm never gonna be able to get this right. And now here I am, twelve years later..." She smiled broadly.

"Now everything's under control?"

Stephanie laughed. "Yeah, right... I remember that back then, Saturdays were a lot different than they are now, because we used to have four girls, we were open until five o'clock, and being like the new girl, you had to come in at the later hours so you'd leave at the later hours, and you got less tables. Progressively, I think we've gotten slower, so now we're down to three girls."

"So what's the best part of the job?" I asked her, already pretty sure—knowing Stephanie—that I knew the answer.

"The customers," she said, confirming my hunch. "I feel like I can really be myself, and if someone as a customer angers me, I know that I don't have to worry that I'll get in trouble if I let them know they're doing something wrong."

"For instance?"

"Well, like there's this customer who comes in all the time," she replied, "and he's fun, you know. But if he says, 'Where's my coffee?' I can say, 'You didn't even sit down yet. Will ya sit down and hold on a second?' Instead of"—in a sing-song voice—"'Oh, I'll be right with you, sir.'" She laughed. "He does it all the time," she said fondly. "He comes in and shouts out his order before he even sits down. And of course I know what he's gonna get every day, too, so it's not like it's any different. I mean, I could have it ready for him by the time he gets here."

"So, Stephanie," I said, changing the subject, "you teach sixth grade, right?"

"Right," she said brightly.

"So how good was the training that you got here for teaching sixth graders?"

I expected her to laugh, but she took my question seriously. "Really, I think it's just people skills," she reflected. "And the same thing goes for teaching as for being a waitress: you either have it or you don't. There's some people that could be very intelligent and could be the nicest person in the world, but they don't have that skill that you have to have—especially with a place like this, where's it's a fast turnover and you have to be quick. So it's more common sense than anything else. I mean, we've had people that went to some really good universities that worked here, and they just couldn't do it. You have to have something in you to be a waitress in a place like this."

"And that's transferable to working with sixth graders?" I asked.

"Not necessarily just sixth graders," Stephanie replied. "I think it's just being up in front of a group of people and being able to command that, and being able to socialize and talk to them in a way where you feel comfortable— that's what you need."

"And you feel that way with your class?"

"Absolutely."

So if the customers were the best part of the job, what part, I asked Stephanie, was the worst?

She had to think about that one. "Hmm... I guess one bad thing would be working really, really hard on a table—and then not getting a tip."

"Has that ever happened?"

"Absolutely," Stephanie replied. "Let's say if I'm working a five-day week, maybe one time during that week I'll get stiffed. So it doesn't happen a lot, but it does happen. And usually it happens when it's a big table—like when you bust your butt on a table with seven people and get a dollar. That really hurts your spirits."

"I can imagine," I said. "I wonder if that's deliberate, or..."

"A lot of times, I think people don't get it," Stephanie said. "Especially when people have children, they feel that it's just a little person that's not eating as much, so they don't have to tip as much. But in my opinion, when you have kids..."

"It's a mess," I laughed, thinking of our two-year-old grandson Liam who loved to come to Fred and Pete's for the pancakes and French toast, and loved to play "Gimme Five" with Rich Erkoboni.

"Right," she said.

I asked Stephanie whether she ever ate here herself.

"All the time," she said enthusiastically. "That's one of the great things about Tommy. He doesn't have any problem with us eating his food and not having to pay for it."

"What's your favorite thing on the menu?"

"The Reuben," she replied instantly. "I don't eat it very often because it's so fattening, but the Reuben is definitely, hands-down, the best thing on the menu. With sour kraut and Swiss cheese, and I make my own Russian dressing out of the ketchup, mayo and pickles here. And the BLT is really, really good, too," she added.

"Everything's good," Midge called from behind the counter.

"Everything here *is* good," Stephanie agreed.

"As long as it doesn't have any animals in it, right, Midge?" I called. Midge had once told me that she was a vegetarian, and it had become a standing topic of conversation between the two of us.

"No animals!" Midge called back.

Stephanie laughed. "Midge is crazy," she said, shaking her head. "I love working with her. She always makes me laugh."

"So did you grow up here in Hamilton?" I asked.

"Yes!" Stephanie said proudly. "I was born here and lived in the same house my entire life, right over on Klockner Road. I just moved out last year, and now I'm looking to buy my first house."

"No kidding! Here in the Township?"

"No," she said, "I'm moving to Browns Mills. Because my fiance and his family, they all live there, so we're down there all the time anyway."

"How far is that?" I asked.

"Thirty-five minutes," Stephanie replied. "It's gonna be a drive going to school, but I don't mind it. It's the country, and I love it, so..."

"It's funny," I said. "Midge lives out in the country, and Anne's talking about moving down to Burlington..."

"Cheese omelet, Anne!" Stephanie suddenly called over my shoulder. "Sorry," she apologized, turning back to me.

"No, that's OK," I said. "We're winding up anyhow. Is there anything else you want to tell me about Fred and Pete's—or about yourself?"

"About Fred and Pete's?" she said, pausing to think. "As long as this place is here, I'll be here," she declared. "Of course I'm here a little bit for the money, but this keeps me grounded. I work five days a week with little kids, but I come here and I go from adolescents to geriatrics."

"And what's the difference?"

"I have to be a lot more professional," Stephanie answered.

"With the kids or with these guys?" I asked.

"With the kids," she laughed. "With the kids. Here I can be myself. That's why I think I'll be here until he closes the place—just because it makes me feel good to be here." Her eyes shone as she started to get up to go back to work. She shook my hand. "I really love this job!" she said. "And you can put that in the book."

WITHOUT HIS BOSTON RED SOX CAP

Tuesday, August 3, 2010. When I was in for breakfast this morning, sitting at the counter with Dave Stout, Anne gave us some very sad news. Bob Lee had passed away on Sunday, just two days ago. It wasn't a complete surprise, of course, given what Bob himself had told me when I first met him here at Fred and Pete's almost two years ago when I was first starting to work on the book. He told me then that he'd been diagnosed with idiopathic pulmonary fibrosis five years earlier and that ninety-five percent of the people who had it died within two to five years after diagnosis. By hanging in there for seven years, he'd beaten the odds big time, and he knew it. Still, it's a terrible loss, and I felt a kind of ache in my gut on hearing the news.

Anne was showing us the obit in this morning's Trentonian when Bob's close buddy Jim Fennelli walked in. The two of them—Bobby and Jimmy—always sat together, either at the counter or in a booth, and you rarely saw one without the other at Fred and Pete's. But this morning, Jim looked stricken, holding his glasses with one hand and wiping his eyes with the other. He'd just heard, he said, on his way in. Maybe somebody in one of the white chairs told him, I don't know. He sat down heavily beside Dave, and Anne handed him the Trentonian. He read the entire obit—it was a long one—without a word. Then he turned to Dave and said, "You know his brother Lucky? Says here his name is Larris—Larris "Lucky" Lee." Dave nodded. It was hard for any of us to say anything.

After breakfast, I picked up a copy of the Trentonian and read the obit myself. It said, "Robert L. 'Bobby' Lee, 74, of Hamilton Township, died Sunday at Robert Wood Johnson Hospital in Hamilton. Born in Trenton, he was a lifelong Hamilton Township resident. Bob was a painting contractor in central New Jersey for more than 50 years and was proprietor of R.L. Lee Co. He was a member of St. Raphael's Church and was formerly active in Painters Local No. 10, local politics, Hamilton Stamp Club, American Philatelic Society, White Horse Fire Co., Hamilton Elks, Musicians Local No. 62, Boy Scout Troop No. 37, an original Babe Ruth Baseball member, and the New Jersey National Guard

696th 50th Armored Division. His main interests were family, business, the stock market and harness racing"—and, I would have added, hanging out with Jimmy at Fred and Pete's.

There was a nice picture of Bob at the top of the obit, wearing a checked shirt and a big smile, but there was something strange about it that I couldn't put my finger on. I kept looking at it and looking at it, then suddenly I realized what it was: it was the first time in the two years that I'd known him that I'd ever seen Bob Lee without his Boston Red Sox cap.

MEGHAN

Monday, August 30, 2010. It's 5:30 in the afternoon, and Tommy Pyle and a couple of other guys are sitting out front, despite the ninety-plus degree heat. Fortunately, with the ceiling fans on high, it's a lot cooler inside. Cash is behind the counter, starting to clean up, and Meghan's taking today's menu down from the wall. Israel looks like he's just finished cleaning the grill, and John Wilwol, wearing a surprisingly new-looking Spirit of '76 t-shirt, is pushing a broom between the tables, patiently sweeping the day's harvest of used straws, napkins, and scratch-offs into a battered dustpan. I ask Meghan if this is still a good time for me to interview her, and she says sure, so I decide to press my luck and ask Cash whether he could do his interview now, too. To my astonishment and great relief, he says yes. Partly because of their hours and also because of their busy schedules, Meghan and Cash have been two of the most difficult interviews to schedule, and now it looks like I'm going to get a two-fer!

In spite of the heat, Meghan, whose last name is Norton and who has her brunette hair up in a clip, is dressed like a petite female version of Johnny Cash, wearing a black Fred and Pete's t-shirt and black pants; while Cash, whose real name is Volodymyr and who keeps his hair cropped very short, has on an olive-colored Steinert t-shirt, brown pants, and a stained white butcher's apron that he puts on whenever he's working the deli counter. The digital sign on the wall over the lottery machine says that the Pick Six is now at $7.5 million, the Mega-Millions is at $12 million, the Jersey Cash Five is at $130,000. It occurs to me that twelve million dollars would come in pretty handy right about now, but I'd settle for seven and a half—or even, in a pinch, for the $130,000. You could buy a lot of Swiss omelets for that kind of money.

After the last few customers straggle out the door and Meghan finishes adding up her tips for the afternoon (which comes out to considerably less than $130,000), she joins me in one of the booths and I switch on the tape recorder.

"All right, Meghan," I began, "so how long have you been working here?"

"Six years," she promptly replied. "Since I was fifteen. Now I'm twenty-one. I turned twenty-one in December."

"Congratulations!" I said. "Feels good to be a grown-up, doesn't it?"

"It's OK," Meghan said with a shrug, "except now I've gotta pay for everything."

I laughed, and asked her whether she had any brothers or sisters. She told me that she had a twenty-three-year-old brother and a seventeen-year-old sister. "She used to work here, but she quit," she added.

"And what about your parents?" I asked.

"Well," she said, "you know my dad comes in here every morning. He used to work for ETS"—the Educational Testing Service—"but now he's on disability, because he got hurt on the job. And my mom teaches fourth grade at Robinson Elementary."

"And you want to be a teacher, too, right?"

Meghan smiled. "Uh-huh."

"What do you want to teach?" I asked her.

"Kindergarten—or pre-school," she replied brightly. "I love little kids!"

"How come?"

Meghan shrugged. "They just love me," she said. "They love their teacher when they're little like that. I don't want older kids, because they're mean. At school, some people were mean to their teachers, and I'm not a mean person, so I don't think I could do it."

"Well, this is probably good training for kindergarten, isn't it?"

"That's true," she chuckled. "There are some people here that are like little kids."

But she said she liked working here, and when I asked her why, she had the same answer as everyone else. "I like the people," she said. "Everyone's always nice to me. I've never had any trouble with anyone. I mean, some people are crazy, but that's just..." She thought for a moment. "That's just Fred and Pete's," she said. "I like Tommy, he's always nice to me. And all the other waitresses are so nice to me—I just love it. And plus the money's good," she added.

"And what about Johnny Woo?" I asked her.

Meghan broke into a big smile. "Oh, he's my favorite!" she beamed. "He's like my second dad, I guess. He's just... I don't know, I've grown attached to him. When he got hurt, I went to visit him. He walks me out to my car, he always gives me presents on every holiday—a present for me, and I give him something. He's like a part of my family... I love him, you know."

I nodded.

"I have a lot of friends here," Meghan went on. "Like Tommy Suits—he's best friends with my dad. They're all the time on the phone—sports, sports, sports... Anyhow, he's really nice, too."

I asked Meghan whether she was into sports herself.

"No," she said, shaking her head.

"You don't like baseball?" I said in amazement. "I mean, it seems like your dad talks about baseball all the time."

"And football," Meghan noted. "If it's not baseball, it's football. Eagles and Phillies, all the time. It's fun, though," she said fondly.

"And what's your mom like?" I asked. "I've never met her."

Meghan smiled. "Oh, my mom's nice. She used to work at American Cyanamid up by the mall on Quakerbridge Road before that got closed down, but they paid for her to go to school to get her teaching degree. She said that's what she had always wanted, and that's what made me want to become a teacher, because I used to go in and help her in the classroom with the kids, and I really, really liked it. So that's why I want to be a teacher." She paused to take a breath. The words were pouring out so fast that I had a hard time keeping up.

"So how much longer til you get your degree?" I asked.

"I have one year left," she replied. "I'll be a senior this year."

"At Rider?"

"William Patterson," Meghan said. "I'm getting my preschool through fifth grade certification. And it's really nice because Rider was expensive or I would have went there. But William Patterson has a program through Mercer County, so I got my associate's degree through Mercer County, and the professors from William Patterson come down here. Because that's two hours away, you know. So we have classes online and we have classes on the weekends. Which I don't really mind. I have class every Saturday from 1:00 to 3:30, but I don't care."

"So how much are you working here?"

"Four days a week," Meghan replied. "I work the 2:00 to 6:00 shift during the week, and during the weekend 8:00 to 2:00."

"And I guess you like this shift," I remarked.

"Um-hm," she said. "It's the same people every day. Even on the weekends— it's the same people, and they get the same thing every day. I sometimes wonder why they don't ever order anything else, but then when I go to my favorite restaurant, I always get the same thing, too."

When I asked Meghan how she felt about the state of the world these days, she said that for her it boiled down to just one thing: jobs. Specifically, would she be able to find a teaching job when she graduated from college next year?

"Teachers are losing their jobs," she said gloomily. "Some of my mom's friends lost their jobs, stuff like that—which makes me think it may be hard for me to find a job. I mean, I love working here, and I'd probably keep working here weekends, but I don't want to be a waitress forever. I want to move out— and I want a new car—so that's why I really want to find a job."

"You have your own car now?"

Meghan nodded. "A Honda Civic. But it's a '97."

"So it's got some miles on it."

"Uh-huh," she said. "And it needs an oil change. It's overdue... But so I'm really scared I'm not going to find a job. That's what I'm most worried about. I'm scared for my mom to lose her job," she added, biting her lip. "And Stephanie, too, because she teaches. I'm thinking, Oh my God, I hope she doesn't lose her job... So that's my biggest worry..." She sighed. "I mean, nobody can find jobs. Like my brother's friends, they all graduated from college but they can't find jobs—and they all have business degrees."

I didn't want to end our conversation on a downer, so I asked Meghan whether there was anything else she wanted to tell me about Fred and Pete's.

She thought about it for a minute and then she smiled. "One of the things we do is we have birthday parties here," she said. "Like John, his birthday's on Valentines Day, so we have a Valentines Day party for him."

"Oh, that's great!"

"It usually always falls on the weekend, which is fun, too," Meghan went on. "I love buying him presents; we decorate his table... I'll always remember stuff like that. It's one of my favorite things to do."

I asked her whether she celebrated her birthday here.

"My birthday?" she said. "Oh yeah, people give me food and flowers and everything—it's really nice. I know that sometimes I say that I hate my work and my job, but the truth is I really do love it. I left here once and got a job at a daycare, because I thought that'd be good experience, but then I came back. I said, 'I wanna come back here.' I mean, I missed everyone. They're like my family, you know. I have a whole big family here, so..."

I nodded. "I know..."

Meghan choked up a little. "I don't want to leave. Like I already miss Theresa. She's only working here one day a week now, and I miss her already."

"She's only working one day a week? I said, surprised. "How come?"

"She only works Tuesdays now," Meghan explained, "because she's working at Victoria's Secret for school—it's like an internship to get more experience as a buyer. So she doesn't work on Sunday with me, and I already miss her. And she misses everyone, too. We all miss each other when we're gone. Like when I was just on vacation, I was bored. I was like, 'I can't wait to get back to work and hear all the gossip.'"

I laughed.

"Everyone knows everything about everyone," Meghan said. "I'll come in and they'll say, 'Oh, I heard you went out last night,' and I'm like, 'How the heck do you even know?' And they'll say, 'Oh, your father told us.' And I'm thinking, 'OK, I'm not telling my dad anything...'" She chuckled. "But I love it. I wouldn't work anywhere else."

"Well, that's a great note to end on," I said, reaching for the tape recorder. "Unless there's anything else you want to add..."

"No," she said. "Just that I love Fred and Pete's—make sure you put that in there. And I love everyone, especially John. He's my favorite, Johnny Woo. Be sure you put that in there in capital letters. TELL HIM I LOVE HIM FOREVER AND EVER!"

"You got it," I smiled. "Thanks, Meghan."

CASH

A few minutes later, John's walking Meghan out to her car, and Cash is cleaning up some last-minute stuff behind the counter. Then he locks up—just like Tom Armenti did when I interviewed him almost two years ago—and he takes a seat across from me in the front booth. He's a big guy, with an open, friendly face, and he seems totally relaxed, in spite of the tape recorder. And just like when I interviewed Tom, we're the only ones in the place now, and it's strangely quiet for Fred and Pete's, except for the whirring of the fans overhead and the occasional clunk of the ice machine.

"Thanks a lot for staying on after work to do this," I began, and he nodded with a slight smile. "So I know that your real name is Volodymyr," I said. "How did you get the name Cash?"

"My last name is Kush," he explained. "But when I got the job here, people didn't know what to call me. My buddy Ostap, who was also Ukrainian, he said, 'You know, we'll make it easy for people. Instead of Kush, we'll call you Cash. It's easy for people to remember and easy to pronounce.'"

And not a bad name if you're the guy working the lottery machine, I thought. I asked Cash when he had first come to this country.

He thought for a moment. "I believe it was 1999," he said. "I was seventeen back then—give or take ten years."

I laughed. "So where did you first live when you came to the States?"

"I came to Hamilton."

"Really?" I was surprised. "Directly to Hamilton?"

Cash nodded. "And since then I stayed in Hamilton."

"No kidding! Well now, first of all, why did you leave the Ukraine, and secondly, how did you wind up in Hamilton?"

"My parents always wanted to go to some better place to make better living, so the USA was their number one pick," Cash explained. "We didn't really know if we was going to come to the United States because there was a game, which is the green card game. It's a lottery game. What you do is you fill out an application, you send it out to Kiev—which is the capital of Ukraine—and they have a random selection. They just pick any random applications and that's how we won."

"Even better than *that* lottery," I said, pointing at the machine.

"Better than the Pick Six lottery, I would imagine," Cash agreed. "Although for that kind of money, you can live in Ukraine, too," he added with a laugh.

I asked him what his parents had done back in the Ukraine before moving here, and he said his father was a driving instructor at the local college, and his mother had been a teacher—same as Meghan's mom.

"Do you have any brothers or sisters?" I asked.

"I have one sister," Cash replied. "An older sister. We all came over together."

"And you were seventeen. So did you go to high school?"

He nodded. "I went to Nottingham for two years. I barely made it, because I didn't speak much English and I really didn't have such good grades for that reason."

"But you managed it."

"I managed it, yeah," Cash said. "And then I went to Mercer County. And I finished Mercer County as a law enforcement major."

"No kidding! I didn't know that," I said. "So how did you wind up here at Fred and Pete's?"

"Well, at that point I was looking for a job," he recalled. "Like any teenager, you go jumping from one place to another, so I worked five, six different jobs. But one of my buddies, who was a Ukrainian like I said before, he was leaving for Ukraine for a month or two, and Tommy needed some help here. So Ostap says, 'Do you want to try it?' And I said, 'I don't know. I'm not sure if I can do it or not.' Because he said you gotta answer phones, you gotta talk to people, you gotta do catering jobs—and since I didn't speak much English, I was kind of afraid."

"When was this?" I asked.

"I guess about three years after I came over. So I'd been here for a while."

I nodded. "I remember Ostap," I told him. "He used to work the grill, and he made the best western omelets."

"Well, you didn't try mine yet!" Cash laughed. "Anyhow, that's how I ended up here. I thought I would just keep it for a month or two until he came back. But when he came back, I just stayed here—although I don't do it full time any more."

"Oh, I know," I said. "You're working at Steinert now, right?"

"Hamilton West," he corrected me. "I did work at Steinert doing field maintenance for a while but now I'm at Hamilton West as a custodian. I work second shift, Tuesday through Saturday. That's why I'm only here Mondays now."

"How's that working out?"

"It's hard to tell," Cash replied. "This is my third week only, and I never in my life worked second shift before."

"Do you think you'll ever go back to law enforcement?"

He nodded. "That definitely is my goal."

I asked Cash what he did here now.

"Here at Fred and Pete's? Everything that needs to be done in the deli," he replied. "From taking catering jobs, to orders to go, making sandwiches. And the lottery machine's a big deal, you know—the biggest probably in the state."

"Is that right?" I had no idea.

"Yeah, one of the biggest," Cash said. "We had the most Pick Six winners here—between us and I believe there's a place on Route 130, another deli there. Same people come in all the time, you know. Oh, and I do cookouts," he added. "A lot of cookouts. Me and Tommy and whoever he needs, we'll go and cook for anywhere from fifty to two hundred people. So it's a big thing. And in the summer, we get really, really busy. Holidays, too. And salads are big here. Half of the crew's in the back of the kitchen peeling potatoes."

I asked Cash whether there were any places like this back in the Ukraine.

He shook his head. "No, not quite the same, not really. People don't really hang around there. Here, you see people that have been coming round twenty, thirty years. In Ukraine, you don't see that. They do have delis, but you don't see the exact same people going to the same place two, three times a day. It's not a very common thing."

"So have you gotten to know any of the customers here?"

"Absolutely!" Cash exclaimed. "Every time I go someplace outside work, I always see people that I meet at Fred and Pete's. It's unbelievable. I'll be walking along at the mall, and I go, 'I know this guy, I know this guy...' Or if I go to the Italian-American Festival, I know half the people there. It's unbelievable. You go to school—you know, Mercer County—and you always see people that go to Fred and Pete's. It's like you can't get enough of them. You see them at Fred and Pete's—and then you see them everywhere else!"

I laughed and told him, "You know, I interviewed somebody for this book who's a big fan of yours—ninety years old."

Cash gave me a quizzical look. "Ninety years old?"

"She just turned ninety," I said. "Her name is Heidi Krall. She's Dave Stout's mother-in-law."

"Oh, OK," he said, a big smile lighting up his face. "She's a nice lady—sure!"

"She thinks you're wonderful."

"Is that right?" Cash said, obviously pleased. "I always liked her, too. She would always put on a nice smile when she'd see me, and I would just smile back at her, you know. She's cute!"

I asked him whether he knew that she had once been a famous opera star at the Metropolitan Opera in New York.

"I heard something like that," he said, "but I didn't really know her name, to be honest with you. But when you told me she was Dave Stout's mother-in-law, I knew who you meant. She comes in once in a while, but not too often any more."

"Well, she thinks you're wonderful," I said.

Cash blushed and looked a little bashful. "It's good to hear when people talk good about you," he murmured.

I asked Cash what he liked about working at Fred and Pete's.

He looked thoughtful. "Getting to know the same people," he said. "Even though there's no younger generation that comes in here regularly and it's mainly people that are senior citizens, I like all the different kinds of personalities here. Everybody's different here. Nobody's the same. And we have fun here," he added. "It's work, but you don't hate when you come in here. You know everything about everybody here, you know what's going on—it's almost like a family here."

"And what about this country?" I asked him. "You've been here more than ten years now. How do you feel about being here in the United States?"

"Let's put it this way," he replied. "I definitely got accepted here. My first and second year, I didn't like it that much. I don't think anybody does, being that you're in a new country and you've left everything behind you. You know, the language, the traditions, the holidays—you're talking about two completely different countries. So it was hard at first, getting to know other people. And back then, let's put it this way, there wasn't as many Ukrainians my age as there is now, and so I didn't really like it at first. But back then I was young, and I didn't really think too much about what life was going to be like in the future for me."

I nodded.

"But then maybe six, seven years ago, I changed my mind into I definitely want to be here for good," Cash declared. "I mean, if I had to go back to Ukraine..." He shook his head. "I don't even go back that often. I've been back twice in all that time, and I really don't even want to go back. I mean, the last two visits, that's about it."

I asked him what it was in particular that he liked about this country.

"Let's put it this way: one thing I *don't* like is the weather," he grinned. "Humidity is a big thing, and I'm not used to humidity. I can take hot weather, but not humidity. Every time we get a lot of humidity, I'm like, 'Oh, I wish I was back home now.' But in particular, what do I *like*?" He paused and scratched his chin. "I think if you live in New Jersey it's very convenient, because in the wintertime you can go skiing—and I do a lot of skiing. In the summertime, there is the beach—you can go down to the shore and Atlantic City, New York City... I mean, everything's around, so I definitely do like it, if you talk about Jersey itself."

"You also got into body-building, right?" I said, remembering what Tom Armenti had told me.

"Yeah," Cash replied with a shrug, "although I was a little heavier before than I am now that I'm married. It doesn't necessarily mean that I don't go lift anymore—I'm still into lifting—but I guess I had a little more free time on my hands back then. I entered a few competitions, just for fun. I didn't really feel like making anything out of it, or getting really, really heavy into it—even though I *was* a little heavy into it, but nothing to where you would make it a career..."

"You mean you weren't planning to run for governor of California?"

Cash laughed. "Exactly," he said. "It was for fun. I figured, 'I'm young,' and I wasn't married back then. But I'm still into it, doing my thing. Not as much dieting as I used to do, though, because I was like a health freak back then. I would stay clean, not for months, but for years and years. Like to eat pizza would be *unbelievable*."

"Oh really?" Hard to imagine not eating pizza in New Jersey.

He nodded. "I remember I would sit down with people and they would be saying, 'Oh, I like Domino's, I like Pizza Hut,' and I'm thinking to myself, I would just like *any* pizza—I could care less."

I laughed.

"I mean, I'm shaking my head to myself," Cash went on. "I cannot believe these people are actually arguing about which place has better pizza. For me, *any* dough with cheese will be perfect!"

"So what about the state of the world?" I asked him. "You know, the big picture."

Cash sighed. "Big picture? Well, first of all, I'm definitely not looking into 2012," he declared. "Let's put it this way: I don't know if it's gonna happen or not, but that's the least of my concerns. If it's gonna happen, it's gonna happen to all of us." I assumed that he must be referring to the apocalyptic predictions that the world was going to come to an end on December 21, 2012—12/12/12—I vaguely remembered having seen promos for the movie.

"Other than that," Cash continued, "there's still wars going on out there. You can't stop it, and I don't think you can prevent it. I mean, ever since humanity, there's always been wars, so that's definitely not a good thing. But does it worry me? Absolutely, because the United States gets involved in any war. It doesn't necessarily have to be an enemy, but it seems like they have to be there. That's probably one of the biggest concerns for me. Granted, if there's a need for help, the United States will be one of the first countries to help others, and that's a good thing. But if there's a war going on, they're also going to be there."

"What about the Ukraine?" I asked. "Do you worry at all about the future of the Ukraine?"

Cash looked thoughtful. "I should say yes," he said slowly. "Probably not as much as I used to, but I still have a lot of family left there. My cousins... And my grandmother, she's still alive..."

I asked him where in the Ukraine he had come from.

"It's a little town, pretty much the same size as Hamilton," Cash replied. "It's called Striy, although if you Google it, you'll see many different spellings. It's in the western part of the country, and it's pretty much like Hamilton. But sure, I worry about them. I mean, you can't bring your whole family here, but I would rather have them to have like we have here."

"Is there a Ukrainian community here in Hamilton?" I asked.

"There's a *big* Ukrainian community here," Cash declared proudly.

"Here in Hamilton?" I had no idea.

"Sure!" he cried. "You have three Ukrainian churches here. One's on Deutz Avenue, one's on Adeline, and there's another one in Yardville. It's a big community, plus there's the Ukrainian-American Cultural Center on Jeremiah, off of Lalor. As a matter of fact, yesterday was a picnic—we were celebrating the independence of Ukraine, which was in 1991. I want to say we had two hundred people, maybe. Mainly Ukrainians. I'd say 99 percent. Pretty awesome!"

IF IT AIN'T TOO LATE

Tuesday, September 21, 2010. I've just finished breakfast, sitting between Jim Fennelli and Leroy Stout, when Little Manny Tramontana comes bustling up to me and asks me if I'm still working on that book about Fred and Pete's. I tell him that I've finished the interviews and that I'm just writing them up, and he says, "I got one more guy you gotta meet."

He grabs my arm and pulls me along with him to the other end of the counter, where he introduces me to a grey-haired guy with a mustache and a blue windbreaker by the name of Henry Poreda. "He lives in Vegas now," Manny tells me. "Runs a saloon out there. But he used to own Brothers Saloon down the street—you know, where Charlie Brown is now. It was a great place. And every time he comes back here to Hamilton, he comes here to Fred and Pete's—ain't that right?"

Henry nods and smiles and hands me a card with his name on it that says: "Sonny's Saloon and Casino: Home of the World Famous Diamond Chinese Restaurant." On the flipside is a picture of Frank Sinatra, Sammy Davis Junior and Dean Martin.

"So you gotta put him in the book," Manny says, "if it ain't too late."

It isn't.

GIMME FIVE

Another thing I want to put in the book: one of Fred and Pete's younger patrons is our two-year-old grandson Liam, who lives in Brooklyn. He loves Fred and Pete's.

Every time he comes for a visit and we drive past it on our way to the playground at Veteran's Park, he calls out, "Fred and Pete's! Fred and Pete's!" from his car seat in the back, and sometimes he'll add, "Richie! Go Fred and Pete's, see Richie!" That's Rich Erkoboni, who made a big impression on Liam by stealing his nose and playing Gimme Five with him but always pulling his hand away whenever Liam tries to slap it.

Liam also asks for Tony (Golowski), who always comes up and says hello whenever he sees him in his high chair, and Kay, the waitress who usually brings him his pancakes or French toast (his two favorite items on the menu).

Along with the pancakes and French toast, Liam likes to lean way back in his high chair and point to the ceiling fans slowly whirling overhead. "Fan! Fan!" he'll tell me— until he sees Rich walk in. Then it's "Richie! Play Gimme Five! Richie!" And Rich, bless his heart, is always happy to oblige.

BOBBY MARCHETTI

Thursday, September 2, 2010. Dressed in grey work clothes with "Hamilton Township School System" emblazoned in red letters above his shirt pocket, with a full head of neatly combed grey hair, Bobby Marchetti is definitely one of the regulars, although he usually comes in during the early shift. I've actually interviewed him once before, the morning that I came in at 5 a.m. and interviewed Joe Gresko, but the battery on my recorder ran out that morning and most of Bobby's interview was inaudible. So today, seeing as Bobby's here at a slightly more civilized hour—about 6:30 a.m.—I'm trying again, even though he's only got a few minutes before he has to take off for work. We're in one of the booths and he's finishing up his breakfast as we talk.

"So Bobby, what do you think of this place?" I asked him, kicking off the interview.

"This place here," he replied with a straight face, his voice surprisingly deep, "we've got some of the most intelligent people here you could ever meet. Their IQ is about a quarter of an inch."

"Is that why you keep coming back?"

Bobby nodded gravely. "That is why I keep coming back. And I was voted the valedictorian of Fred and Pete's at one time," he added.

"Is that right?" I laughed. "So what happened? Did you get a free cup of coffee for that?"

"I get comp sometimes," he replied. "Like in Atlantic City, they comp you. Tommy comps me for the correct answers on things."

I asked Bobby what he usually had for breakfast, and he told me the same thing as today: an egg and cheese omelet.

"What kind of cheese?" I asked.

"American," Bobby replied. "White American—I don't like the orange."

"And how long have you been coming here?"

"Let's see... About thirty-five years," Bobby said.

"Since you were five years old?"

"Ah," he groaned, "I'm sixty-seven."

"Are you really?"

"Yeah."

"You don't look it," I said, and that was the truth. He looked more like fifty.

"I don't?"

"Nah."

"That's good," Bobby declared. "It's the environment here."

I asked him whether he was from Trenton originally, and he said he was. "I grew up on Roebling and Division," he said. "I moved out here about 1976. Right now, I work over at Steinert High School. Before that, Heinemann Electric." Same as Rich Erkoboni, I thought.

"So what do you think of the kids at Steinert?" I asked him.

"The kids are getting better and better," Bobby replied gruffly. "They've by-passed all of us. I ain't gonna tell you which *way* they by-passed us, but they did. But they ain't teaching them right any more—ain't that right, Tommy?"

Tom Armenti had just walked up, and he nodded in agreement. "They can't frickin' add," he said despairingly.

Bobby shook his head. "They can't do percentages, they can't add, they can't write—everything they do, they print. They got the phone in one ear and the music in the other ear..." He started laughing, and then cried out, "There's something wrong! They're ruining my country!"

I laughed, and then asked him, "So Bobby, what do you *think* about your country these days?"

"I think the whole country needs some discipline," he declared. "That's what we need: old-fashioned discipline!"

"What does that mean?" I asked.

"It means you get a crack in the head once in a while," Bobby said. "That'll straighten you out. They think they need counseling—they don't need counseling. That's what's ruined us: all this counseling! And too many meetings!"

"That's the truth," I laughed.

"The work place has more meetings than the Pentagon!" Bobby exclaimed, and then, in a stage whisper, asked me, "How'm I doing? Am I doing good?"

"You're doing real good," I assured him with a laugh. "So tell me, what do you do at Steinert?"

"Me? Well, I tutor the kids during lunch—whatever they don't get in the classroom, I straighten them out out there," Bobby explained. "And I take out the garbage, like a *stunod*—whereas I should be sitting in the front office and giving directives—and I clean up the joint that our little children mess up. And as for the state of the world," he suddenly added, "the air conditioner in my car ain't working, and it's been ninety-five every day!"

Israel overheard him from behind the counter and told him that he'd fix his air conditioner for him for twelve hundred dollars.

"Twelve hundred dollars?" Bobby cried. "I'll wait for the end of the month and I'll put the heat back on. But right now, I gotta get to work. It's almost seven."

"Well, teach 'em well," I said as Bobby got up out of the booth. "They're the future—remember that."

"Yeah, the future," he grunted, making a face.

MARIO

It's seven o'clock now and Israel is cooking up a lot of bacon on the grill, and the salty-sweet smell fills the air. Noreen's having breakfast with Kent, but now Kent gets up to go to work with Bobby, and pretty soon Noreen gets up and heads out the door, too. "Have a good day!" I call after her. She waves and says, "You too!" Then a guy in a green jacket makes his way up to the lottery machine, and Anne yells, "Jerry!" She turns to me with a big smile and says, "That's Jake's son Jerry!" So I go up and shake Jerry's hand, tell him who I am, and tell him how much I liked and admired his father. Then I tell him that I'm writing a book about Fred and Pete's and that his dad is going to be in it. He says he's glad to hear it and wants to be sure he gets a copy when it comes out.

I take a seat at the counter and order my breakfast, waiting to see if Mario's going to show up today. Mario Brescio is definitely one of the regulars and I've been wanting to interview him for some time now. But at first he wasn't crazy about the idea. So eventually I talked to his wife, and she said she'd talk to him about it—and then a couple of days ago she said he'd do it. So I kept looking for him every morning until yesterday when Vicki told me that he'd been coming in earlier lately, more like seven o'clock. So here I am, keeping an eye on the door.

Finally, at about 7:15, he walks in, looking a little like Mark Twain and wearing a grey sleeveless t-shirt. But not just any t-shirt. In bold red, white and green lettering, it proudly proclaims: HARD-WORKING, GOOD-LOOKING, SUPER OUTGOING, ATTITUDE-HAVING, HAND-GESTURING, TRADITION-KEEPING, LOVING AND ROMANCING MAGNIFICENT ITALIAN!

As we settled into a booth in the back, I read Mario's t-shirt out loud so that I could get it on tape and then said, "OK, Mario, the interview's over. I mean, what more can you tell me besides that?"

"It's over," Mario agreed. "Fast, huh?"

I laughed. "Listen, Mario, I really appreciate your doing this," I told him. "You're the last guy in the book. The last interview. I got Marchetti a few minutes ago, so you're the only one left on my list."

"You got Marchetti?" Mario muttered, sounding somewhat surprised. "He's half nuts. I'm the other half. So now you got the whole thing. You got 'em all."

I laughed again, and asked Mario where he'd grown up.

"South Trenton," he replied. "We lived at 221 Bridge Street. By Market Street, Union Street... Before they ripped everything out. It's all gone. They cleaned it out. They put the turnpike through there. Twenty-nine, one-twenty-nine—something like that."

I nodded. "I know where you mean," I said, and I told him that I was in a band that used to play in a bar on South Broad not far from there.

"Oh yeah?" Mario raised an eyebrow. "South Broad? That wasn't far. Centre Street, Lamberton Street, Bridge Street, Second Street... Those were the good old days, boy. The '40's, '50's..."

I asked him when he was born.

"September the eighth, 1932," Mario replied proudly. "I'll be seventy-eight next week. September the eighth."

"Congratulations!" I said. "Were you the oldest?"

"No," he replied, "my sister, she's eighty, eighty-one. She lives in Michigan. And I had an older brother, but he died."

"So you were the youngest?"

Mario nodded. "The youngest nut."

"And what about your parents?" I asked. "What did your dad do?"

"I didn't even know my father," Mario replied heavily. "I was two years old when he died. He was twenty-nine. My mother was twenty-nine, too—I was seven years old when *she* died."

"Oh my God," I murmured. "How did your dad die at twenty-nine?"

"I have no idea."

"They never told you?"

Mario shook his head wearily. "They never told me," he sighed. "I didn't have a clue what was going on."

"And then your mother died when you were seven?"

"Yeah," Mario said sadly. "She was twenty-nine, too. So my aunt raised us. And you know what they are. No good, man. I couldn't wait to get outta there."

"Is that right? Was she too strict?" I asked.

"Yeah," Mario muttered. "You know how they do. They just took you over for the money. They'd pay 'em."

"So how old were you when you left home?"

"Let's see..." Mario thought for a moment. "Sixteen? Seventeen?"

"And what did you do?"

"Fucked around, you know—do this, do that. Anything," Mario replied.

"But you lived on your own?"

"Yeah," he nodded. "I couldn't wait to get out of there, man."

"She's not alive any more, I take it."

"Nah, she's dead." Mario shook his head. "I had to quit Trenton High in tenth grade—I had no clothes to wear. So I said, 'Fuck it,' and I quit. Tenth grade I got outta there. Then I got drafted when I was twenty-one, in 1953."

"And you became a paratrooper, right?" I said, remembering an earlier conversation that we'd had on the subject. "How did that happen?"

Mario scowled. "I was from New Jersey, right? So I figured I'd go to Fort Dix for basic training." He paused and then said, "I never seen Fort Dix. They sent us to Kilmer—Camp Kilmer—for two weeks, and then I went on a train to Fort Campbell, Kentucky, for sixteen weeks of basic. That was an airborne base, you know."

"Is that what you signed up for?"

"No!" Mario exclaimed indignantly. "But about the fourteenth week of basic, this major comes around and he says, 'Any of you guys like to go airborne?' So who do you think puts his hand up?"

I laughed.

"Two weeks later, they grabbed us and sent us to Fort Benning jump school," he went on. "So then I had three weeks of basic training over there, jumping out of airplanes. You had to make five jumps before they'd give you your wings. But it was good," he added proudly. "I was in shape, man."

"You remember the first time you jumped?"

"Oh yeah," Mario replied with feeling. "You don't forget that."

"Tell me about it," I said.

"Well, you go through jump school, you're gonna jump," he said. "You start with the tower—a thirty-five foot tower—you gotta make PLF's"—parachute landing falls—"you gotta do this, you gotta do that—you know, it's training, man. You are in shape. Then they put you in the plane and you make your first jump. They take you up thirteen hundred feet. That's the highest we'd jump. But it's like thirteen thousand—same thing."

"Except you have less time," I said.

"That's right," Mario chuckled. "And then the fourth or fifth jump I made, both chutes opened on me—the main and the reserve. I'm hanging by my ass, and I'm thinking, 'Oh, I'm dead, I'm dying.' But I worked my way free and landed. When I got there, they come running up to me: 'What the hell was that?' And I said, 'I dunno, but I worked my way free and I landed all right.'"

"Jeez..."

"Then I was in Japan," Mario continued. "I was there a year, and I made seventeen jumps there."

"But you didn't have to go to Korea?"

Mario shook his head. "No," he said. "We were ready to go to Korea. They kept us in Japan for a year. In case Korea kicks up again, we're there."

"A little different from Trenton, huh?" I remarked.

"Oh yeah," Mario said.

"Did you get to go off base at all?"

"Once in a while, we'd go into town," he recalled. "I was in the MP's there, too, you know. Town patrol, the bars... That wasn't bad. Eight hours, and then you'd go back to base. The cafeteria was always open, so you could go there twenty-four hours a day and eat..."

"Kind of like Fred and Pete's," I said.

"Yeah, kinda," Mario chuckled. "And then I was ready to come home, but I said, 'I wanna make one last jump—you'd get fifty dollars a jump, you know. And I broke my ankle. I landed wrong. So I was in the Army hospital there for two months, until they finally got me outta there and put me on a plane to Midway, then Hawaii—stayed there two weeks in Tripler Army Hospital. Then they flew me out to California, and after that I was in a hospital in Pennsy"—Pennsylvania—"for another two months..."

"All because of your ankle?" I said. "You must've really messed it up..."

"Aw," Mario groaned, "they put metal pins in it—they're still in there. Metal screws... I was in there for another month and a half and then they finally discharged me, and I went home." He took a long sip of coffee.

"So then what?" I asked.

"Oh, I did a little bit of this, a little bit of that, you know," Mario replied. "And then I went iron-working. And I stayed in there a while. About ten, fifteen years. I did rod work, buildings, highrises..."

"Here in Trenton?"

"All over. Trenton, but we'd go here and there, you know. Wherever they'd send you."

"And you were in a local?" I asked.

Mario nodded. "Local 68."

"So what kind of shape were you in?" I asked him.

"I was big," Mario replied proudly. "An animal. I've lost a hundred pounds," he added glumly. "Yeah, I had some shit, man."

I asked Mario about his family, and he told me that he'd been married to his present wife, Marian, for thirty-five years. He said that he'd been married once before, that he had four children from his first marriage, and one daughter from his current marriage. "She's twenty-seven now," he said. "You ever meet her? She's been in here. You've probably met her. Her name's Adrianne. I call her Munchie," he added fondly.

"How about your other kids?" I asked. "Do you ever see them?"

"Oh yeah," Mario beamed. "Mike, he was here yesterday. He just opened up a big photography business. He takes pictures—high school football, that kind of thing. He bought a big building on Broad Street. Nice place. And Mario, he's doing good, too. He used to write to the editor all the time—he's pretty smart, Mario is."

"Like his dad?"

"Nah, smarter than that," Mario said.

I asked Mario why, after fifteen years, he'd quit iron-working.

"I retired," he said emphatically. "In '92. So I been retired, what, eighteen years? I was getting too old for that shit. Because that's work, man. You gotta be in shape to be an iron-worker. Up on those high-rises—oh, boy..."

"You ever have any accidents up there?"

Mario shook his head. "No, thank God," he muttered. He paused, and for a moment he seemed to be looking right through me. "You gotta walk around like a monkey up there," he said, "and you gotta watch what you're doing, or else..." He whistled like the sound of Wiley Coyote dropping off a cliff in a Roadrunner cartoon. "A lot of guys got hurt up there," he added softly. "Because you're just hanging on, baby—terrible." His gaze dropped to the table.

"So when did you first start coming here?" I asked him, changing the subject to something less terrifying.

"Oh Christ," he said, "I used to come here a lot, back when Freddy was still here—Tommy's father. And Pete. You know, Fred and Pete—the originals. Those were the good old days, man."

"So what do you think of this place?"

"Oh," he replied languidly, "it ain't bad. It's like a zoo, but what are you gonna do?"

I chuckled. "So what do you like about it?"

Mario shrugged. "The people, the shit that goes on here, you know... Idiots, fuckin' bedbugs... Fred and Pete's, boy," he added, shaking his head again as if he were marveling at the very idea.

"What do you eat here?" I asked him. "Is there anything in particular that you like?"

"Yeah," he said, "me and my wife used to come here a lot for their fish and chips every Friday—that's very good. And then I'm here every morning. I'll come here and bullshit an hour, two hours, and then go home—do what I gotta do. Every day the same thing."

"So what do you do every day?"

"Oh, I got a lot of work at home to do—cut the grass, fix the roof, wash the dishes, everything. She's working all the time," Mario explained, "so I help her. And she pays me," he added, totally deadpan. "I tell her, 'Give it up, I'm twenty dollars short. I did the dishes, I did this, I did that.' So she throws me a twenty."

I cracked up.

"You ask her," he said. "I don't work for nothing. And she's been over there for what? Thirty-eight years now?"

"Where?"

"Robert Wood," Mario said, meaning Robert Wood Johnson Medical Center, which used to be Hamilton Hospital. "She's a nurse. Doing endoscopies. And they do colonoscopies, throats, all of that. Thirty-eight years."

"So she was a nurse when you got married?"

"Oh yeah," he replied, nodding. "I think she's the oldest one at Robert Wood. Thirty-eight years. Good old Robert Wood."

"So Mario, tell me about the harmonica," I said. "When did you first start playing?" I'd first heard him play one morning a few weeks before Christmas. I was at the counter quietly eating my breakfast, when suddenly I'd heard somebody playing a truly moving rendition of "Silent Night"—on a harmonica, of all things. And when I turned around, I was amazed to see that it was none other than Mario, sitting at a table behind me, playing for some of his friends in the booths. From "Silent Night" he went straight into "Jingle Bells" and then a couple of others. He was really good.

"Oh, quite a while ago," he said. "You know how it started? I used to work for Lipp Brothers, the furniture store in Trenton—a big store—delivering furniture, you know. And the guy I worked with, this one time we were sitting in the truck waiting for something—I don't remember what the hell it was—so he pulls out this harmonica, and I say, 'You play that thing?' And he says, 'Yeah,' and he starts playing. And I say, 'Hey, that's pretty good. How the hell did you learn that?' And he says, 'I just picked it up and started blowing in it.' He was pretty good, and so I decided to buy a harmonica for myself. I played with it, messed around, tried to play a song, and then I put it away. 'Fuck it,' I said. 'I can't play this.' But then I picked it up again, carried it with me everywhere I went, until I started playing it. Then I got better, better..."

"Yeah," I told him, "you really sound terrific. You blew my mind the first time I heard you play."

"They all like it," Mario said. "Everywhere I go, they want me to play. 'Come on, man,' they say, 'where's your harmonica?'"

"Well, one of these days, you've gotta play for my grandson," I said. "He's two years old, and he would love it."

"Oh yeah?" Mario said, arching his brow. "Sure, I'll play him a few syllables."

I asked Mario my standard question about the state of the world, and his response was characteristically blunt: "It's fucked up," he said.

"How so?"

"The people that are running it are idiots," he declared. "Like Obama..."
Mario shrugged. "But I don't even worry about it, I don't even care. What do I
care what they do, what they don't do? It ain't like it was in the '40's and '50's,
that's for sure. You see all this shooting and stabbing and robbing and murder.
It never used to be like that. They're idiots today."

Not much more to say on that score, so I asked Mario if he was still going
in for his blood transfusions at the hospital.

"Yeah," he replied wearily. "Something was wrong with the bone marrow—
it's not producing. So I have to get a pint now and then, you know. It's starting
to get better, though," he said, brightening. "They said it will over time."

"Well, that's good," I said.

"I hope," Mario added. "He thinks it's going to get better, though. He says
it's not no cancer or nothing. It's just the bone marrow ain't producing like it
used to. And that's where you get the blood. It happens to a lot of people. So you
gotta go maybe once a month or twice a month to put blood in. I actually got
around nine pints already. You take two pints and it takes six hours. It's terrible.
I hate it."

"You just sit there?"

Mario nodded. "You just sit there watching television," he said, shaking
his head in frustration. "Christ, I never was sick a day in my life—until I got to
my seventies. Seventy-five, seventy-six... It's discouraging. See, I was an animal.
I used to pick people up like they were a loaf of bread. But I can't do nothing
no more." He heaved a deep sigh and looked across the table at me. "Don't get
old, man."

"Yeah," I said. "But you're doing all right. You get those infusions, hang out
here at Fred and Pete's, and just do what your wife tells you."

"That's all," Mario agreed with a shrug, and then a faint smile crossed his
face. "What else are you gonna do?"

STUFF CABBAGE

Monday, December 14, 2009. Susie's out of town visiting her mother in Florida, so I've been coming to Fred and Pete's more than usual. In fact, today I've finally made the trifecta: breakfast, lunch and now dinner. Actually, I might not have come in for dinner, except that Theresa mentioned when I came in for lunch that all her usual customers weren't going to be having dinner tonight because they were going to some restaurant for dinner—something they did once a year. "All the old men go," she said fondly, and then added brightly, "but me and Meghan are gonna crash it." That's when I told her that I'd come in for dinner.

It's a few minutes after five when I get there—pitch black outside already, but then of course it's only about a week until the shortest day of the year. "Oh!" Theresa says when she sees me. "You really did come in!" John Wilwol and Tommy Pyle are in one of the booths, a little more dressed up than usual. "You guys going to the dinner?" I ask, and John nods. Tommy gets a call on his cell phone and moves to the next booth to take the call, so I slide in across from John. Then Fred Wright comes in, dressed in a suit. He's surprised to see me there. "I didn't know you came in for dinner," he says. I tell him it's so that Theresa would at least have one paying customer, since everybody else was going to the outside dinner. "You going?" I ask him. Of course he is. I tell him that I've got his chapter out in the car, if he'd be willing to take a look at it. "So you don't get sued?" he asks. I laugh and tell him I just want to make sure it's accurate. John tells me he read his earlier today, and the only thing he found wrong was that it was the police who would stop by when his mother made donuts, not the priests. I tell him that I must have thought he said priests because he grew up so close to Holy Angels. "Yeah, that's true," he says. "Corner of Marshall and Lalor."

I go out to my car and get the manila envelope with Fred's chapter in it, and he seems impressed when I hand it to him—as if he hadn't been quite sure until now that I was really writing this book that I'd interviewed him for. He asks me what I'm going to do about getting it published, and I tell him I'll probably self-publish it, since I'm not sure I want to go through all the hassle of finding a commercial publisher. And he says that if

I want, he can publish it through his office—same as he publishes for the Supreme Court. He means it, and I am genuinely moved by his offer.

Meanwhile, Theresa comes by and asks me if I want anything to eat. "We're out of the stuffed cabbage," she says, and goes up to the paper menu that's tacked up on the wall and crosses off STUFF CABBAGE. "The meatloaf is good, though, if you like meatloaf," she tells me. So I order the meatloaf and a glass of water. "We have tomato soup or I can fix you a salad," she says. I take the tomato soup. Good on a cold night like this.

John's just having something to drink, and Tommy Pyle is pretty excited, talking a mile a minute on his cell phone. "He talking to his broker?" I ask John. "I don't know," John says. "Talking to some guy about baseball." I finish the tomato soup, which is nice and hot, and Theresa brings me the meat loaf. It's a generous portion, complete with green beans and some nice looking potatoes.

Just then Tom Armenti comes in from the kitchen, all revved up. I get the impression that he's just come back from a catering run, and that he rushed to get back here in time for the dinner. "I gotta loosen up," he says, and without another word he drops down on the floor and starts doing push-ups—eighty of them, without breaking a sweat. "So what time are we supposed to be there?" he asks as he jumps back up. John tells him they're supposed to be there at 6:30, and Tommy Pyle says, "Yeah, but we won't eat til seven." I ask John where they're going, and he says it's an Italian place across from the Hibernian Club. I ask him if he likes Italian food, and he says he does but they'll probably have American food, too.

Meanwhile, Rich Erkoboni has come in and taken the seat at the table across from Fred Wright. He looks great. He's wearing a checked jacket over a black sweater, a gold chain, dress pants, and black loafers with tassels. "Man, look at those shoes, will ya?" Fred says. "You can see your face in them." Rich waves him away. They're forever busting each other's chops. Meanwhile, Tom Armenti goes back into the kitchen and comes out with a gigantic bottle of Merlot. "You guys bringing anything?" he asks. It must be a BYOB place.

It looks to me like they're ready to go. And sure enough, a minute later, Cash, who's been working the counter, turns off the front lights. "Time to go," John says, and they all get up and start toward the front door. As each of them heads out the door to their cars, I realize that this really is a special night and that there's a kind of buzz in the air—and even though I'm not going with them, I'm really glad I stopped in tonight.

THAT MAY BE

It's a balmy morning—Memorial Day, 2010—and I'm sitting on one of the white plastic chairs out front talking with John Bella, who's wearing a classy green shirt with palm trees on it. We watch as an old Plymouth station wagon with flag decals plastered all over it pulls up in front of the Italian Peoples' Bakery next door and an exceptionally large blonde wearing a star-studded tiara climbs out and goes inside.

"Must be going to the parade," John says.

"Nice day for it," I say.

"Yeah," John agrees, "but I'd rather be in the Islands."

He asks me if I've ever been to Bermuda, and I tell him no. "You gotta go," he says. "It's one of my favorite places."

I nod, but then I tell him that I'd rather go back to Alaska. "You wouldn't believe it," I say. "Incredible mountains, rivers, waterfalls, moose, eagles, grizzlies, and the biggest damn glaciers you ever saw..."

John nods and closes his eyes. "That may be," he says serenely. "But they ain't got Fred and Pete's."

ACKNOWLEDGMENTS

First of all, my heartfelt thanks to Tom Armenti, without whom there wouldn't *be* a Fred and Pete's to write about. And thanks also, Tom, for going along with my crazy idea of writing this book, for letting me freely interview your staff and your customers, and for sitting still long enough yourself to tell me the amazing story of this amazing place that has meant so much to so many people. And finally, thanks most of all for always making me feel welcome at Fred and Pete's, day in, day out, year in, year out—no matter how little sleep you've had the night before and no matter how badly Maryland may have lost to Duke.

My thanks also to:

Annie Pecan, for feeding me breakfast all these years, for helping to restore my faith in the human race, for inspiring me to write this book, and for helping me distribute and collect all those draft chapters so that the people I interviewed could read them and get back to me with their corrections.

Bobby Lee, for your generous spirit and your unfailing kindness—you were a true gentleman in every sense of the word.

Bobby Marchetti, for your infinite wisdom.

Dave Stout, for your dedicated service to our country in the jungles of Viet Nam, for your many amazing (but usually true) stories, for generously sharing your plastic spoons with me, and for introducing me to your remarkable brother LeRoy—and your equally remarkable mother-in-law Heidi.

Elaine "Midge" Morrissy, for always making me laugh, for coming up with the perfect title for this book, and for always bringing me ice water, even when I don't ask for it.

Fred Wright, for consistently cracking me up, for helping me appreciate the finer things in a Mercedes, and for your very kind offer to help me get this book out.

Gary Amico, for keeping the faith when others have lost theirs, and for still making the best tomato pies anywhere—period!

Gonzalo Vargas, for patiently washing all those thousands of dishes that we all eat and drink from, day in, day out.

Guy Norton, for your passion for the game, and for choosing Jackie Robinson.

Heidi Krall, for all the beautiful music.

Israel Chavez, for all those hundreds—thousands?—of Swiss omelets that have kept me going all these years.

Jack Reid, for making sure that the kids in the neighborhood get to school safely each morning, and for your courageous service to our country all those years ago on the frozen battlefields of Korea.

Jake Wig, for your friendship, for the old cowboy songs, and for those little handmade forest critters that I still keep as a reminder of our many mornings at the counter.

Jerry Sowa and Maria Sinibaldi, for all the good times.

Jim Fennelli, for all the stories, and for being such a good friend to Bobby Lee.

Joe Persicketti, for being a good guy and always saying hello, no matter how busy you are behind the counter.

John Bella, for making me laugh, and for steadfastly trying to maintain a modicum of decorum out front, no matter how hopeless the task.

Johnny "Woo" Wilwol, for being a true friend.

Kay Neutzman, for your wonderful smile and for refilling my cup before I even know it's empty.

Kathy Kapp, for your boundless enthusiasm and for kindly putting me in touch with your husband John to get my mower fixed—he did a terrific job!

LeRoy Stout, for keeping Dave more or less under control, and for always being so easy to talk to.

Liam, for being so well behaved.

Mario Brescio, for always speaking your mind, for playing the best damn harmonica in the State of New Jersey, and for finally (with a little encouragement from Marian and Adrianne) agreeing to be interviewed—and then actually getting it back to me!

Marvin Block, for just being Marvin. What more can I say?

Meghan Norton, for being such a nice person and such a good friend to John.

Nick Massaro, for keeping your head when all those about you (including me) are losing theirs.

Noreen Armenti (together with Brooke and Kent), for your unstinting patience and support over all the years since Tom took the place over, without which there would be no Fred and Pete's.

Rich Erkoboni, for patiently playing Gimme Five with our grandson Liam, no matter how many times he asks, and for always holding the fort out front, no matter how frickin' cold it gets.

Stephanie Caldwell, for somehow always managing to get my breakfast to me on Saturday mornings, no matter how nuts it gets.

Theresa "Lushka" Carney, for helping us all feel young again—or at least a little less old—and for those cute little faces that you always put on our checks.

Tim Desmond, for being so consistently funny in spite of it all.

Tommy "Suits" Pyle, for being such an all-around great guy, and for helping me to finally understand what makes the Phillies such a great team.

Tony Golowski, for your kindness to our grandson, for all the money you've raised in all those golf tournaments for all those worthy causes, and for that great umbrella you sold me for just $2.50—it actually works!

Vicki Ranfone, for never losing your cool back there behind the counter, no matter how many hoagies you have to make, and for your continuing generous contributions to everyone's favorite charity, Philadelphia Park.

Volodymyr "Cash" Kush, for being such an all-around good guy, and for getting me to finally read Pushkin.

Also, special thanks to Gaines Hill and Lindsay and Beth and the rest of the gang at CreateSpace who have been so patient and so professional in seeing me through my first venture in self-publishing; to Bill Grogan, for his continuing inspiration, encouragement and support; to my father, Steve Jellinek, who read some of the early sections of the manuscript and promised to read the whole thing if I ever got it published; and to Susie, for never once giving me a hard time about all the hours that I spend at Fred and Pete's, and for always being there for me, no matter what.

Finally, my sincere apologies to anyone who wanted to be interviewed but whom I wasn't able to include in this book. There are so many great people and so many great stories in Fred and Pete's that if I had included them all, this book could have given *War and Peace* a run for its money (*Fred and Peace,* or maybe *War and Pete's...*?) But who has the time nowadays to read anything as long as *War and Peace*—much less to write it? That said, my hope is that even if you aren't actually in the book, these stories have helped you to remember—or, if you've never been there, to get a feel for—this very special place, and some of the very special people who make it what it is.

Paul Jellinek
Mercerville, NJ
October 2010

Made in the USA
Middletown, DE
19 May 2020

95401612R00156